Rewriting Language

COMPARATIVE LITERATURE AND CULTURE

Series Editors
TIMOTHY MATHEWS AND FLORIAN MUSSGNUG

Comparative Literature and Culture explores new creative and critical perspectives on literature, art and culture. Contributions offer a comparative, cross-cultural and interdisciplinary focus, showcasing exploratory research in literary and cultural theory and history, material and visual cultures, and reception studies. The series is also interested in language-based research, particularly the changing role of national and minority languages and cultures, and includes within its publications the annual proceedings of the 'Hermes Consortium for Literary and Cultural Studies'.

Timothy Mathews is Emeritus Professor of French and Comparative Criticism, UCL.

Florian Mussgnug is Reader in Italian and Comparative Literature, UCL.

Rewriting Language
How Literary Texts Can Promote Inclusive Language Use

Christiane Luck

First published in 2020 by
UCL Press
University College London
Gower Street
London WC1E 6BT

Available to download free: www.uclpress.co.uk

Text © Christiane Luck, 2020

Christiane Luck has asserted her right under the Copyright, Designs and Patents Act 1988 to be identified as author of this work.

A CIP catalogue record for this book is available from The British Library.

This book is published under a Creative Commons Attribution Non-commercial Non-derivative 4.0 International license (CC BY-NC-ND 4.0). This license allows you to share, copy, distribute and transmit the work for personal and non-commercial use providing author and publisher attribution is clearly stated. Attribution should include the following information:

Luck, C. 2020. *Rewriting Language: How Literary Texts Can Promote Inclusive Language Use*. London, UCL Press. https://doi.org/10.14324/111.9781787356672

Further details about Creative Commons licenses are available at http://creativecommons.org/licenses/

Any third-party material in this book is published under the book's Creative Commons license unless indicated otherwise in the credit line to the material. If you would like to re-use any third-party material not covered by the book's Creative Commons license, you will need to obtain permission directly from the copyright holder.

ISBN: 978-1-78735-669-6 (Hbk)
ISBN: 978-1-78735-668-9 (Pbk)
ISBN: 978-1-78735-667-2 (PDF)
ISBN: 978-1-78735-670-2 (epub)
ISBN: 978-1-78735-671-9 (mobi)
DOI: https://doi.org/10.14324/111.9781787356672

Contents

Acknowledgements vi

Introduction 1

1. Linguistics and literature 14
2. Problematising the linguistic status quo – *The Left Hand of Darkness* and *Häutungen* 53
3. Proposing linguistic neutrality – *The Cook and the Carpenter* and *Woman on the Edge of Time* 75
4. Reversing the linguistic status quo – *Egalias døtre* 98
5. 'It's good to make people realise … double standards' – *Evaluating the impact of literary texts thematising sex/gender and language* 121

Conclusions 167

Works cited 184

Index 193

Acknowledgements

This book would not have been possible without the help and support of mentors, colleagues, friends and family. No project takes place in isolation and a lot of people have encouraged me over the years – by taking an interest in my research, listening to my ideas and concerns, and reviewing my work. While I am unable to thank everyone personally, I would like to express my gratitude to those who have played a key part in the creation of this book.

First of all, I would like to thank my PhD co-supervisors, Dr Geraldine Horan and Professor Susanne Kord, whose expertise, feedback and support have been invaluable over the course of this project. Susanne and Geraldine have always been open to my approach and ideas: with their guidance I have been able to experiment and thereby develop as a researcher and writer. I particularly appreciate their constructive reviews of my work, highlighting potential problems as well as different perspectives. In extension, I would like to thank my PhD examiners, Professor Felicity Rash and Professor Georgina Paul, as well as my anonymous reviewers. Their constructive criticism and detailed feedback helped me to further develop my thesis into a publishable body of work. I would also like to thank the staff at UCL Press for helping me to transform my manuscript into a book.

Meeting other PhD students and making friends has provided a supportive context for conducting my research. My friendships with Mathelinda Nabugodi, Liz Harvey-Kattou, Magali Burnichon and Gabriella Caminotto have provided much-needed camaraderie in all its highs and lows. Over the years, Gabriella, Magali, Liz and Mathelinda helped me immensely with tips, advice and a friendly ear – thank you! I would also like to thank my friend Lauren; our discussions around literature, sex/gender and language have been very insightful. Lauren has always been supportive of my research; as have my friends Rachel Watts, Mareike Brendel and Satu Viljanen. I really appreciate the many hours spent providing advice as well as distraction – new ideas often emerged after a shared outing or break.

My partner Jack Fisher has shouldered most of the emotional support over the years, and I would like to thank him in particular. Jack has always encouraged my work, providing feedback on chapter drafts, listening to my ideas and reassuring me when I felt disheartened. This research project has stimulated much discussion – sometimes antagonistic on my part – and I really appreciate Jack's patience and understanding. Our open exchanges provided a valuable experimental space and allowed me to clarify my position. Moreover, Jack's insights as a technical and creative writer helped me to clearly structure and express my thoughts.

My research project was self-funded and I would like to thank my employers UK-German Connection, the Learning Enhancement and Development department at City, University of London, and The Brilliant Club for their flexibility and support. Flexible working hours and the opportunity to further develop my research, writing and teaching skills have been invaluable. In addition, I would like to thank the Jackson Lewis Scholarship committee; receiving a scholarship allowed me to pay for materials and expenses to conduct my focus group study. I would also like to thank my most recent employer, the Communication and Engagement department at the University of Central Lancashire. My flexible working arrangement enabled me to find the time to revise my thesis for book publication.

Access to a wealth of materials and to quiet working spaces has also played a fundamental role in the completion of this research – I would like to thank the librarians and staff at the public and university libraries I have visited over the years. Senate House Library, The British Library, Dulwich Library and Manchester Central Library have been some of my favourite research and writing spaces, and have allowed me to develop ideas as well as concentrate on processing them.

Thank you also to all my focus group participants – their contributions have provided invaluable insights into reader perspectives on my selected texts. I have only been able to offer some homemade cake in return for their time; their commitment is therefore doubly appreciated. In fact, I believe it is their responses that render this book particularly fruitful.

Last but not least, I would like to thank my parents Gisela Luck and Wolfgang Luck who have always supported my endeavours. My father is unfortunately no longer alive but I know he would be proud of me, as he always has been.

Introduction

Activists and linguists have been highlighting the issue of biased language use since the 1970s. Empirical research has supported the need for more inclusive language. As a result, some English and German linguistic practices – and formal usage, in particular – have changed. However, broader revisions are yet to be made, and many inclusive adaptations remain either ignored or contested. The key question motivating my research is: 'How can English and German speakers be more widely convinced of the importance of inclusive language?' In this book, I provide one possible answer: I propose that literary texts can help to sensitise readers to the impact of biased language use and thereby promote wider linguistic change.

I employ an interdisciplinary approach to explore the validity of my suggestion and do so in three distinct stages: First, I create a theoretical framework for literary texts thematising the issue of sex/gender and language. I identify three distinct approaches: 'Problematising the linguistic status quo'; 'Proposing linguistic neutrality'; and 'Reversing the linguistic status quo', and categorise texts accordingly. Secondly, I analyse the effectiveness of each approach from a linguistic and philosophical perspective – with one key thinker providing the context for my discussion. Thirdly, I assess the impact of the three approaches on readers with a focus group study. Together, these three perspectives allow me to provide solid evidence for the value of literary texts. On the basis of these findings I argue that literary texts are a useful tool to sensitise readers to the importance of inclusive language.

My work builds on previous research; a key text being Anna Livia's 2001 *Pronoun Envy: Literary Uses of Linguistic Gender*. Livia analyses 'written texts in English and French ... that in some way problematize the traditional functioning of the linguistic gender system' (Livia 2001, 5). The author elaborates: 'I concentrate on French and English because it is in these languages that the most daring experimental works have been produced' (Livia 2001, 5). Moreover, she focuses 'on written texts … because many morphological indicators of gender in French are only apparent in the written form' (Livia 2001, 5). Our projects overlap in terms of our shared interest in the literary, and specifically written, problematisation of the issue of sex/gender and language. As do our choice of texts: three of the novels she evaluates in her chapter on 'Epicene Neologisms in English', namely *The Left Hand of Darkness*, *The Cook and the Carpenter* and *Woman on the Edge of Time*, form a key part of my own analysis. However, our approaches also diverge fundamentally from the outset. One central difference is the linguistic focus; in contrast to Livia, my working languages are English and German. I assess literary texts in these two languages because of their shared linguistic heritage. English has been shaped by German – Germanic tribes such as the Jutes, Angles and Saxons invaded and settled in Britain from the fifth century onwards (Durkin 2012, n. pag.) – while the global status of English today influences developments in the German language.

However, it is the differences in communicating sex/gender that are of most interest for my discussion: while English predominantly relies on social connotations, German additionally employs grammatical gender. This makes them fruitful for comparison. In effect, it is this comparative approach that forms the heart of my study and marks another difference to Livia's work. I analyse texts written in English and German as well as texts in translation. I am therefore less concerned with linguistic origin than with the texts' effectiveness at problematising the linguistic status quo in each language. Nevertheless, my choices are firmly guided by Livia's central criterion. The texts I assess equally 'test the reader's comprehension, demonstrating both the flexibility and the limits of the gender system' (Livia 2001, 10). Moreover, '[t]hey also test the imagination, so that what is produced is not a blueprint for linguistic change but a challenge' (Livia 2001, 10). Additionally, the final lines of Livia's conclusion effectively mark the beginning of my project. 'The hegemonizing power of cultural gender is indisputable', she states, '[w]hat is demonstrated by the texts examined here is that the possibilities for subverting that hegemony through grammatical gender and other means are equally impressive' (Livia 2001, 202). Continuing Livia's train of thought, I add a sociological perspective, namely a focus group study, to the literary and linguistic analysis. By providing an insight into reader responses, I offer empirical evidence for the impact of literary texts.

Justification of texts

Literary

My selection centred on literary texts that profoundly engage with the issue of linguistic representation. Ursula K. Le Guin, Verena Stefan, Marge Piercy, June Arnold and Gerd Brantenberg challenge social and linguistic norms in their writing. Fiction is understood to be a powerful tool, as Verena Stefan comments in the 1994 introduction to *Häutungen*. Encountering the literary problematisations of women's subordination shaped her own understanding. '1972 begann ich wieder zu lesen', she states, '[u]nd gemeinsam mit anderen Frauen stellte ich fest …, in welcher Mangelsituation wir lebten' (Stefan 1994b, 8) [I started reading again in 1972, and together with other women I realised how deficient our situation was][1]. As a result, she explains, '[e]*in buch zu schreiben war damals die geeignetste form, für die sache der frauen zu handeln*' (Stefan 1994b, 10, emphasis in original) [To write a book was therefore the most appropriate way to act for the women's cause at the time]. Stefan therefore considers writing an effective form of activism. Ursula K. Le Guin agrees. As she remarks in an interview with Jonathan White, '[o]ne of the functions of art is to give people the words to know their own experience. There are always areas of vast silence in any culture, and part of an artist's job is to go into those areas and come back from the silence with something to say' (Freedman 2008, 101). Fiction, according to Le Guin, can provide a voice to those who have been silenced. And while the impact of this voicing may be contested, '[f]iction and poetry can't change anything', as Marge Piercy remarks in an interview with Monica J. Casper, Piercy also contends that it has the potential to 'change someone's consciousness' (Casper 2014, n. pag.). Sensitising a reader can be the first step toward altering their perception of the world, as Stefan's own reading experience illustrates.

The selected texts for my discussion belong to the genre of narrative fiction and are, moreover, perspectival. That is, they enable readers to access the narrator's perceptions from a first person or third person perspective. Verena Stefan's *Häutungen* seems to be at odds with this criterion as it is a hybrid between a fictional and autobiographical narration. This, following narrative studies, could potentially compromise perspective-taking. However, despite its autobiographical leanings, Stefan's narration is akin to *The Left Hand of Darkness*. By employing devices such as symbols and metaphor it effectively mirrors a literary text. Additionally, the narrated events and experiences are recognisable to many female readers, thereby encouraging perspective-taking. The texts I have chosen were originally published between 1969 and 1977; in effect, almost 50 years before the present day. Questions might be: 'Why not choose more contemporary writers?'; and 'Are these texts not outdated?'. My response is twofold: first, *The Left Hand of Darkness*, *Häutungen*, *Woman on the Edge of Time*, *The Cook and the Carpenter* and *Egalias døtre* are all iconic texts. These early engagements with, and challenges to, linguistic norms provide a useful foundation for current and future research. Furthermore, all originate from a distinct time of social upheaval, in particular second-wave feminism, and therefore provide a valuable insight into concerns at the time and their progress since.

This leads me directly to my second reason. As I show throughout this book, while language use has changed in many formal contexts, inclusive language remains contested. As the responses of my focus group participants illustrate, English and German speakers today often do not notice the linguistic status quo. Moreover, they are as confused by neutral terminology as readers might have been several decades earlier. The texts therefore remain highly relevant. The literary experiments of the 1960s and 1970s symbolise a strong belief in the possibility of change. Art was considered a key driver both in communicating the artificiality of social norms and initiating social change. Le Guin, Stefan, Piercy, Arnold and Brantenberg all highlight the potential of literary texts. By providing a space to experiment and imagine, these authors played a key role in sensitising readers to the issue of sex/gender and language. And as the reader responses in my focus group study highlight, they continue to do so today.

Philosophical

The philosophical frame for each literary approach and evaluation was selected on grounds of suitability. However, Gottfried Wilhelm Leibniz, in particular, might be queried as potentially outdated in light of more recent theory. My choice was guided by the intention to illustrate the long history of thought on language and imagination. Leibniz's *salva veritate* principle already confirmed in 1686 that two terms need to be fully replaceable in order to be considered one and the same. If they are not, such as 'man' and 'human', as I show in Chapter 2, they cannot be employed interchangeably. Leibniz's thought is therefore fruitful for framing Le Guin's and Stefan's literary problematisations, as well as reader responses today. Equally insightful is Ludwig Wittgenstein's work. Wittgenstein's 1953 *Philosophische Untersuchungen* might be a more recent text, but his relevance could still be questioned. My response is that Wittgenstein's thought is revolutionary in terms of its exploration of the link between language and imagination. In fact, his notion 'eine Sprache vorstellen heißt, sich eine Lebensform vorstellen' [to imagine a language means to imagine a form of life] provides a sound basis for arguing that linguistic change is not only necessary but also possible. And while a caveat is a wider acceptance by the speech community, the linguistic status quo is exposed as malleable. This provides a valuable context for Piercy's and Arnold's literary experiments, as well as the focus group findings. Finally, Sigmund Freud's 1905 work on humour – with particular focus on wordplay – illustrates the potential of playful engagement with language. Rather than being rejected as farcical, humorous language is shown to be a useful tool to sensitise speakers. As such, Freud's work highlights the potential of Brantenberg's satiric problematisation; illustrated also by the text's impact on readers today.

Definitions of key terms

Sex/gender

The terms 'sex' and 'gender' need to be clarified as they play a central role throughout. This is not as simple a task as it may initially seem. First of all, 'sex' holds several meanings. While the term is primarily defined as '([c]hiefly with reference to people) sexual activity, including specifically sexual intercourse', it also holds the meaning '[e]ither of the two main categories (male and female) into which humans and most other living things are divided on the basis of their reproductive functions' (Oxford Dictionaries (OD 2016, n. pag.). Disregarding the first and focusing on the second definition, it is this division of human beings 'on the basis of their reproductive functions' that leads to 'sexism'; that is, '[p]rejudice, stereotyping, or discrimination, typically against women, on the basis of sex' (OD 2016, n. pag.). Closely related to this notion of 'sex', and 'sexism', is the concept of 'gender', which is defined as '[t]he state of being male or female (typically used with reference to social and cultural differences rather than biological ones)' (OD 2016, n. pag.). That is, 'gender' is here understood to refer to the sociocultural behaviours associated with a certain sex. However, complicating matters further, this separation of biology and culture is far from clear-cut. For one, 'gender' is also defined as '[t]he members of one or other sex' (OD 2016, n. pag.), which, in fact, renders the term equivalent to 'sex'. In many instances therefore, someone might be referring to a person's 'gender' when in fact they mean this person's 'sex' – which is problematic on several accounts. First, this conflation creates confusion as to whether bodies or behaviour, or a combination of both, are at the centre of the argument. And secondly, it enshrines the notion that both are essentially interlinked; that 'biology is destiny'.

As Rhoda Kesler Unger argues in her 1979 article 'Toward a Redefinition of Sex and Gender', the two terms need to be separated to avoid the above conflation. Unger bases her assessment on the fact that psychological studies all too often equated biology with culture, an equation that could be avoided with clearer terminology. 'The distinction between sex and gender', she states, 'can assist in the generation of research hypotheses that do not assume the former is necessarily the basis for the latter' (Unger 1979, 1093). As a result, she adds, 'it [is] less likely that psychological differences between males and females will be considered explicable mainly in terms of physiological differences between them' (Unger 1979, 1093). Unger's argument contributed to the linguistic and conceptual separation of bodies and behaviour, as is visible in the definitions of 'sex' and 'gender' today. However, as the *Oxford Dictionaries*' entries also highlight, this divide, while still present, is once more becoming obscured. In fact, as David Haig argues in his study 'The Inexorable Rise of Gender and the Decline of Sex: Social Change in Academic Titles, 1945–2001', '[t]his distinction [between sex and gender] is now only fitfully respected, and gender is often used as a simple synonym of sex' (Haig 2004, 87). When analysing the titles of more than 30 million articles, the author noticed a clear shift. For example, Haig found, while '[f]or the years 1945–1959, 1,685 … SCI titles out of 1,162,909 contained sex but only five … contained gender', '[f]rom about 1980, gender began a steady increase in frequency, partly at the expense of sex' (Haig 2004, 89–90). Explaining these results further, Haig states, '[a]mong the reasons that working scientists have given me for choosing gender rather than sex in biological contexts are desires to signal sympathy with feminist goals, to use a more academic term, or to avoid the connotation of copulation' (Haig 2004, 94–5). In this sense, 'gender' has for many effectively become the replacement term for 'sex'.

At the same time, however, the very distinction between 'sex' and 'gender' is potentially an issue. As Penelope Eckert and Sally McConnell-Ginet argue in *Language and Gender*, 'there is no obvious point at which sex leaves off and gender begins, partly because there is no single objective biological criterion for male or female sex' (Eckert and McConnell-Ginet 2003, 10). They elaborate, 'the selection among … criteria for sex assignment is based very much on cultural beliefs about what actually makes someone male or female' (Eckert and McConnell-Ginet 2003, 10). The authors' understanding is based on Judith Butler's 1990 inquiry into sex/gender in *Gender Trouble: Feminism and the Subversion of Identity*. In fact, Butler questions the understanding of 'sex' in purely biological terms: '[a]re the ostensibly natural facts of sex discursively produced by various scientific discourses in the service of other political and social interests?' (Butler 2007, 9). Continuing along this line of thought, Butler proposes that 'gender' might in fact create 'sex'. She states, 'gender is also the discursive/cultural means by which "sexed nature" or "a natural sex" is produced and established as "prediscursive," prior to culture' (Butler 2007, 10). As a result, 'sex' is far from a mere biological category; culture seems to produce bodies as much as behaviours. While this seems to justify an inclusive use of 'gender', that is encompassing 'sex' to some extent, 'gender has come to be adopted as a simple synonym ... for sex by many writers who are unfamiliar with the term's recent history' (Haig 2004, 95). Consequently, such usage might be confusing or misleading. Taking these potential issues into account, I use the compound 'sex/gender'. This is useful because first, it acknowledges that both terms are at once distinct and interrelated, and secondly, it highlights a central link between 'sex' and another type of 'gender', grammatical gender, with language the key focus of this book.

The term 'grammatical gender' has its own potential problems and needs to be clarified accordingly. First of all, English is considered a 'natural gender language ... where gender-associated information is conceptually and semantically embedded and is not overtly marked on a grammatical level' (Sato et al. 2013, 792), as Sayaka Sato, Pascal M. Gygax and Ute Gabriel explain in 'Gender Inferences: Grammatical Features and their Impact on the Representation of Gender in Bilinguals'. German, on the other hand, is a 'grammatical gender language ... [in which] both animate and inanimate nouns are morphologically marked for gender' (Sato et al. 2013, 793). Grammatical gender, in particular, is generally understood as unrelated to biology – the separation between 'Genus' [gender] and 'Sexus' [sex] in German highlights this. As the *Oxford Dictionaries*' online platform states, '[it] is only very loosely associated with natural distinctions of sex' (OD 2016, n. pag.). However, as I show, terms used in reference to human beings, such as nouns, pronouns, names and titles, are in fact predominantly associated with one sex/gender. Consequently, grammatical gender and physical bodies are far from separate entities; this is visible also in the dual German use of 'Geschlecht' [sex/gender]. In contrast to 'Genus' and 'Sexus', 'Geschlecht' can encompass both grammar and biology. Sato et al. highlight this link by distinctly referring to 'grammatical and biological gender' (Sato et al. 2013, 793), but I believe the compound 'sex/gender' is able to make the case for this connection more clearly. I therefore refer to 'sex/gender and language'. Similarly, I employ 'male' and 'female' to highlight the sexed/gendered nature of grammatical properties. The phrase 'male generic terms' helps to illustrate that supposedly neutral terms, such as the English noun and the German pronoun 'man', are indeed specific.

However, overall I intend to use 'sex/gender' sparingly as I am aware that a compound can be challenging if overused. Therefore, I employ 'neutral' or 'specific', instead of 'sex/gender-neutral' or '-specific', to avoid oversaturation. Equally, I refer to 'the linguistic representation of women and men' as a synonym for 'sex/gender and language' – which leads me on to two more central terms: 'woman' and 'language'.

Woman

The term 'woman' is defined as '[a]n adult human female', with 'female' defined as '[o]f or denoting the sex that can bear offspring or produce eggs, distinguished biologically by the production of gametes (ova) which can be fertilized by male gametes' (OD 2016, n. pag.). However, like the definitions for 'sex' and 'gender', this understanding is far from straightforward. As Butler points out, '[i]f one "is" a woman, that is surely not all one is; the term fails to be exhaustive' (Butler 2007, 4). Specifically, 'gender is not always constituted coherently or consistently in different historical contexts'; and moreover, 'gender intersects with racial, class, ethnic, sexual, and regional modalities of discursively constituted identities' (Butler 2007, 4). In short, 'woman' seems too narrow a concept to encompass the diversity of a 'female' experience. However, as Butler adds, a term is certainly needed to signal the disparate treatment of the sexes. '[T]he political task is not to refuse representational politics – as if we could', she says; '[t]he juridical structures of language and politics constitute the contemporary field of power; hence, there is no position outside this field' (Butler 2007, 7). In fact, Butler believes that the issues inherent in the term 'woman' can be useful to further debates on sex/gender and its intersection with other forms of oppression. 'The assumption of its essential incompleteness permits that category to serve as a permanently available site of contested meanings' (Butler 2007, 21), she states. I employ 'woman' with awareness of its potential limitations. However, I believe it is important at this point in history to be able to name the experience of being 'female' and the bias associated with it. My intention is here not to universalise this experience or reassert any essential difference, but to analyse and challenge the hierarchy of the sexes/genders. To do so, I require a consistent and, moreover, a recognisable term.

Language

Another term that needs clarification is 'language'. Defined as '[t]he method of human communication, either spoken or written, consisting of the use of words in a structured and conventional way' (OD 2016, n. pag.), it is important to state which type of language I am referring to. I focus on written language – more specifically, written language employed in literary texts. Moreover, I evaluate literary texts narrated from a first person or third person perspective. While the constructed nature of written language differs from the spontaneity of speech, it presents key advantages. In line with Livia's explanation, it is in writing that English and German linguistic experiments become visible and pertinent. What might be lost or ignored in a conversation, such as the use of a neutral pronoun, is able to act as a key feature in a written text. And through consistent usage, I believe, readers are able both to acclimatise to linguistic experiments and reflect more profoundly on their significance. I work with literary texts in particular, as they, in contrast to theoretical or rhetorical texts, tell a story with the help of fictionalised characters, settings and events. They essentially paint a picture rather than providing the nuts and bolts of an argument. This aesthetic experience, as I explore throughout this book, has a profound impact on readers.

However, this stylistic distinction is the only one I am making; the particular genre of the selected texts is less significant. As my focus is on texts that problematise the linguistic representation of women and men, I analyse work that meets this criterion. Consequently, the presented texts range in genre from confessional writing and science fiction to satire. A particular focus is on how texts engage with nouns, pronouns, names and titles. To clarify, I am here most interested in the lexical meaning of words; that is, '[t]he meaning of a word considered in isolation from the sentence containing it' (OD 2016, n. pag.). However, I follow Vyvyan Evans's understanding, as laid out in *How Words Mean: Lexical Concepts, Cognitive Models, and Meaning Construction*, that '[w]ord meaning ... is always a function of a situated interpretation' (Evans 2010, 23). And this interpretation, I argue, is guided by sociocultural notions. I am therefore investigating both the denotations and connotations of terms in relation to sex/gender.

In my analysis I consult a range of linguistic traditions and approaches: reference to historical linguistics allows me to provide an insight into how the meaning of words has developed, while the findings of psycholinguistic studies illustrate how speakers understand terms today. A comparative linguistic perspective enables here a deeper understanding, as it highlights both similarities and differences between the two languages. This comparison, as I show throughout, provides fruitful insights.

Chapter outline

In Chapter 1, I introduce key thinkers from the English- and German-language context, such as Robin Lakoff and Senta Trömel-Plötz, as well as their contemporaries. I focus on research on nouns and pronouns, in particular. To place theoretical debates in a wider research context, I present empirical findings from the 1970s to recent years. Early studies include Sandra L. Bem and Daryl J. Bem's 1973 'Does Sex-Biased Job Advertising "Aid and Abet" Sex Discrimination?' and Josef Klein's 1988 'Benachteiligung der Frau im generischen Maskulinum – eine feministische Schimäre oder psycholinguistische Realität?'. More recently, Jane G. Stout and Nilanjana Dasgupta's 2011 study 'When *He* Doesn't Mean *You*: Gender-Exclusive Language as Ostracism' and Dries Vervecken, Bettina Hannover and Ilka Wolter's 2013 'Changing (S)expectations: How Gender Fair Job Descriptions Impact Children's Perceptions and Interest Regarding Traditionally Male Occupations' investigated the impact of male generic terms. The chapter concludes with examples of recent language use, illustrating that while linguistic change has taken, and is taking, place, inclusive language remains contested. Following on from this, I present findings from narrative theory and research. Wolfgang Iser's argument that fiction enables readers to see norms in a new light, and moreover that this experience shapes understanding, is here central. This premise is supported by empirical research, such as Melanie C. Green and Timothy C. Brock's 2000 study 'The Role of Transportation in the Persuasiveness of Public Narratives', and Hans Hoeken and Karin M. Fikkers's 2014 research 'Issue-Relevant Thinking and Identification as Mechanisms of Narrative Persuasion'. These findings provide the basis for my proposal that literary texts can help to sensitise readers and thereby further promote inclusive language use.

In Chapters 2 to 4, I evaluate English- and German-language literary texts thematising sex/gender and language in relation to my premise.

In particular, I assess how texts engage with the issue and how effective they are in their engagement. I identify three distinct approaches employed by authors and group the texts into the following clusters: 'Problematising the linguistic status quo', 'Proposing linguistic neutrality' and 'Reversing the linguistic status quo'. My analysis of the effectiveness of each approach is framed by a philosophical and an etymological perspective. The philosophical evaluation allows me to assess the wider relevance of the literary problematisations, while an etymological discussion of key terms enables me to highlight that language has been, and continues to be, subject to change.

In Chapter 2, 'Problematising the linguistic status quo', I assess Ursula K. Le Guin's 1969 *The Left Hand of Darkness* and Verena Stefan's 1975 *Häutungen*. Le Guin, I argue, consistently employs 'he' and 'man' to highlight that these terms are rarely understood inclusively. Stefan takes a more direct approach and openly questions the generic use of male nouns and pronouns. In doing so, I propose, Le Guin and Stefan problematise the ability of male terms to represent both sexes/genders. I frame the authors' probing of this dual representation by discussing Gottfried Wilhelm Leibniz's *Allgemeine Untersuchungen über die Analyse der Begriffe und Wahrheiten*. Leibniz argues that words are employed to convey concepts and ideas, and fail if they do not communicate clearly. This notion of 'failure' is explored further by an etymological study of male generic terms. Complementing the empirical results presented in Chapter 1, I show that many of these nouns and pronouns have neither an inclusive origin nor core meaning. In conclusion I argue that *The Left Hand of Darkness* and *Häutungen* effectively illustrate this incongruence to the reader. Furthermore, by challenging the linguistic status quo, I suggest, they pave the way for more experimental texts.

June Arnold's 1973 *The Cook and the Carpenter* and Marge Piercy's 1976 *Woman on the Edge of Time* take centre stage in Chapter 3, 'Proposing linguistic neutrality'. Arnold and Piercy both use epicene pronouns to refer to characters – Piercy imagines a future egalitarian society employing 'person' instead of 'he' or 'she', while Arnold proposes 'na' as used by the members of a separatist community. The use of neutral language, I argue, is tied to proposing a society in which sex/gender no longer matters. I integrate Ludwig Wittgenstein's *Philosophische Untersuchungen*, and especially his concept 'eine Sprache vorstellen heißt, sich eine Lebensform vorstellen', into my discussion to evaluate this suggestion from a wider philosophical perspective. For Wittgenstein, language enables the comprehension of a certain 'form of life', and consequently a change in language could allow for a new conception. An etymological study provides evidence of past and current understandings of key nouns and pronouns. In conclusion, I propose that by allowing readers to experience linguistic neutrality, *The Cook and the Carpenter* and *Woman on the Edge of Time* encourage them to think beyond current linguistic practices.

In Chapter 4, 'Reversing the linguistic status quo', I assess the English and German translations of Gerd Brantenberg's 1977 *Egalias døtre*. Brantenberg uses reversed versions of male generic terms and thereby, I argue, highlights how damaging a biased language can be. I propose that the English and German versions of Brantenberg's novel successfully make the case for each language. The novel employs wordplay, such as 'housebound', instead of 'husband', and 'Herrlein', instead of 'Fräulein', to engage the reader. By using humour, I suggest, the translations of *Egalias døtre* can be seen to have liberating potential. To assess this proposal from a theoretical perspective, I discuss Sigmund Freud's *Der Witz und seine Beziehung zum Unbewussten*. Freud believes humour allows readers to laugh at figures of authority and consequently experience a feeling of liberation. The impact of this experience remains contested, however, and I evaluate the function of humour from various perspectives. The discussion of key terms, such as 'woman' and 'wife', provides an etymological frame, and highlights that these can hold unexpected origins and meanings. The English and German translations of *Egalias døtre*, like *The Left Hand of Darkness/Häutungen* and *The Cook and the Carpenter/Woman on the Edge of Time*, I conclude, sensitise readers to the issue of sex/gender and language. Additionally, I suggest, the reversal of male generic terms prompts readers to consider more inclusive terminology.

Chapter 5 evaluates the impact of the three approaches on readers. With a focus group study I assess how readers respond to the literary texts, with particular focus on the nouns and pronouns employed to represent women and men. Furthermore, I explore whether literary texts can help to sensitise readers to, and potentially encourage them to become more supportive of, inclusive language. I conducted a pilot focus group to test my materials, and two focus groups with native English speakers and two with native Germans. Each group was presented with an excerpt from Le Guin's *The Left Hand of Darkness*, Arnold's *The Cook and the Carpenter* and Brantenberg's *Egalias døtre* in either language. I collected data using a semi-structured topic guide and the results were analysed with grounded theory. The findings of this study highlight the relevance of literary texts in raising awareness of the issue of sex/gender and language. Moreover, the data shows that literary texts encourage readers to reflect on the impact of dominant linguistic practices.

These results feed into my wider assessment and link back to my earlier contention that fiction is a powerful tool to illustrate and challenge wider social norms and issues. In particular, I explore the educational potential of literary texts in relation to sex/gender and language, addressing how they can help to sensitise readers to linguistic norms and prompt them to consider, and employ, alternatives. Based on my findings, I discuss the possibilities and limitations of the three literary approaches. Moreover, I suggest how the evaluated texts could reach a wider audience and thereby further promote inclusive language use. Additionally, I clarify the type of linguistic revision I would like to see for the English and German language, and point out fruitful avenues for future research.

Note

1. Translations are my own unless indicated otherwise.

1
Linguistics and literature

The feminist critique of language is a relatively recent historical phenomenon, but over the past 50 years it has had a profound impact on the understanding of and attitudes towards the issue of sex/gender and language. In this chapter I present historical debates in the English- and German-language context as well as empirical findings. I explore discussions around the significance of nouns and pronouns in particular, as these form the central focus of my argument. As I show, while certain linguistic practices have adapted in line with inclusive language proposals, others remain either ignored or contested. This lays the foundations for my investigation into the potential of literary texts to promote inclusive language use.

Linguistic background: English

Lakoff and Spender

It is difficult, if not impossible, to pinpoint the exact moment when the representation of women and men came to the forefront of linguists' minds. In fact, it was not necessarily a professional interest that started the inquiry, but a heightened awareness of the role of language in society. During the civil rights movement in the United States in the 1960s, different social groups – different in terms of their disparate treatment from the (white, male) norm – began to question the way they were represented linguistically. Derogatory and belittling terms, such as 'boy' to address a man of colour or 'bitch' to refer to a woman, were obvious targets, but soon language in general took centre stage. Questions from a female perspective included, for example: why was 'doctor', a supposedly neutral term, usually pronominalised with 'he' rather than 'she'? And why were human beings generically referred to as 'man' but never as 'woman'? In short, why were men linguistically portrayed as *the* representatives of humanity? Alongside the demand for a more equal place in society, disaffected groups, with women the particular focus of this book, also demanded a more equal place in language. This was especially important to those who saw a direct link between the terms employed for women and a society that assigned them an inferior position. Language was here considered not only a reflection of societal bias but also a tool to perpetuate it. Two thinkers who made key contributions to the early feminist critique of language are Robin Lakoff and Dale Spender. There have been many other influential voices; however, I focus on Lakoff's and Spender's work as it encapsulates the different positions on the link between language and reality.

Lakoff's 1973 essay 'Language and Woman's Place', which formed the basis for her later book is, according to Lenora A. Timm, a 'pioneering work' (Timm 1976, 251). Nevertheless, it is not without its problems. To name but three of Timm's criticisms: Lakoff's 'methods of analysis', 'definition of terms and concepts (or lack thereof)' and 'use of freewheeling … generalizations' (Timm 1976, 245). Lakoff's approach might cause some concern; however, in 'Language and Woman's Place' she makes several central observations, inspiring generations of researchers to come. First, Lakoff links societal power to language: '[t]he language of the favored group, the group that holds the power, along with its non-linguistic behavior, is generally adopted by the other group, not vice-versa' (Lakoff 1973, 50). The author therefore identifies a connection between linguistic disparity and social positioning. Secondly, societal power structures are not only reflected in language use but also in meaning. As Lakoff comments, '[o]ften a word that may be used of both men and women …, when applied to women, assumes a special meaning that, by implication rather than outright assertion, is derogatory to women as a group' (Lakoff 1973, 57). The term 'professional' is one of her examples: a male professional is generally considered an expert who happens to have a sex/gender. On the other hand, if a professional is female, she is often perceived in relation to her sex only.

Spender agrees with Lakoff's observation. As she states in her 1980 work *Man Made Language*, '[t]o be linked with male is to be linked to a range of meanings which are positive and good: to be linked to minus male is to be linked to the *absence* of those qualities' (Spender 1980, 23, emphasis in original). In a social context in which men are the 'favoured' group, and furthermore, in which women are primarily categorised as sexual beings, the logic is that a professional 'minus male' can only be a prostitute.[1] In such a context women are marked by their sex/gender. Lakoff elaborates: 'in the professions the male is unmarked, we never have *man (male) doctor*' (Lakoff 1973, 60, emphasis in original), while English speakers were, and still are, familiar with the reverse: 'woman doctor' or 'lady doctor'. These '[l]inguistic imbalances' (Lakoff 1973, 73) are of key concern; in contrast, however, the generic use of 'man' is less significant to Lakoff's mind. She believes that male generic terms 'of course refer to women members of the species as well' (Lakoff 1973, 74). At this point both theorists' positions begin to diverge substantially. Lakoff argues, 'I don't think it [the use of 'man'] by itself specifies a particular and demeaning role for women, as the special uses of *mistress* or *professional* ... do' (Lakoff 1973, 74, emphasis in original) and explains, 'it does not indicate to little girls how they are expected to behave' (Lakoff 1973, 74–5). Spender, on the other hand, holds the opposite position: '[h]e/man makes males linguistically visible and females linguistically invisible ... so that it seems reasonable to assume the world is male until proven otherwise' (Spender 1980, 157, emphasis in original). 'He' and 'man', the author argues, essentially imply male-as-norm – the unmarked use of 'man' is therefore as problematic to Spender as professional terms are to Lakoff.

Lakoff explains why she makes this distinction: 'we should be attempting to single out those linguistic uses that, by implication and innuendo, demean the members of one group or another' (Lakoff 1973, 73). Presumably the use of 'man' and 'mankind', to her mind, do not. However, as Spender points out, '[t]hrough the use of *he/man* women cannot take their existence for granted: they must constantly seek confirmation that they are included in the *human* species' (Spender 1980, 157, emphasis in original). The need to 'seek confirmation' for their humanity could consequently cause women equal 'psychological damage' (Lakoff 1973, 73), as Lakoff terms it, as degrading language. However, Spender's critique also raises concerns, according to Maria Black and Rosalind Coward. The authors comment that Spender fails to reflect on 'many apparently non-gender specific terms that bear no resemblance to the exclusively masculine *man*, [which] occur in utterances where the same pattern of exclusive reference ... is also found' (Black and Coward 1999, 108, emphasis in original). In short, linguistic representation matters as a whole; that is, unmarked 'man' is as significant as unmarked 'doctor' and terms of degradation.

While Lakoff and Spender disagree on which nouns are most in need of revision, they share an understanding of what is frequently deemed the most controversial aspect of Spender's work: the origins of androcentric language. Lakoff believes that men's societal position has filtered down into language, that 'this lexical and grammatical neutralization [of 'man' and 'mankind'] is related to the fact that men have been the writers and the doers' (Lakoff 1973, 74). Spender agrees that '[women] have not had the same opportunity to influence the language, to introduce new meanings where they will be taken up, to define the objects or events of the world' (Spender 1980, 52–3). In effect, both concur that men's linguistic position is linked to their position in society. However, Spender takes this interplay between language and reality one step further: 'because males have primarily been responsible for the production of cultural forms and images ... it would be surprising if language were to be an exception' (Spender 1980, 31). This equation of social and linguistic power is for many, including Black and Coward, a step too far. It implies the ability to communicate pre-language, the authors comment, and '[o]ne wonders how, without already having a language, the patriarchs around the linguistic conference table managed to communicate to each other their plans about such a complex and sophisticated system' (Black and Coward 1999, 106). One could argue that 'man-made' does not necessarily have to mean made from scratch. In fact, Spender's proposition could equally be interpreted to refer to a more gradual linguistic influence, for example in the form of societal power being translated into language.

Nevertheless, both theorists agree that social hierarchies shape linguistic representation. The key question that really divides Lakoff and Spender, however, is whether women's and men's position in language is simply a historical relic or whether it impacts on speakers' understanding today. Lakoff argues that 'it is very seldom the case that a certain form of behavior results from being given a certain name, but rather, names are given on the basis of previously-observed behavior' (Lakoff 1973, 75). Consequently, the unmarked and marked interpretations of 'professional' are down to observation only. This is problematised by Spender on two accounts. First, she questions who observes and to what effect, and secondly, she queries the division of category and behaviour. In relation to the first point Spender states that '[n]ew names ... have their origins in the perspective of those doing the naming rather than in the object or event that is being named' (Spender 1980, 164). Considering the 'favoured' societal position of men, it seems plausible that official observing and naming, at least, took/takes place from a predominantly androcentric perspective. Furthermore, it seems likely that this observation was/is based on men, 'taking themselves as the centre, the reference point' (Spender 1980, 54). In reference to her second point she elaborates, '[o]nce certain categories are constructed within the language, we proceed to organize the world according to those categories. We even fail to see evidence which is not consistent with those categories' (Spender 1980, 141). According to Spender, categories determine human beings' behaviour beyond their initial implementation. Consequently, speakers might expect a 'male doctor' when the term is unmarked and a 'prostitute' when encountering a 'female professional'.

This is where we get to the heart of the disagreement between Lakoff and Spender: the link between linguistic and social change. Lakoff believes that '[l]inguistic imbalances ... are clues that some external situation needs changing, rather than items that one *should* seek to change directly' (Lakoff 1973, 73, emphasis in original), while Spender argues that 'because their meanings are primarily those of minus male, women continue to be devalued. By such an interrelated process is the subordination of women in part created and sustained' (Spender 1980, 23–4). Lakoff takes the position that social change precedes a change in language – 'social change creates language change, not the reverse' (Lakoff 1973, 76). Spender, on the other hand, considers both to be interlinked: '[a]s more meanings are changed so will society change and the sexist semantic rule be weakened; as society and the sexist semantic rule changes so will more meanings change' (Spender 1980, 31). Nevertheless, despite this divergence Lakoff and Spender agree on the impact of language on speakers. Lakoff refers to the 'psychological damage' of derogatory terms, while Spender believes words 'help to structure a sexist world in which women are assigned a subordinate position' (Spender 1980, 31). Both theorists therefore consider language to have a tangible effect on speakers' perceptions – and understanding that is based on the Sapir–Whorf hypothesis.

The Sapir–Whorf hypothesis

The notion that language influences thought is not unique to Edward Sapir nor Benjamin Lee Whorf. In fact it goes back to thinkers of the Enlightenment period such as Wilhelm von Humboldt. In his 1810/11 *Schriften zur Sprache*, he already stated that '[j]ede Sprache setzt dem Geiste derjenigen, welche sie sprechen, gewisse Grenzen' (von Humboldt 1973, 13) [every language creates certain intellectual boundaries for its speakers]. Language is, von Humboldt elaborates, 'ein selbständiges, den Menschen ebensowohl leitendes, als durch ihn erzeugtes Wesen' (von Humboldt 1973, 13) [an independent entity that guides human beings as much as it is created by them]. Sapir, a linguist who studied American Indian, Indo-European and Semitic languages, built on this understanding. Based on his observations of different linguistic systems, he states in his 1933 essay 'Language' that '[l]anguage is heuristic … in the much more far-reaching sense that its forms predetermine for us certain modes of observation and interpretation' (Mandelbaum 1949, 10). Sapir agrees with von Humboldt that language shapes our comprehension of the world, and further, shapes it in correspondence with the norms of a given society. Thus '[l]anguage is a great force of socialization, probably the greatest that exists … a common speech serves as a peculiarly potent symbol of the social solidarity of those who speak the language' (Mandelbaum 1949, 15). Created, and employed, to communicate a particular world view, language, according to Sapir, reinforces this world view by the very act of communicating. As the author states in his 1929 'The Status of Linguistics as a Science', '[w]e see and hear and otherwise experience very largely as we do because the language habits of our community predispose certain choices of interpretation' (Mandelbaum 1949, 162). In short, speakers are unable to understand their environment, be it natural or cultural, extralinguistically but are bound by the particular preconceptions laid down in language. As '[f]or the normal person every experience, real or potential, is saturated with verbalism' (Mandelbaum 1949, 11), Sapir believes that this predisposition is difficult, if not impossible, to circumvent:

> Human beings do not live in the objective world alone, nor alone in the world of social activity as ordinarily understood, but are very much at the mercy of the particular language which has become the medium of expression for their society. It is quite an illusion to imagine that one adjusts to reality essentially without the use of language and that language is merely an incidental means of solving specific problems of communication or reflection. The fact of the matter is that the 'real world' is to a large extent unconsciously built up on the language habits of the group. (Mandelbaum 1949, 162)

Whorf, a student of Sapir's, took the notion of linguistic coercion as his starting point, and located further evidence through his investigations of the Hopi language. As he comments in his 1936 essay 'An American Indian Model of the Universe', the world view of Hopi speakers is different from that of English speakers precisely because their language presents different conceptions, with time and space a central example. Taking these differences as the foundation for his argument, Whorf comments in his 1940 'Science and Linguistics': '[w]e dissect nature along lines laid down by our native languages. The categories and types that we isolate from the world of phenomena we do not find there because they stare every observer in the face' (Carroll 1956, 213). To paraphrase, established categories, such as time and space, guide speakers to label their perceptions in correspondence. This guiding function of language, according to Whorf, is laid down in the 'linguistic system' (Carroll 1956, 212), such as grammar. Therefore grammar, he argues, 'is not merely a reproducing instrument for voicing ideas but rather is itself the shaper of ideas' (Carroll 1956, 212). As a result, speakers of a certain language seem trapped: they are coerced to categorise according to one particular world view and essentially unable to create any new categories. Whorf sees the cause for this inability in 'the difficulty of standing aside from our own language … and scrutinizing it objectively' (Carroll 1956, 138). In short, speakers are unable to perceive language and its implications.

In its strongest form, the Sapir–Whorf hypothesis proposes that language determines thought, an understanding that attracted criticism from its very inception. One immediate counterargument offered by Julia M. Penn in *Linguistic Relativity Versus Innate Ideas: The Origins of the Sapir–Whorf Hypothesis in German Thought* is that '[t]he proponent … must be prepared to accept the logical consequences of [her/]his position, i.e. that there is no prelinguistic thought in the individual and that human thought was not originally responsible for the creation of language' (Penn 1972, 18). Sapir himself expresses doubt whether this really was the case. As he states, '[l]anguage is primarily a cultural or social product and must be understood as such' (Mandelbaum 1949, 166). And as language is closely interlinked with society it therefore cannot exist prelinguistically. The strongest version consequently seems dubious even to its co-originator. However, as Penn highlights, a more general concern around the theory is 'deciding just what "the" Whorf hypothesis is' (Penn 1972, 13). Whorf, maybe in anticipation of such a question, provides further clarification in his 1940 'Linguistics as an Exact Science':

> [T]he 'linguistic relativity principle,' … means, in informal terms, that users of markedly different grammars are pointed by their grammars toward different types of observations and different evaluations of externally similar acts of observation, and hence are not equivalent as observers but must arrive at somewhat different views of the world. (Carroll 1956, 221)

Language directs towards different understandings of the world, according to Whorf – his use of 'somewhat different', rather than 'definitely different', confirms that along with Sapir he positions himself at the lesser end of the determinist scale. However, to critics of Whorf's work it is the very notion of difference that is problematic. For example, reviewers take issue with the evidence Whorf used as the foundation for his theories. One criticism by Alan Garnham and Jane Oakhill, for example, points out that 'Whorf translated Native American languages into English in a "simplistic, word-by-word" fashion' (Tohidian 2009, 69). Equally, Ekkehart Malotki's *Hopi Time: A Linguistic Analysis of the Temporal Concepts in the Hopi Language* (1983) illustrates that Whorf's identification of differences between English and Hopi is problematic. The basis of linguistic relativity therefore seems questionable to begin with.

Nevertheless, many researchers were inspired by the Sapir–Whorf hypothesis and decided to investigate further. And as its strongest form is generally rejected, studies focused on exploring what Iman Tohidian terms in 'Examining Linguistic Relativity Hypothesis as One of the Main Views on the Relationship between Language and Thought': '[t]he weak version ... [which says] that language *influences* thought' (Tohidian 2009, 70, emphasis in original). This 'weak' version, according to the author, is divided into two sub-versions: first, the notion that 'language influences perception' and secondly, the concept that 'language influences memory' (Tohidian 2009, 70). Tohidian highlights that both weaker forms are supported by early evidence. Language influencing memory is backed by Hogan Carmichael and Walter Carmichael's 1932 study of the link between labels and images in memory; and language influencing perception is supported by Eric Lenneberg and John Roberts's 1956 investigation into colour comprehension by English and Zuni speakers. However, despite these results, the weak versions of the Sapir–Whorf hypothesis are not without problems either. Tohidian asks, for example, 'what is language influencing – all thoughts or certain types of thought? If the latter, then what sort of thoughts are influenced?' (Tohidian 2009, 72). To provide a partial answer, Whorf's own understanding of language is useful: '[it] first of all is a classification and arrangement of the stream of sensory experience which results in a certain world-order' (Carroll 1956, 55). According to Whorf, then, language shapes thought in relation to certain categories, which, in turn, shape a particular world view.

Earl Hunt and Franca Agnoli agree with this labelling function of language in 'The Whorfian Hypothesis: A Cognitive Psychology Perspective'. They state that '[l]anguage provides the coding system for transmission of an idea from one person to another. The codes must refer to prototypes' (Hunt and Agnoli 1991, 386). This notion of prototypes is of particular interest to feminist linguists. If prototypes represent one sex/gender rather than the other, many argue, they lead speakers to equate this *one* sex/gender with the prototype for humanity. In short, as categorisation is essential for human understanding and equally shapes this understanding in turn, the category 'man', if used to refer to all human beings, skews interpretation. As Sally McConnell-Ginet argues in 'Prototypes, Pronouns and Persons', '[l]ive human beings are generally perceived as women or as men, not as androgynes' (McConnell-Ginet 1979, 77). Consequently, '[d]efinite singular generics that represent some human prototype are only with difficulty interpreted as gender-indefinite' (McConnell-Ginet 1979, 65). As speakers are unable to imagine a neutral being, they imagine a particular human being, a prototype. Fatemeh Khosroshahi's 1989 study 'Penguins Don't Care, but Women Do: A Social Identity Analysis of a Whorfian Problem' provides some empirical evidence. The author presented participants, who were traditional or reformed language users – that is, they employed male generic or inclusive terms – with paragraphs including 'he', 'he or she' or 'they', and asked respondents to draw the associated mental image. Khosroshahi found that '[t]he number of male images was much higher than the number of female images' (Khosroshahi 1989, 513). And while '*[h]e or she* and *they* did not differ significantly in the number of female … and generic images', '*he* evoked the lowest number of female images' (Khosroshahi 1989, 515, emphasis in original). In fact, 'he' was rarely interpreted generically: only '19%' (Khosroshahi 1989, 516) of the images, according to Khosroshahi's study, were of women. In line with McConnell-Ginet, 'he' seems to be linked to the prototype 'male'.

Furthermore, the language use of the four different groups of respondents is telling. As Khosroshahi reports, 'whereas reformed- and traditional-language men did not differ significantly in the number of female, male, and generic images that they generated …, reformed women produced significantly more female figures … than traditional women' (Khosroshahi 1989, 514). To paraphrase, women who are aware of the impact of male generic terms chose to counteract this bias, whereas men with equal awareness did not. Both female and male traditional language users, on the other hand, interpreted 'he' according to its dominant denotation and connotation. The author reflects, 'if we consider the *weak* form of the Sapir–Whorf hypothesis, … we can restate our conclusion in this form: *all groups conformed to Whorf's thesis except the men who had reformed their language*' (Khosroshahi 1989, 520, emphasis in original). In short, all groups interpreted in correspondence with their understanding of categories and therefore their world view, except for the male group with reformed linguistic practices. While Khosroshahi's conclusion may not be particularly forceful – '[c]hanging language does not necessarily produce alteration at the cognitive level, but it doesn't seem to hinder it either' (Khosroshahi 1989, 522–3) – her study makes an important point nevertheless. In fact, it provides evidence that language influences thought, in line with the Sapir–Whorf hypothesis.

Empirical evidence

> A number of Lakoff's unsupported assertions about women's language could be reformulated as hypotheses, then tested in a controlled experiment or checked for validity against data gathered in natural speech situations. This strikes me as the only sensible way to arrive at a *valid* description of linguistic features which are characteristic of women in this society or elsewhere. (Timm 1976, 251, emphasis in original)

As Timm states in her review of Lakoff's work, without empirical evidence it is difficult to come to any conclusions about the impact of the linguistic representation of women and men. Furthermore, it is difficult to argue for linguistic change to level any disparity. Two pivotal studies of the 1970s tried to advance the debates and put feminist linguistic contentions to the test: Sandra L. Bem and Daryl J. Bem's 1973 'Does Sex-biased Job Advertising "Aid and Abet" Sex Discrimination?', and Joseph W. Schneider and Sally L. Hacker's 1973 'Sex Role Imagery and Use of the Generic "Man" in Introductory Texts: A Case in the Sociology of Sociology'. Published in the same year as Lakoff's essay, both studies question how the generic use of 'man' shapes understanding.

Bem and Bem investigated whether the phrasing of job advertisements impacts on participants' motivation to apply. The authors found that the use of 'lineman' and 'frameman' meant 'no more than 5% of the women were interested' while 'lineworker' and 'frameworker' resulted in a clear increase: '25% of the women were interested' (Bem and Bem 1973, 13–14). 'And when the ads for lineman and frameman were specifically written to appeal to women [i.e. by using 'linewoman' and 'framewoman'], nearly half (45%) of the women in our sample were interested in applying for one or the other of these two jobs' (Bem and Bem 1973, 14). Women seem to be able to picture themselves in the roles relative to whether or not they are linguistically represented. Schneider and Hacker's study backs these findings. Asking introductory sociology students to submit pictures that represented typical topic titles such as 'Social Man', 'Urban Man', 'Political Man', 'Industrial Man' and 'Economic Man'

(Schneider and Hacker 1973, 14), the results showed that '[a]mong all respondents, about 64 percent of those students receiving "man"-linked labels submitted pictures containing men only, whereas only about half of those receiving labels without the term submitted male-only pictures for the five labels' (Schneider and Hacker 1973, 14). Participants interpreted the term 'man' as specific and selected images accordingly.

Janice Moulton, George M. Robinson and Cherin Elias's 1978 study 'Sex Bias in Language Use: "Neutral" Pronouns That Aren't' extended this investigation to the use of pronouns. Participants were asked to create a story on the basis of a given pronoun, and the authors found that 'when the pronoun *his* was used, 35% of the story characters were female; for *their*, 46% were female; and for *his or her*, 56% were female' (Moulton et al. 1978, 1034, emphasis in original). This indicates that pronouns equally influence interpretation. Furthermore, the choice of 'he' appears to skew interpretation toward male. Moulton et al. consider this bias to be a form of *'parasitic reference'* (Moulton et al. 1978, 1035, emphasis in original), '[t]o the extent that coming more readily to mind confers an advantage, females are disadvantaged when they are part of a population referred to by a parasitic "neutral" term' (Moulton et al. 1978, 1035). This is further supported by Wendy Martyna's 1980 study 'The Psychology of the Generic Masculine', which asked children and young people to complete sentences with a pronoun of their choice. She reports that '[w]hen the person was presumed male …, *he* was used 96 percent of the time. When the person was presumed female, *she* was used 87 percent of the time' (Martyna 1980, 71, emphasis in original). Martyna concludes, '[t]he pronoun was picked to match the gender of image received, and thus seems to be a gender-specific rather than a generic term' (Martyna 1980, 72).

Janet Shibley Hyde's 1984 study 'Children's Understanding of Sexist Language' further investigated how children perceive the generic use of the pronoun 'he'. Participants were asked to create a story based on a sentence containing 'he', 'he or she' or 'they', with the following results: '[w]hen the pronoun was "he" or "his," overall 12% of the stories were about females; when it was "they" or "their," 18% were female, and when the pronoun was "his" or "her" ("he" or "she"), 42% of the stories were about females' (Hyde 1984, 700). Mykol C. Hamilton's 1988 'Using Masculine Generics: Does Generic *He* Increase Male Bias in the User's Imagery?' supports Hyde's results. Participants were asked to complete sentences with either the 'traditional, formal; *he*' or 'unbiased' pronouns (Hamilton 1988, 788, emphasis in original), and prompted to reflect on who they imagined. The results showed that 'across subject sex and dependent measures, subjects in the unbiased condition displayed less male bias than did subjects in the masculine generic condition' (Hamilton 1988, 793). Further, 'male subjects display[ed] more male bias ... than female subjects' (Hamilton 1988, 793). Again, male generics seem to evoke male-as-norm, and especially for male participants.

Two studies conducted in the 1990s, John Gastil's 'Generic Pronouns and Sexist Language: The Oxymoronic Character of Masculine Generics' and Sik Hung Ng's 'Androcentric Coding of *Man* and *His* in Memory by Language Users', provide further evidence. Gastil investigated what image comes to mind when reading various pronouns in general sentences – the author found that '*he* is the least generic pronoun of the three considered' (Gastil 1990, 638, emphasis in original). Ng evaluated the link between male generic terms and male bias, with results showing that '*[m]an* and *his* were found to be coded in memory primarily in the masculine linguistic category. Their membership in the feminine linguistic category was marginal' (Ng 1990, 462, emphasis in original). Allen R. McConnell and Russell H. Fazio's 1996 study 'Women as Men and People: Effects of Gender-Marked Language' adds to this by investigating whether the use of 'a man-suffix, a no-suffix, or a person-suffix occupation title' evoked a certain type of person (McConnell and Fazio 1996, 1005). The authors also explored whether the presumed sex/gender of the referent matched certain characteristics. McConnell and Fazio found that 'man-suffix titles result in assessments consistent with masculine stereotypes (and less consistent with feminine stereotypes) and person-suffix titles result in assessments consistent with feminine stereotypes' (McConnell and Fazio 1996, 1008). The use of male generic terms therefore evokes a certain sex/gender alongside expected behaviours, which maintains male-as-norm on two levels: biologically and socially.

This double bias is explored by Marise Ph. Born and Toon W. Taris in their 2010 study 'The Impact of the Wording of Employment Advertisements on Students' Inclination to Apply for a Job'.[2] Neutral job titles were matched with 'gender-specific' descriptions, and participants asked to reflect on their level of interest. The results showed that 'women were less inclined to apply if a masculine profile ... rather than a feminine profile was given' (Born and Taris 2010, 495). However, '[f]or men, the inclination to apply did not depend on whether a masculine or a feminine profile was presented' (Born and Taris 2010, 495). Furthermore, the authors found that '[w]omen were sensitive to the gender-typicality as well as the presentation form of these requirements, whereas men were indifferent' (Born and Taris 2010, 497). Born and Taris summarise that '[w]omen are possibly substantially more aware of their own gender than men ... This phenomenon is generally recognizable in minority group members, who are more aware of their lower status than majority group members' (Born and Taris 2010, 497).

Jane G. Stout and Nilanjana Dasgupta's 2011 study 'When *He* Doesn't Mean *You*: Gender-Exclusive Language as Ostracism' built on these results by 'examin[ing] the theorized link between linguistic bias and group-based ostracism' (Stout and Dasgupta 2011, 759). Respondents were asked how they perceived job descriptions formulated in 'masculine gender-exclusive terms', 'gender-inclusive terms' or 'gender-neutral terms' (Stout and Dasgupta 2011, 759). The results showed that 'participants in the gender-exclusive condition perceived the description to be more sexist' and 'women expected to feel more ostracized in the work environment' (Stout and Dasgupta 2011, 760). Additionally, 'women in the gender-exclusion condition reported significantly less motivation to pursue the job' and 'less identification with the job' (Stout and Dasgupta 2011, 761). The use of exclusive language, such as generic 'he', seems to indicate to potential female applicants that the job is not for them. On the other hand, 'men reported being more motivated after reading gender-exclusive language' (Stout and Dasgupta 2011, 761), the authors report. In conclusion, they state that '[a]lthough the language objectively seems passive and unintentional, our work suggests that it is experienced by women as rejection. ... linguistic cues can subtly inform women that their group does not belong in the given situation' (Stout and Dasgupta 2011, 766).

Caleb Everett confirmed the need for linguistic visibility further in his 2011 study 'Gender, Pronouns and Thought: The Ligature Between Epicene Pronouns and a More Neutral Gender Perception'. Comparing the impact of exclusive and neutral language use, he located androcentric bias in male participants, in particular. Karitiâna speakers, who employ epicene pronouns, and English speakers were asked to provide a name for a neutral visual stimulus, with the results showing that 'for each language, male respondents tended to use fewer female names than female respondents' (Everett 2011, 146). This might be because of each sex/gender selecting names in correspondence with their group; however, 'Karitiâna speakers['] ... construal of the figures, at least as reflected in a naming task following a clause-length description, is markedly less androcentric than the construal evinced by English speakers' (Everett 2011, 147). The author concludes that 'it appears that English speakers may have a more androcentric construal of certain gender-neutral stimuli than speakers of languages with epicene pronouns' (Everett 2011, 149), providing additional evidence for the impact of language on imagination. Chiara Reali, Yulia Esaulova, Anton Öttl, and Lisa von Stockhausen's 2015 study 'Role Descriptions Induce Gender Mismatch Effects in Eye Movements during Reading' provides a valuable illustration of the effect of linguistic change. Participants were asked to read sentences containing a job description and a linked pronoun, and the authors found that 'gender mismatch was reliable only for the female condition, which produced an impairment in the sentence processing when followed by a masculine pronoun' (Reali et al. 2015, 8). It seems the increasing linguistic visibility of women – as in pairings of traditionally male occupations with the female pronoun – is having an impact on respondents. While groupings such as 'doctor, she' might be more familiar today, 'nurse, he', on the other hand, continues to jar readers' processing abilities. This is confirmed by a follow-up questionnaire in which participants stated that '[they] found it particularly difficult to associate the representation of a male referent to a female occupation' (Reali et al. 2015, 8) – perhaps owing to the perceived devaluation of 'man' by a 'female' term. To challenge stereotypes, linguistic visibility is therefore crucial for both sexes/genders, even more so for women who continue to be under-represented.

Linguistic background: German

Trömel-Plötz and Pusch

Senta Trömel-Plötz obtained her PhD in the United States and was strongly influenced by the problematisation of women's and men's linguistic representation. Her 1978 essay 'Linguistik und Frauensprache' transferred the feminist critique of language to the German-language context. Similar to Lakoff and Spender, Trömel-Plötz believes that the societal power structure is reflected linguistically: '[e]s ist nur plausibel, daß eine weitreichende gesellschaftliche Diskriminierung sich auch sprachlich niederschlägt' (Trömel-Plötz 1978, 50) [it is only plausible that extensive social discrimination is also represented linguistically]. Furthermore, she considers this linguistic reflection of society an act of discrimination in itself: '[d]ie Diskriminierung besteht gerade sehr oft darin, wie eine Frau angeredet oder nicht angeredet wird' (Trömel-Plötz 1978, 50) [discrimination manifests itself very often in the way women are addressed or not addressed]. In effect, like Lakoff and Spender, the author proposes that language both mirrors society – with men as the privileged or 'favoured' group – and puts women at a disadvantage.

However, German, owing to its grammatical structure, employs additional means to communicate the disparate treatment of the sexes/genders. It is not only social gender that leads to assumptions in the German language, but grammar also. As a result, nouns employed to represent women and men, such as 'der Zuhörer, er' [the listener (masc.), he], Trömel-Plötz argues, are both grammatically and conceptually male.

As 'male' is considered generic, particular adaptations are necessary to evoke 'female'. So while the English, 'the listener, he', can be adjusted to 'the listener, she' via a shift in pronoun, 'der Zuhörer, er', as Trömel-Plötz explains, has to be extended to 'die Zuhörerin, sie' (Trömel-Plötz 1978, 51–2) [the listener (fem.), she]. As the suffix '-in' highlights, any modification essentially implies a deviation from the norm, with the author concluding that 'das maskuline grammatische Geschlecht und der Mann als Referent [sind] die Norm … und die femininen Formen mit der Frau als Referent die Abweichung. Der Mann dominiert auch in der Sprache' (Trömel-Plötz 1978, 56) [the masculine grammatical gender and man as the referent are the norm … and the feminine forms with woman as the referent the deviation. Man also dominates in language]. And this hierarchy extends to innovations; while linguistic deviation is the norm for women, male terms are rarely linked to a female original. As the author shows, a possible 'Kindergärtnerin – *Kindergärtner' [nursery teacher (fem.) – nursery teacher (masc.)] is reconfigured entirely: '*Erzieher*' [nursery teacher (masc.)], with 'Krankenschwester – *Krankenbruder' [nurse (fem.) – nurse (masc.)]: '*Krankenpfleger*' [nurse (masc.)] another example (Trömel-Plötz 1978, 56, emphasis in original). Trömel-Plötz comments: '[h]eute reflektiert unsere Sprache und unser Sprechen die Ungleichheit zwischen Frauen und Männern in unserer Gesellschaft' (1978, 63–4) [our language and speech today reflect the social disparity between women and men]. This disparity is understood to be part of wider social injustice: 'Sprechen … [ist] ein Großteil unseres Handelns' (Trömel-Plötz 1978, 64) [speech is a major component of our action]. Consequently, Trömel-Plötz, in line with Spender, believes that linguistic revision is key to social change.

This position was controversial, and as it was published in *Linguistische Berichte*, a prominent journal, it received considerable attention. For instance, Hartwig Kalverkämper, in his 1979 response to Trömel-Plötz, opposes her argument per se. In the opening to his essay 'Die Frauen und die Sprache', he appeals to 'Wissenschaft' [science] to underpin his argument: '[d]abei geht es mir nicht darum … mich an dem plakativen Geschlechterstreit und Rollenkampf direkt zu beteiligen …; es geht mir vielmehr darum, die linguistische Wissenschaftsposition, die methodologischen Implikationen des Beitrags unter die Lupe zu nehmen' (Kalverkämper 1979, 56) [I am not interested in participating in the blatant battle of the sexes; I am concerned with analysing the linguistic and scientific position, and the methodological implications of [Trömel-Plötz's] contribution]. Kalverkämper aligns his critique with linguistics as a science – which, he believes, is everything Trömel-Plötz's approach is not. First, he argues that semantics is 'logisch inspiriert' (Kalverkämper 1979, 58) [inspired by logic] while Trömel-Plötz's methodology shows 'Verlorenheit der Gedankengänge' (Kalverkämper 1979, 60) [incoherent trains of thought]. Secondly, Kalverkämper '[geht] die Problemlage, ein sprachliches Phänomen, linguistisch an' (Kalverkämper 1979, 65) [approaches the issue, a linguistic phenomenon, linguistically] while Trömel-Plötz's approach is 'unlinguistisch' (Kalverkämper 1979, 60) [unlinguistic]. And finally, the author shows 'Verantwortung vor der Wissenschaft' (Kalverkämper 1979, 60) [responsibility before science] whereas Trömel-Plötz's work is 'unwissenschaftlich' (Kalverkämper 1979, 67) [unscientific]. The core of his opposition relates to Trömel-Plötz's linking of grammar and sex/gender. According to the author, grammatical gender is simply a linguistic feature and therefore entirely unrelated to reality. He explains the unmarked function of male generic terms as follows: 'für solche Fälle der Ausblendung spezieller Merkmale in der Textverwendung sieht das Sprachsystem die Neutralisation vor' [for such cases of disregarding particular features in texts the linguistic system employs neutralisation] and elaborates that neutralisation erases sex/gender 'um die Komplexität der Welt sprachlich zu reduzieren und somit ökonomisches Kommunizieren zu ermöglichen' (Kalverkämper 1979, 58) [to linguistically reduce the complexity of the world and thereby enable efficient communication]. Trömel-Plötz's error, Kalverkämper explains, is that she 'vermischt die außersprachliche Kategorie "Sexus" mit der sprachlichen Kategorie "Genus", indem sie von Gegebenheiten beim Genus auf Gegebenheiten des Sexus schließt' (Kalverkämper 1979, 60) [confuses the extralingusitic category 'sex' with the linguistic category 'gender' by assuming that conditions of gender are linked to conditions of sex]. Consequently, to the author's mind, her work is unlinguistic.

However, Kalverkämper introduces a caveat to his argument: '[d]as soll allerdings nicht kategorisch besagen, daß die Sprachgemeinschaften in Einzelfällen nicht doch eine Beziehung zwischen Genus und Sexus, zwischen Sexus und Genus erstellten' (Kalverkämper 1979, 60) [this does not mean that speech communities have not created a link between grammatical gender and sex, between sex and grammatical gender in certain individual cases]. In effect, grammar and sex/

gender can be interrelated, but only in certain instances such as 'der Vater, er' [the father, he] or 'die Mutter, sie' [the mother, she]. That is, grammar and sex/gender are essentially separate entities in the main. However, as Kalverkämper's argument progresses this seems not strictly the case either. According to the author, 'Genus' and 'Sexus' correspond in other instances as well: '[d]ort, wo eine Spezifizierung, Differenzierung, schärfere Genauigkeit zur Darstellung der außersprachlichen Wirklichkeit vonnöten ist …, wird eben auch unterschieden, meist mit Hilfe der Determination durch Kontext und/oder Situation' (Kalverkämper 1979, 60) [where a specification, differentiation, stronger accuracy is needed to represent the extralinguistic reality …, it is distinguished, predominantly with the help of determining the context and/or situation]. The sex/gender of 'Zuhörer', for example, would be revealed via context. If the context is lacking in detail, terms are to be interpreted as 'male' first and foremost. The author explains in reference to job titles: '[e]rst in einer Zeit, in der Frauen in öffentliche Stellen, in die verschiedensten Berufssparten drängen, wird man sich der Notwendigkeit bewußt, für die neuen Inhaberinnen dieser Stellen neue Berufsbezeichnungen zu suchen' (Kalverkämper 1979, 61) [only once women enter the public sector, and diverse lines of employment, will speakers realise the necessity to find new job titles for the holders of these roles]. In extension, this rule could be applied more widely in a social context that favours 'male', confirming Trömel-Plötz's argument. Therefore, women need to become linguistically visible to counteract this underlying premise.

Kalverkämper's response inspired Luise F. Pusch to counter. In her 1979 essay 'Der Mensch ist ein Gewohnheitstier, doch weiter kommt man ohne ihr', she contends that 'TRÖMEL-PLÖTZ "verwechselt" nicht Sexus und Genus, sondern sie analysiert gezielt die Beziehungen zwischen der grammatischen Kategorie Genus und dem Sexus der Referent/inn/en' (Pusch 1979, 96, emphasis in original) [TRÖMEL-PLÖTZ does not 'confuse' sex and grammatical gender but analyses the relationship between the grammatical category gender and the sex of the referent]. Indeed, Pusch believes Kalverkämper misunderstood Trömel-Plötz to begin with, since '[e]s geht … eindeutig um ein referenzsemantisches Problem, um die Frage nämlich, ob Aussagen mit Personenbezeichnungen *aller* Art …, *tatsächlich* in der postulierten Weise funktionieren' (Pusch 1979, 94, emphasis in original) [it is clearly a reference-semantic issue, the question namely, whether statements including referents of *all* kinds …, *actually* function in the postulated manner]. To Kalverkämper's argument that representing women and men equally is 'cumbersome' and 'unwieldy'

Pusch responds as follows: '[e]s geht überhaupt nicht um sprachliche "Ökonomie" oder "Schwerfälligkeit", sondern um die Aufrechterhaltung der überkommenen sozialen Klassifizierungen, die in den Anrede- und Bezeichnungsasymmetrien ihren sprachlichen Niederschlag finden' (Pusch 1979, 97) [it is not about linguistic 'economy' or 'clumsiness' at all, but about the maintenance of social classifications, which are reflected in asymmetrical titling and referencing conventions].

While Kalverkämper's position remains powerful, at the time the debate was shaped by Trömel-Plötz and Pusch. Together with Ingrid Guentherodt and Marlis Hellinger they edited a special edition of *Linguistische Berichte* that laid down the cornerstones of the German feminist critique of language. It succinctly sets out the key points:

> Sprache ist sexistisch, wenn sie Frauen und ihre Leistungen ignoriert, wenn sie Frauen nur in Abhängigkeit von und Unterordnung zu Männern beschreibt, wenn sie Frauen nur in stereotypen Rollen zeigt und ihnen so über das Stereotyp hinausgehende Interessen und Fähigkeiten abspricht, und wenn sie Frauen durch herablassende Sprache demütigt und lächerlich macht. (Guentherodt et al. 1980, 15)

> [Language is sexist when it ignores women and their achievements, when it only represents women as dependent on or inferior to men, when it only shows women in stereotypical roles and thereby denies them other interests and capabilities, and when it humiliates and ridicules women through condescending language.]

This understanding has inspired a wealth of research into the representation of women and men in German, which continues to this day.

Empirical evidence

Josef Klein's 1988 study 'Benachteiligung der Frau im generischen Maskulinum – eine feministische Schimäre oder psycholinguistische Realität?' is one early German study to evaluate the link between language and perception. Klein investigated whether there was empirical evidence for Trömel-Plötz's or Kalverkämper's position by presenting participants with a male generic term, 'der Einwohner' [the inhabitant (masc.)], and asking them to select the most suitable referent. The results showed that '[v]on der Gesamtgruppe werden 69 % der Lücken durch Nennung eines männlichen Vornamens oder der Anredeform

"Herr" und nur 20 % durch Nennung einer entsprechenden weiblichen Form ausgefüllt' (Klein 1988, 315) [participants chose a male first name or the title 'Mr' 69% of the time, and the female equivalent only 20% of the time]. In a follow-up study the author used forms to allow for women's linguistic visibility. Nevertheless, Klein again found that:

> [O]bwohl die grammatische Struktur der feminin/maskulinen Doppelform die Testpersonen geradezu aufdringlich darauf stößt, daß der jeweiligen Personengruppe Frauen in gleichem Maße wie Männer angehören, bleibt auch hier das Übergewicht männlicher Geschlechtsspezifizierung und damit eine deutliche Prädominanz der Assoziation 'Mann'. (Klein 1988, 316)

> [Even though the participants are reminded explicitly by the grammatical structure of the feminine/masculine dual-form that women are equally part of the group as men, the sex specification 'male' and the association 'man' remain distinctly predominant.]

Consequently, the premise male-as-norm seems to impact on participants' ability to imagine female 'inhabitants' in both instances. However, '[d]as generische Maskulinum hat allerdings eine deutliche Verstärkerwirkung. Bei seiner Verwendung liegt der Vorsprung männlicher Geschlechtsspezifizierung … im Durchschnitt um 18 % höher' (Klein 1988, 319) [male generic terms increase the sex specification 'male'. If these terms are used, male specification increases on average by 18%], according to Klein. '[Die] primäre … Assoziation "Mann"' (Klein 1988, 319) [the primary association 'man'] might be evoked by both male generic and forms, but seems associated with male generics in particular.

Lisa Irmen and Astrid Köhncke's 1996 study 'Zur Psychologie des "generischen" Maskulinums' supports Klein's findings.[3] The authors presented participants with sentences in which a key term was underlined, and asked them to decide whether the term corresponded with a certain category. The results showed that '[d]er Itemtyp GM-F [generisches Maskulinum-Frau] wurde in der Regel mit "nein" beantwortet' (Irmen and Köhncke 1996, 159) [the correspondence of a male generic term with women as category was generally answered by 'no']. A second group of respondents was presented with a highlighted term as above, this time followed by an image. The authors found that: '[d]ie verhältnismäßig langen Zeiten für die Bestätigung der Frauen-Bilder nach einem "generischen" Maskulinum sprechen für den maskulinen Bias dieses Personenbezeichnungstyps' (Irmen and Köhncke 1996, 163) [the relatively long confirmation times for female images after a male 'generic' term indicate a male bias of this type of referent]. Karin M. Frank-Cyrus and Margot Dietrich's 1997 'Sprachliche Gleichbehandlung von Frauen und Männern in Gesetzestexten: Eine Meinungsumfrage der Gesellschaft für deutsche Sprache' provides further evidence. The authors investigated how male generics, neutral terms and forms are perceived by respondents – with the results that '88 % der Antwortenden finden Frauen beim Gebrauch generischer Maskulina ungenügend berücksichtigt ... 60 % halten sie sogar für überhaupt nicht berücksichtigt' (Frank-Cyrus and Dietrich 1997, 62) [88% of the respondents thought women were insufficiently addressed when male generic terms were used ... 60% thought they were not addressed at all]. A comparison with the other two versions is telling: '44 % der Antwortenden [haben] die Berücksichtigung von Frauen in der geschlechtsneutralen Fassung positiv bewertet' (Frank-Cyrus and Dietrich 1997, 63–4) [44% of respondents rated the consideration of women as positive in the neutral version], while forms resulted in '96 % der Antwortenden [bewerteten] die Berücksichtigung von Frauen positiv' (Frank-Cyrus and Dietrich 1997, 64) [96% of respondents rated the consideration of women as positive].

Friederike Braun, Anja Gottburgsen, Sabine Sczesny and Dagmar Stahlberg's 1998 study 'Können *Geophysiker* Frauen sein? Generische Personenbezeichnungen im Deutschen' adds to this by assessing how male generic, neutral and forms are perceived in a stereotypical context. The authors found that 'in der Bedingung Beidnennung ... wurde ein signifikant höherer Frauenanteil geschätzt als in der Bedingung neutrale Sprachform' (Braun et al. 1998, 273) [in the condition 'form' ... a significantly higher proportion of women was estimated than in the neutral condition]. In effect, forms not only triggered a higher estimation of women in female-specific contexts, '[d]er Wert in der Beidnennungsbedingung überstieg tendenziell auch den der maskulinen Sprachform' (Braun et al. 1998, 273) [the number in the condition 'form' generally exceeded that of the male generic condition]. A follow-up study provided more evidence, with results showing that '[i]n der Beidnennung ... wurde ein signifikant höherer Frauenanteil geschätzt als in der neutralen Sprachform ... und der maskulinen' (Braun et al. 1998, 277) [in the condition 'form' ... a significantly higher percentage of women was estimated than in the neutral condition ... and the male condition]. Braun et al. summarise as follows: 'das generische Maskulinum [evozierte] Schätzungen von 17 % bis 65 %. Die Neutralform erreichte als niedrigsten Wert 23 % und als höchsten 53 %. Bei Beidnennung lagen die Schätzungen zwischen 27 % und

74 %' (Braun et al. 1998, 280) [male generic terms evoked estimations of 17% to 65%. The lowest percentage for neutral terms was 23% and the highest 53%. For the condition 'form', estimations ranged between 27% and 74%]. Being linguistically visible seems to result in higher conceptual availability.

Klaus Rothermund's 1998 study 'Automatische geschlechtsspezifische Assoziationen beim Lesen von Texten mit geschlechtseindeutigen und generisch maskulinen Text-Subjekten' extends the empirical investigation into language and imagination. Assessing the time required to associate a female or male subject with a male generic term, the author found that '[f]ür die Singular-Formen des GM [generischen Maskulinums] findet sich eine signifikante Interaktion von *GM* und *Testphrasentyp* ..., die darauf zurückgeht, daß das GM im Singular hauptsächlich männliche Assoziationen auslöst' (Rothermund 1998, 190, emphasis in original) [for singular forms of male generic terms, male generics and test phrases show a significant interaction ..., which is due to singular male generic terms evoking predominantly male associations]. However, Rothermund reflects that this association is evoked only when singular forms are employed; the plural seems to lessen male connotations. To explore this further, Rothermund conducted a second study evaluating the association time for singular/plural male generic terms, with results showing that '[a]uf Beschreibungen, die das GM im Singular enthielten, wurden verstärkt männliche Assoziationen gebildet; für die im Plural dargebotenen GM-Phrasen fand sich ein Überhang weiblicher Assoziationen' (Rothermund 1998, 194) [for descriptions in singular male generic terms, male associations were more strongly evoked; for plural male generic phrases a predominance of female associations were found]. Consequently, participants seem to interpret a referent's sex/gender on the basis of grammatical gender. As the author confirms, '[m]öglicherweise geht das Umkippen ... zu einer weiblichen Repräsentation in der Pluralform auf die begleitend eingesetzten Artikel und Pronomen zurück' (Rothermund 1998, 195) [the shift to a female representation in the plural form might be linked to the corresponding article and pronoun].

Dagmar Stahlberg, Sabine Sczesny and Friederike Braun's 2001 study 'Name Your Favourite Musician: Effects of Masculine Generics and of their Alternatives in German' evaluated the perception of male generic, neutral and split forms via a questionnaire on 'favorite heroes in novels, real life, and history and their favorite painters, musicians, and athletes' (Stahlberg et al. 2001, 466). The authors found that 'masculine generics ... triggered fewer female responses than alternative formulations'; furthermore, 'female participants mention[ed] more women than male participants' (Stahlberg et al. 2001, 466). This reminds us of empirical results for the English language context: group membership, as delineated by sex/gender, has additional consequences for the perception of women – with men more likely to imagine other men. In a follow-up experiment Stahlberg et al. introduced 'Binnen-I' forms, such as 'PolitikerInnen', to evaluate their impact on speakers' perceptions. The results showed that '[m]asculine generics triggered the fewest female responses, whereas feminine-masculine word pairs and especially capital *I* forms made participants respond with more female names' (Stahlberg et al. 2001, 467, emphasis in original). The more explicitly women are referred to, the easier speakers seem to be able to imagine them.

Ute Gabriel and Franziska Mellenberger's 2004 study 'Exchanging the Generic Masculine for Gender-Balanced Forms – The Impact of Context Valence' repeated Stahlberg et al.'s experiments with an adapted questionnaire. Focusing on the noticeable difference in response between women and men, the authors found that 'female personalities were named more often by female participants ... than by male participants' (Gabriel and Mellenberger 2004, 275). Additionally, the impact of the linguistic version, that is male generic, neutral or split/pair, was significant as 'more female personalities were named if the gender-balanced form was used than if the masculine was used as a generic' (Gabriel and Mellenberger 2004, 276). This was particularly the case for male participants 'who chose almost no female personalities when the masculine-generic was used' (Gabriel and Mellenberger 2004, 276). Female respondents, on the other hand, similar to their English language counterparts, were more likely to name other women, especially if women were mentioned explicitly. However, group membership is not only signalled by terms, as highlighted by Lisa Irmen and Nadja Roßberg's 2004 study 'Gender Markedness of Language: The Impact of Grammatical and Nonlinguistic Information on the Mental Representation of Person Information'. Evaluating the influence of stereotypes, the authors found that '[f]or the stereotypically masculine nouns, reading times for feminine, masculine, and neutral continuations differ significantly between tasks: neutral as well as masculine continuations speed up compared to feminine continuations' (Irmen and Roßberg 2004, 283). It seems readers save cognitive time when perceiving a match between male grammatical gender and stereotype but lose time when not. In short, the link between grammar, sex/gender and stereotype puts women at a conceptual disadvantage. A follow-up experiment extended the above by using split terms, for example 'Telefonisten und Telefonistinnen' [operators], and unmarked forms, for example 'Alleinerziehende' [single parents]. The results show that 'masculine continuations are read faster than feminine continuations … compared to feminine and neutral continuations, reading times for masculine continuations speed up' (Irmen and Roßberg 2004, 290). While the norm might still be male, '[r]esults for the splitting forms confirm the assumption that an unambiguous gender-balanced grammatical input should prepare the reader equally well for all gender-related and unrelated continuations irrespective of the thematic subject's stereotypical gender' (Irmen and Roßberg 2004, 291). In summary, the authors state, '[t]he assumption that formal grammatical gender generally does not contribute biological gender information to mentally represented person information is not confirmed by the results' (Irmen and Roßberg 2004, 296).

Alan Garnham, Ute Gabriel, Oriane Sarrasin, Pascal Gygax and Jane Oakhill's 2012 study 'Gender Representation in Different Languages and Grammatical Marking on Pronouns: When Beauticians, Musicians, and Mechanics Remain Men' provides further support. Investigating the impact of stereotype and plural pronouns, the authors found that whereas 'in English, the mental representation of gender when reading role names is solely based on the stereotypicality of those role names' (Garnham et al. 2012, 493), the results for German show that 'the presence of a pronoun morphologically identical to the feminine singular ['sie'] seems to have facilitated positive answers to continuation sentences about women' (Garnham et al. 2012, 494). The authors conclude 'combining grammatical cues that do not match … seems to distract readers from forming a specifically male gender representation' (Garnham et al. 2012, 498). Again, grammatical gender is not understood neutrally; furthermore, it can be employed strategically to evoke women. Dries Vervecken, Bettina Hannover and Ilka Wolter's 2013 study 'Changing (S)expectations: How Gender Fair Job Descriptions Impact Children's Perceptions and Interest Regarding Traditionally Male Occupations' investigated the impact of male generic terms and its alternatives on children's imagination. Reminiscent of Hyde's 1984 English-language study, participants were presented with job titles in male generic or pair form and asked to imagine a film character. As Vervecken et al. report, '[i]n the pair form condition, children – regardless of their sex … – assigned more female first names to movie characters acting in stereotypically male domains than in the generic masculine form condition' (Vervecken et al. 2013, 212). Furthermore, '[g]irls generally assigned more female names than did boys' (Vervecken et al. 2013, 212), again highlighting the impact of group membership. In the follow-up experiment the authors additionally asked: *'Who can succeed in this occupation?'* (Vervecken et al. 2013, 213, emphasis in original), with the following results: '[w]hen stereotypically male occupations had been presented in pair forms, children of both genders perceived women's and men's success in a more balanced way than if occupational titles had been presented in generic masculine forms' (Vervecken et al. 2013, 213). A third study asked children to rate *'How much would you like to be…?'* (Vervecken et al. 2013, 214, emphasis in original); the authors found that 'girls indicated more interest in male occupations presented in pair forms rather than generic masculine forms …, boys' interest remained unaffected by the linguistic form' (Vervecken et al. 2013, 215). The results show that girls benefit from inclusive language use, and furthermore, that boys are not impaired by it.

Lisa Kristina Horvath and Sabine Sczesny's 2015 study 'Reducing Women's Lack of Fit with Leadership Positions? Effects of the Wording of Job Advertisements' backs these findings from the perspective of work. Asking participants to assess a fictional applicant's aptitude for a low and high status position, based on advertisements for a leadership position, the authors found that '[f]emale applicants were perceived as significantly less suitable for the high-status position than male applicants when the masculine form was used …; this difference was marginal for the masculine form with (m/f)' (Horvath and Sczesny 2015, 322). On the other hand, '[i]n the word pair condition, female and male applicants were rated as similarly suitable' (Horvath and Sczesny 2015, 322). Not only is self-efficacy at stake, but also hiring decisions could be informed by whether or not occupations are phrased in inclusive language. Horvath and Sczesny conclude that 'women's perceived fit with top management apparently increased when the position was advertised with a word pair in a gender-balanced or symmetrical way, compared with the masculine form (whether combined with (m/f) or not)' (Horvath and Sczesny 2015, 323). The study once more confirms what Pusch already contended in 1980: '[f]ür das Deutsche gilt … die Strategie: Beide Geschlechter benennen – nicht nur das männliche' (Pusch 1980, 73) [for the German language the strategy applies: Name both sexes/genders not only the male].

Current usage and attitudes

Official language use has changed profoundly over the past 50 years. Editorial style guides promote inclusive language, women no longer need to declare their marital status via their title and legislation drafting guidelines advocate unbiased terms. Even national anthems are adapted to allow for the conception of both sexes/genders: revised in 2012, the first verse of the Austrian anthem now states, 'Heimat großer Töchter und Söhne' (Bundeskanzleramt Österreich 2012, n. pag.) [Home of great daughters and sons]. Where previously Austria was referred to as 'Heimat bist du großer Söhne' [Home are you of great sons], the 'Bundeshymne' includes 'Töchter' today. However, none of these changes was swift and without opposition. In fact, as I show below, debates about the value and legitimacy of linguistic change continue to this day.

In early 2019, the city of Hannover issued a leaflet on gender-fair language use to ensure that all government communications, such as letters, forms and legal documents, are inclusive. While the guidance is not without its problems – for example, the advocated use of 'Familie Schulz' instead of 'Frau und Herr Schulz (mit Kindern auf Grund von Einschulung o.ä.)' (Landeshauptstadt Hannover 2019, 1) [Family Schulz; Mrs and Mr Schulz (with children because of school enrolment or similar)] subsumes women into the family unit led by Herr Schulz. However, the *Verein Deutsche Sprache* is not concerned with how to best formulate inclusively. In fact, it illustrates a fundamental opposition to linguistic change. The authors call for a 'Widerstand' [resistance] against the 'zerstörerischen Eingriffe in die deutsche Sprache' (Maron et al. 2019, n. pag.) [destructive interventions into the German language]. While empirical studies have shown that language and imagination are indeed linked, the authors insist that '[d]ie sogenannte gendergerechte Sprache beruht ... auf einem Generalirrtum' (Maron et al. 2019, n. pag.) [the so-called gender-fair language is based ... on a fallacy], reminding of Kalverkämper's position some 40 years earlier. According to the *Verein Deutsche Sprache*, grammar and sex/gender are separate entities: the 'zerstörerischen Eingriffe' therefore do not lead to social change but to 'lächerliche ... Sprachgebilde' (Maron et al. 2019, n. pag.) [ridiculous constructions] and 'Verzerrungen der Sprache' (Maron et al. 2019, n. pag.) [contortions of language]. Inclusive language, so the position of the authors, is untenable on both linguistic and social grounds.

In contrast, the *Gesellschaft für deutsche Sprache* (GfdS) argues that language does matter. 'Ein wichtiger Aspekt, um die Gleichbehandlung sicherzustellen, ist eine geschlechtergerechte Sprache' (GfdS 2019, n. pag.) [an important aspect to ensure equal treatment is a gender-fair language], the authors state. However, they also have reservations – in this case about the 'Sichtbarmachung des dritten Geschlechts' (GfdS 2019, n. pag.) [visualisation of the third sex/gender]. Gender-fair language needs to fulfil certain criteria; according to the authors, it has to be 'verständlich', 'lesbar', 'vorlesbar', 'grammatisch korrekt' and ensure 'Eindeutigkeit und Rechtssicherheit' (GfdS 2019, n. pag.) [understandable, legible, readable, grammatically correct, and guarantee unambiguousness and legal certainty]. The *Gesellschaft für deutsche Sprache* has reservations about the 'Gendergap (_)' and 'Gendersternchen (*)', in particular, which are considered in need of 'einer gründlicheren Sprachanalyse' (GfdS 2019, n. pag.) [a more thorough linguistic analysis]. Effectively, inclusive language has to comply with 'heute gültigen Regeln' (GfdS 2019, n. pag.) [currently valid rules] to be useful for the speech community.

References to linguistic norms feature also in the English-language context. The discussions around neutral drafting of UK Government bills are an interesting case in point. Since 2007, guidelines advise that 'he' should no longer be employed as an inclusive term for 'he and she' in legislation. Prior to that, as Christopher Williams's 2008 study 'The End of the "Masculine Rule"? Gender-Neutral Legislative Drafting in the United Kingdom and Ireland' shows 'the Capital Allowances Act 2001 contains 48 occurrences of *he* and zero of *she*; the Incomes Tax (Earnings and Pensions) Act 2003 contains 20 occurrences of *he* and zero of *she*' (Williams 2008, 146, emphasis in original). The official explanation, as quoted by Williams, maintained '[i]n principle, we would like to draft using gender-free language. In practice, however, we are uncertain of how easy this will be to achieve without making the law more clumsily expressed, and as such harder to grasp' (Williams 2008, 146), again reminding of Kalverkämper. In the intervening years, inclusive language has become more widespread. Nevertheless, it remains contested, as a 2013 debate in the House of Lords on 'Legislation: Gender-neutral Language' indicates.

In the debate, Lord Scott of Foscote provides several examples of the use of 'they' and its perceived incorrectness. He argues that '[t]he clarity of the language of the protocol is certainly not assisted by the use of grammatically inappropriate plural pronouns coupled with references to a single person' (House of Lords Hansard 2013, n. pag.). While Lord Scott seems concerned with the 'unambiguousness and legal certainty' of language akin to the *Gesellschaft für deutsche Sprache*, he also includes an emotive perspective. He states that '[t]he drafting ... is not only unacceptable and unnecessary but is, I suggest, an insult to the lovely English language' (House of Lords Hansard 2013, n. pag.). Moreover, he argues, '[t]o prostitute the English language in pursuit of some goal of gender equality is, I suggest, unacceptable' (House of Lords Hansard 2013, n. pag.). The English language – 'lovely' and 'prostituted' – seems in need of protection from 'zerstörerische Eingriffe'. Consequently, in line with the *Verein Deutsche Sprache*, he advocates against linguistic change. His viewpoint might not be supported by the House; the final comment by Lord Gardiner of Kimble confirms that 'the Government remain committed to producing high-quality legislation that is clear, accessible and free from ambiguity. We believe that gender-neutral drafting is perfectly compatible with that objective' (House of Lords Hansard 2013, n. pag.). However, opposition persists in official discourse.

The interplay between change and resistance can also be observed in relation to educational materials and job advertisements. Both are significant, as they communicate the possibilities and limitations of each sex/gender in the particular sociocultural context. To assess how women and men are represented in schoolbooks today, Franziska Moser and Bettina Hannover evaluated 18 texts in their 2014 study 'How Gender Fair are German Schoolbooks in the Twenty-First Century? An Analysis of Language and Illustrations in Schoolbooks for Mathematics and German'. In contrast to earlier results, the authors found that 'the proportions of female and male persons were comparably more equal' (Moser and Hannover 2014, 399). However, as Moser and Hannover add, 'in today's books we found males to still be more frequent than females, particularly among adults and in books for mathematics' (Moser and Hannover 2014, 399). A bias toward male-as-norm therefore remains, and continues to shape thinking from a young age. In continuation, job advertisements convey which sex/gender seems most suited to a certain profession. Marek Cieszkowski (Bydgoszcz)'s 2015 study 'Zum geschlechtergerechten Sprachgebrauch am Beispiel deutscher und polnischer Stellenausschreibungen' investigated how inclusively job adverts are worded today. Among 100 descriptions the author identified 'geschlechtergerechte (71 %)', 'geschlechtsspezifische (14 %)' and 'inkonsequente (diskriminierende) ... (15 %)' (Cieszkowski (Bydgoszcz) 2015, 30) [gender-fair (71%), gender-specific (14%) and inconsistent (discriminating) ... (15%)]. While inclusive terminology is certainly predominant, 29% of the descriptions remain exclusive or discriminatory. Equal linguistic representation in both schoolbooks and job advertisements remains an ongoing project.

The premise that linguistic change is 'awkward' and 'hinders communication' might be one factor why some change is slow and opposition remains. To evaluate whether this argument has substance, Christopher Blake and Christoph Klimmt's 2010 study 'Geschlechtergerechte Formulierungen in Nachrichtentexten' assessed 'Lesbarkeit und sprachliche Ästhetik' of inclusive and exclusive terms (Blake and Klimmt 2010, 295) [readability and linguistic aesthetics]. The authors presented participants with a newspaper article worded in 'generisch maskuline[n] Formen', 'Binnen-I-Formen', 'Paarformen' or 'genusneutrale[n] ... Formulierungen' (Blake and Klimmt 2010, 296) [male generic forms, Binnen-I forms, pair forms or neutral wording]. Blake and Klimmt found that '[s]owohl in Relation zur generisch maskulinen Artikelversion als auch bezogen auf den absoluten Indexwert bewerten die Versuchspersonen ... auch die Lesbarkeit der Texte mit alternativen Formen positiv' (Blake and Klimmt 2010, 298) [both in relation to the male generic version and the absolute index value, participants rated ... the readability of texts with alternative forms positively as well]. Furthermore, the authors report, '[h]insichtlich der sprachlichen Ästhetik zeigten sich aus Publikumssicht keine bedeutenden Unterschiede zwischen den verschiedenen Textversionen' (Blake and Klimmt 2010, 298) [in relation to linguistic aesthetics, from the audience's perspective there were no significant differences between the text versions]. Neither understanding nor text style seem impaired by inclusive terminology.

This is supported by Vera Steiger and Lisa Irmen's 2011 study 'Recht verständlich und "gender-fair": Wie sollen Personen in amtlichen Texten bezeichnet werden? Ein Vergleich verschiedener Rezipientengruppen zur Akzeptanz geschlechtergerechter Rechtssprache'. The authors asked '[j]uristische Fachleute', 'ältere Personen ("Generation 60 +")' and 'Personen mit nicht-akademischem Bildungshintergrund' (Steiger and Irmen 2011, 302) [legal experts, older people (generation 60+) and people with a non-academic educational background] to complete gaps in a legal text with their preferred term. The subsequent evaluation showed that '[a]llgemein bevorzugten die Teilnehmenden – und zwar unabhängig davon, ob sie Laien oder Fachleute im Bereich Rechtswissenschaft waren – im Text neutralisierende Formulierungen' (Steiger and Irmen 2011, 314) [the participants generally preferred – and independently of whether they were laypeople or experts in law – neutral wording in the text]. Additionally, Steiger and Irmen found, '[d]as GM [generische Maskulinum] verschlechterte ... die Beurteilung dessen, wie stark Frauen im Text berücksichtigt und ob beide Geschlechter gleichmäßig repräsentiert sind' (Steiger and Irmen 2011, 315) [male generic terms decreased ... the assessment of how well a text represents women and of whether it represents both sexes/genders equally]. In effect, respondents both preferred neutral terminology and considered male generic terms discriminatory; thereby providing further counter-evidence to the argument that linguistic change is necessarily 'clumsy' and 'unnecessary'.

Despite positive perceptions, not only official linguistic practices remain contested, but general language users also often fail to employ more inclusive terms. Elisabeth A. Kuhn and Ute Gabriel investigated potential reasons for the lack of inclusive terms in everyday language in their 2014 study 'Actual and Potential Gender-Fair Language Use: The Role of Language Competence and the Motivation to Use Accurate Language'. The authors asked two groups of native German speakers to complete sentences with 'either a gender-fair or gender-biased personal noun' and reflect 'on their motivation to use accurate language' (Kuhn and Gabriel 2014, 218). The authors found that '[s]pontaneous gender-fair language use was lower for university students than for trainees' (Kuhn and Gabriel 2014, 218), even though '[u]niversity students reported a significantly stronger motivation' (Kuhn and Gabriel 2014, 220). The overall results showed that 'people spontaneously used gender-fair language infrequently' (Kuhn and Gabriel 2014, 220). While a prompt to use inclusive terms in a follow-up study increased usage, the authors conclude that 'the participants in both samples used gender-fair forms in less than 70% of the cases' (Kuhn and Gabriel 2014, 221). In effect, whether prompted or not, respondents continued to predominantly employ exclusive terms.

Sabine Sczesny, Franziska Moser and Wendy Wood's 2015 study 'Beyond Sexist Beliefs: How Do People Decide to Use Gender-Inclusive Language?' explored this further. The authors presented native German speakers with a text on a general subject and asked them to complete blanks with a personal noun. The results showed that '[o]n average, participants used gender-inclusive language forms in about 4 of the 10 texts' (Sczesny et al. 2015, 947). A follow-up assessment brought further insight; the authors found that 'participants were more likely to use gender-inclusive language … when they had used it frequently in the past and thus had formed language-use habits' (Sczesny et al. 2015, 948). Additionally, Sczesny et al. discovered that intention also influenced language use to some extent. To investigate how sexist beliefs, in particular, impact on inclusive language use, Sczesny et al. conducted a second study. Employing the same materials as above, as well as three sexist belief measures, the results showed that '[p]articipants used gender-inclusive language forms in about 4 of the 10 texts on average' (Sczesny et al. 2015, 949). However, 'participants with stronger sexist beliefs had less favorable attitudes toward using gender-inclusive language' (Sczesny et al. 2015, 951). Habit again proved a key motivator to use inclusive terms – consequently, Sczesny et al. recommend that 'successful interventions to increase such language use could focus on simple repetition of non-sexist language terms so that these become established habits' (Sczesny et al. 2015, 952). Furthermore, the authors believe, 'interventions could address people's understanding of the consequences of gender-inclusive language as a means of altering explicit intentions to use it' (Sczesny et al. 2015, 952). A combination of repeated usage and increased awareness could therefore help to implement inclusive language use more widely.

In their 2015 study 'Just Reading? How Gender-Fair Language Triggers Readers' Use of Gender-Fair Forms', Sara Koeser, Elisabeth A. Kuhn and Sabine Sczesny explored the impact of exposure to inclusive terms. The authors asked native German speakers to read a text containing 'gender-fair forms', 'masculine generics' or 'passive voice or omissions' and complete blanks, with the results showing that '[p]articipants used gender-fair forms rarely' (Koeser et al. 2015, 346). However, 'presenting gender-fair forms ... revealed an effective strategy to increase readers' own use of gender-fair language' (Koeser et al. 2015, 346). In a follow-up study, Koeser et al. evaluated whether the 'additional text condition, i.e. gender-fair with raised awareness' might further increase usage (Koeser et al. 2015, 349). The authors asked respondents to follow the same instructions as above. Again, '[p]articipants used gender-fair forms infrequently' (Koeser et al. 2015, 349). However, the results also showed that 'women used significantly more gender-fair forms after reading the gender-fair text (without raised awareness)' (Koeser et al. 2015, 349). Men, on the other hand, 'used more gender-fair forms only after reading the gender-fair text with raised awareness' (Koeser et al. 2015, 350). The authors conclude: 'awareness raising might be a promising strategy to increase their [men's] use of gender-fair language' (Koeser et al. 2015, 350). This supports Sczesny et al.'s hypothesis that increasing awareness of the importance of inclusive language promotes usage, and by men in particular.

The importance of raising awareness is also acknowledged by speakers who employ inclusive language. In the 2016 study 'Bucking the Linguistic Binary: Gender Neutral Language in English, Swedish, French and German', Levi C. R. Hord found that people who identify as non-binary felt that societal acceptance of inclusive language was a major hurdle. As Hord's results showed, 'none claimed that neutral language was widely used in society' (Hord 2016, 21). Respondents reflected that 'getting people to use the gender-neutral language we have in English is difficult and tiring' (Hord 2016, 22), and '[t]he linguistic potential and content is there, society poses the actual problem' (Hord 2016, 24). That is, the wider speech community seems to be reluctant to employ inclusive language and needs to be more firmly convinced. In the following section I present the findings of narrative research to explore how literary texts can help to sensitise readers. My premise is that literary texts that thematise the issue of sex/gender and language can be a useful tool to promote inclusive language use.

Narrative studies

> In reading a novel, any novel, we have to know perfectly well that the whole thing is nonsense, and then, while reading, believe every word of it. Finally, when we're done with it, we may find – if it's a good novel – that we're a bit different from what we were before we read it, that we have been changed a little… (Le Guin 1976, 3–4)

As Ursula K. Le Guin states in the 1976 introduction to *The Left Hand of Darkness*, literature can have a powerful impact on readers. With the help of characters and storylines, literary texts – with perspectival texts the particular focus of this book – introduce readers to unfamiliar viewpoints and environments, or, indeed, present familiar people and places in a new light. And though 'the whole thing is nonsense', as Le Guin reflects, readers willingly immerse themselves in this fictional representation. Moreover, they often find themselves changed by the encounter with a text, by the very act of reading.

The impact of literary texts on readers has been explored by narrative scholars. One of the first cornerstones they propose is that far from being passive recipients, readers are active co-creators of meaning. As Wolfgang Iser argues in his 1978 text *The Act of Reading: A Theory of Aesthetic Response*, literary texts 'induce him[/her – the reader] to participate both in the production and the comprehension of the work's intention' (Iser 1978, 24). James W. Polichak and Richard J. Gerrig agree with this perspective; in their article '"Get Up and Win!" Participatory Responses to Narrative' they define the position of the reader as 'side-participant' (Polichak and Gerrig 2013, 75). The authors explain that 'readers bring a well-used repertory of participatory processes to narrative experiences' (Polichak and Gerrig 2013, 75). That is, readers actively participate in the reading process, and moreover do so from a familiar cognitive perspective. As Polichak and Gerrig suggest, 'readers' participation in narratives arises out of the same basic mental operations and emotional responses evolved for comprehending and responding to conversation' (Polichak and Gerrig 2013, 91). Effectively, the narrative is processed as a dialogue that readers witness and reflect on, and which might prompt them to respond or act.

The concept of literary texts as 'a form of communication' is central to Iser's thinking (Iser 1978, ix). And this communication is understood to be instructive; as the author argues, 'fiction is a means of telling us something about reality' (Iser 1978, 53). By holding up a fictional mirror to social norms and conventions, Iser believes, literary texts 'enable us to see that familiar reality with new eyes' (Iser 1978, 181). However, in contrast to non-fiction this instructive process is not made explicit. As the author suggests, 'unlike philosophies and ideologies, literature ... questions or recodes the signals of external reality in such a way that the reader [her/]himself is to find the motives underlying the questions' (Iser 1978, 74). Tying in with Polichak and Gerrig's understanding of the reader as 'side-participant', this co-constructive relationship with the text, according to Iser, leads to the reader 'participat[ing] in producing the meaning' (Iser 1978, 74). Readers mentally build the narrative worlds, and do so within the context of their own experience and sociocultural environment. This knowledge provides 'a referential background against which the unfamiliar can be conceived and processed' (Iser 1978, 38). As a result, literary texts encourage a conversation between 'what is' and 'what could be'.

With the promotion of inclusive language the prime focus of this book, one question is how readers respond to literary texts that experiment linguistically. Gerrig's reflections on innovative language in literature are here insightful. In his 1993 *Experiencing Narrative Worlds On the Psychological Activities of Reading* he argues that 'the use of such innovations mimics the act of collaboration and draws the readers more strongly into the intimate environs of the narrative world' (Gerrig 1993, 124). In effect, according to the author, literary explorations of linguistic representation support the co-constructive nature of the reading process. Rather than being told why and how to employ alternatives, fiction allows readers to experience linguistic problematisations and proposals. From a neurological perspective, this process tunes into the brain's inherent flexibility. As Paul B. Armstrong argues in his 2013 text *How Literature Plays with the Brain: The Neuroscience of Reading and Art*, '[t]he brain's response to novelty and ambiguity gives it a chance to learn about itself' (Armstrong 2013, 89). Through self-reflection, the author continues, readers notice 'what typically happens beneath our notice when we read, and in doing so we can analyze the workings of our brains' (Armstrong 2013, 90). Consequently, literature 'provides a laboratory in which the brain can experiment with its social skills – testing, challenging, extending, and scrutinizing habitual practices' (Armstrong 2013, 144).

However, the impact of fiction is not restricted to promoting self-reflection. Through the encounter with literary alternatives to the linguistic status quo, shifts in perception might also take place. As Iser argues, 'our past still remains our experience, but … in the course of the reading, these experiences will also change, for the acquisition of experience is not a matter of adding on – it is a restructuring of what we already possess' (Iser 1978, 132). For me, encountering the German translation of Gerd Brantenberg's *Egalias døtre* evokes a particularly strong memory of this impact. At the time of reading I was living in an area in which I did not feel safe. My flat was accessed via a small, dark alleyway and I felt nervous leaving during the day and even more so returning home at night. The world presented in the novel, however, opened a door to a different perspective. In Egalia, I did not have to feel this way; in fact, in Egalia, I, as a woman, had nothing to fear. As a consequence of reading the text I walked the streets differently. Furthermore, I began to feel differently about myself and my place in the world. It was of course 'nonsense' to be feeling this way, but this 'nonsense' had a profound impact nevertheless. The novel allowed me to become immersed in an alternative conception of the sexes/genders, and through this immersion I was able to comprehend the artificiality of women's position. I was able to perceive what is generally considered the norm in a different light.

This capacity of perspectival literary texts to evoke a new understanding is supported by empirical studies. First of all, fiction is processed differently, as Rolf A. Zwaan's study 'Effect of Genre Expectations on Text Comprehension' illustrates. In one experiment, the author presented participants with 'excerpts from news stories' or 'excerpts from literary stories', and asked them to evaluate a subsequent statement (Zwaan 1994, 922). The results showed that '[t]he texts were read significantly slower in the literary condition … than in the news condition' (Zwaan 1994, 924). Moreover, '[t]here were higher scores on the surface and textbase levels in the literary condition' (Zwaan 1994, 924). A follow-up experiment supported these findings. Again, the news texts were read faster than the literary stories, and 'the literary readers devoted extra processing resources to surface-level processes … [and] to the construction of a coherent textbase' (Zwaan 1994, 929). Consequently, the author summarises, 'expectations about the genre of a text influence how readers process and mentally represent texts' (Zwaan 1994, 930). Sonya Dal Cin, Mark P. Zanna and Geoffrey T. Fong agree in 'Narrative Persuasion and Overcoming Resistance' that this difference is due to expectations. While readers cognitively prepare themselves to evaluate the pros and cons of a rhetorical argument, they 'expect to be entertained' when encountering a literary text (Dal Cin et al. 2004, 177). As a result, readers disable their critical evaluation skills in order to tap into what Raymond A. Mar and Keith Oatley term 'simulation' of the novel's characters and events. In 'The Function of Fiction is the Abstraction and Simulation of Social Experience', the authors explain that 'while engaging with such products [films, novels, plays, and TV dramas] we undergo a form of experience not found elsewhere, reacting to represented events as if we were a part of them' (Mar and Oatley 2008, 173). Through this modelling process readers are able to access 'complex social information in a manner that offers personal enactments of experience, rendering it more comprehensible than usual' (Mar and Oatley 2008, 173). Consequently, the authors propose, '[n]arrative fiction ... helps us to understand life in terms of how human intentions bear upon it' (Mar and Oatley 2008, 173); that is, by simulating reality in recognisable terms readers are able to access different motivations and experiences.

This simulation, Mar and Oatley believe, results in a heightened impact of perspectival literary texts. 'Whereas expository representations tell us information', they explain, 'literary narratives show us things by having us experience them first-hand' (Mar and Oatley 2008, 177). Fiction allows readers to 'try out' new perspectives and environments, an experience that in turn encourages empathy and understanding. However, not all narratives have the same effect: readers need to be able to become immersed in the fictional events for the simulation to take place. In short, the story and its characters need to be sufficiently engaging. In 'The Role of Transportation in the Persuasiveness of Public Narratives', Melanie C. Green and Timothy C. Brock refer to this process of immersion as 'transportation'. Based on Gerrig's proposals in *Experiencing Narrative Worlds*, the authors understand 'transportation as a convergent process, where all mental systems and capacities become focused on events occurring in the narrative' (Green and Brock 2000, 701). When transportation occurs, all cognitive functions are concentrated on the simulation of the fictional characters and events. Consequently, 'the reader loses access to some real-world facts in favor of accepting the narrative world' (Green and Brock 2000, 702), as was the case during my reading of the translation of *Egalias døtre*. I felt transported into an entirely different world view while reading. Moreover, this experience has had a long-lasting impact; I have not considered the status quo 'normal' since.

This anecdotal experience is supported by Green and Brock's experiments. In a first study, the authors presented participants with a narrative about the murder of a child by a psychiatric patient.[4] When subsequently asking them to complete several measures, including story-specific beliefs and a transportation questionnaire, the authors found that 'there was a significant effect of transportation on the violence index ... with highly transported participants indicating that violence was more likely' (Green and Brock 2000, 706). Additionally, the results showed that 'highly transported participants reported beliefs more consistent with those implied in the story, indicating that psychiatric patient freedoms should be restricted' (Green and Brock 2000, 706). In effect, the level of transportation was directly linked to story-consistent beliefs. A follow-up experiment confirmed these results further. Participants read the same narrative and once more completed several measures, 'with highly transported readers reporting more story-consistent beliefs; the pattern of results was identical to Experiment 1' (Green and Brock 2000, 711). The authors propose that 'transportation is a mechanism whereby narratives may exert their power to change beliefs. The results are noteworthy in that the belief-change dimensions were not explicitly articulated in the story' (Green and Brock 2000, 718). That is, even if beliefs are merely implied they may be sufficient to alter readers' preconceptions about characters and environments. For example, the narrative did not explicitly state that violence may occur at any time, or that psychiatric patients are potentially dangerous; however, the simulation of these notions resulted in a shift of awareness, at least in highly transported readers.

But what enables readers to become transported? Green investigated possible answers in her study 'Transportation into Narrative Worlds: The Role of Prior Knowledge and Perceived Realism'. She asked participants to read a short story about 'a homosexual man who returns to his college fraternity reunion' (Green 2004, 253). The respondents subsequently completed a series of measures, including belief statements and a transportation scale, with results showing that 'individuals with close friends or family who were homosexual ... were more transported into the story' (Green 2004, 257). Additionally, Green found that '[i]ndividuals who were more transported showed more story-consistent beliefs' (Green 2004, 258). Effectively, familiarity seems to impact on transportation, which, in turn, impacts on the reader's beliefs. However, readers need not necessarily be familiar with a certain character or issue to become transported. As Hans Hoeken and Karin M. Fikkers showed in their study 'Issue-Relevant Thinking and Identification as Mechanisms of Narrative Persuasion', readers are also able to simulate experiences and opinions different from their own. The authors asked participants to read a narrative presenting either a positive or negative attitude toward raised tuition fees. After completing a questionnaire measuring their attitudes, engagement and identification, Hoeken and Fikkers found that it was the perspective given by the protagonist that proved most influential. So, '[e]ven when the protagonist expressed a dissimilar attitude, and the antagonist a similar attitude to that of the participants, participants identified more strongly with the protagonist than with the antagonist' (Hoeken and Fikkers 2014, 93). Consequently, it is the protagonist's perspective with which readers identify and which subsequently shapes understanding.

This potential of narratives to modify preconceptions is particularly significant for disadvantaged social groups. As Adam G. Galinsky and Gordon B. Moskowitz highlight in their study 'Perspective-Taking: Decreasing Stereotype Expression, Stereotype Accessibility, and In-Group Favoritism', being able to put oneself in the place of another enables identification and thereby decreases bias. In one study, the authors showed a photograph of an older person and asked participants to reflect on a typical day in this person's life. One third were given no instructions, one third were asked to repress stereotypical responses and the final third 'were instructed to adopt the perspective of the individual in the photograph' (Galinsky and Moskowitz 2000, 711). The authors found that '[b]oth stereotype suppressors ... and perspective-takers ... wrote less stereotypical essays of the elderly than did participants in the control condition' (Galinsky and Moskowitz 2000, 712). Additionally, '[p]erspective-takers ... expressed more positive evaluations of the target individual' (Galinsky and Moskowitz 2000, 712). A second study confirmed these findings. The authors presented participants with a 'list of 90 traits ... and asked [them] to rate how well each trait described them' (Galinsky and Moskowitz 2000, 715), followed by the same task as in the first experiment. The results showed that '[b]oth stereotype suppressors ... and perspective-takers ... wrote less stereotypical essays of the elderly', and that '[p]erspective-takers expressed more positive evaluations' (Galinsky and Moskowitz 2000, 715). Furthermore, '[p]erspective-takers rated the elderly less stereotypically than did participants in the other two conditions' (Galinsky and Moskowitz 2000, 715).

In a final experiment, the authors investigated whether perspective-taking can also impact on the perceptions of social groups as a whole. Participants were assigned to one of four conditions: one group was asked to imagine 'a day in the life of an underestimator', another to take the perspective of an underestimator, a third to reflect on the similarities between overestimators and underestimators, and the final did not complete the writing task (Galinsky and Moskowitz 2000, 718). All completed measures rating 'how well each trait describes both groups' and their 'favorability' (Galinsky and Moskowitz 2000, 718). The authors found that only the 'participants in the perspective-taking condition did not rate the in-group ... any higher than the out-group' (Galinsky and Moskowitz 2000, 719). Additionally, 'taking the perspective of what it is like to be an out-group member increased ratings of the out-group to a level comparable to that of the in-group' (Galinsky and Moskowitz 2000, 719). In effect, taking another's perspective, be they an individual or a group, seems to decrease preconceptions.

Literary texts narrated from a first person or third person perspective encourage identification with the protagonist. Readers are transported not only into the narrative world but also into the main character; they see what she or he sees and feel what she or he feels. The higher the level of transportation, as Green and Brock's study showed, the deeper the immersion into the protagonist's perspective. And the deeper the immersion, the lower the resistance to different viewpoints and ideas. Dal Cin et al. argue that this is what makes literary texts so powerful in promoting change; more powerful, in fact, than rhetorical arguments. They state, '[w]hen presented with a communication advocating a position with which we do not agree, there is a tendency to ignore the message, counterargue the information, or belittle the source' (Dal Cin et al. 2004, 177). On the other hand, 'narratives might be more effective than rhetoric because the former are not seen as persuasive attempts' (Dal Cin et al. 2004, 177). Consequently, the authors propose, 'narratives may be inherently suited to the presentation of messages seeking to change strong attitudes because they "get under the radar" of our efforts to protect these attitudes' (Dal Cin et al. 2004, 177–8). Readers want to become transported into a narrative as this allows them to experience pleasure; to achieve this aim they willingly take on the perspective of the protagonist. By taking on this perspective, readers effectively simulate a potentially different understanding – and this simulation allows the fictional world to become 'real'. This persuasive potential is not restricted to the boundaries of a text; in fact, literary texts can continue to shape understanding long after a story has ended.

As Markus Appel and Tobias Richter show in their study 'Persuasive Effects of Fictional Narratives Increase Over Time', reading fiction can have a long-term impact. The authors presented participants with one of two experimental texts containing true and false assertions. Subsequently, respondents were asked to complete a questionnaire at the time of reading and again two weeks later indicating their agreement. The results show that 'there was a considerable short-term persuasive influence of false information in the fictional narrative, but the influence of false information was even higher at a delay of two weeks' (Appel and Richter 2007, 125). As a result, the authors propose, 'fictional narratives can have a persistent implicit influence on the way we view the world, and ... these effects may last longer than the effects of typical explicit attempts to change beliefs' (Appel and Richter 2007, 129). By 'getting under the radar' then, as Dal Cin et al. argue, literary texts can alter what readers perceive to be 'real'. In the case of this book, this perception relates to attitudes towards the issue of sex/gender and language. In particular, I ask how literary texts can promote inclusive language use.

Of course, '[n]either a theory nor a story explains completely or adequately, there's always something missing', (Tillman 2004, 140) as Lynne Tillman argues in 'Telling Tales'. However, as studies have shown, and Christina D. Weber confirms in 'Literary Fiction as a Tool for Teaching Social Theory and Critical Consciousness', literary texts can be a powerful tool to change perspectives. One of Weber's students comments after encountering both fiction and theory, '[t]heories come to life and have more depth in these stories' (Weber 2010, 358). Additionally, she or he remarks, 'theories become more applicable to every life, meaning ... I can put myself in that particular situation' (Weber 2010, 358). This interplay between text, imagination and reality is effectively put to the test in this book.

Conclusions

The feminist critique of language has had a profound impact on speakers' understanding of and attitudes towards the issue of sex/gender and language. From the first debates ignited by the civil rights movement in the United States the issue has captured the imagination of English- and German-language activists, theorists and empiricists alike. However, despite a wealth of evidence that male generic terms negatively impact on the conception of women, inclusive terminology remains contested. Nevertheless, linguistic change has certainly taken place. Schoolbooks have been revised to represent women and men more equally, job advertisements employ more inclusive terminology and even national anthems have been adapted to reflect an inclusive society. But many general language users continue to refrain from using inclusive language. As studies have shown, linguistic practices are shaped by exposure, habit and motivation. Equally, awareness of the significance of women's and men's linguistic representation seems key to promoting linguistic change.

Based on the findings of narrative theory and research, I propose that literary texts can be a useful tool to make speakers more aware of the importance of inclusive language use. In particular, I investigate how different literary texts engage with women's and men's linguistic representation, and how this engagement can help to influence attitudes. Over the next three chapters I evaluate three approaches employed by literary authors to highlight the issue of sex/gender and language: 'Problematising the linguistic status quo', 'Proposing linguistic neutrality' and 'Reversing the linguistic status quo'. I begin by evaluating two early texts that question dominant linguistic practices: Ursula K. Le Guin's 1969 *The Left Hand of Darkness* and Verena Stefan's 1975 *Häutungen*. These texts lay the foundation for my argument.

Notes

1. As R. W. Holder's 2008 *Dictionary of Euphemisms* highlights, this understanding remains relevant to this day. He states: '[g]iven the antiquity of their *trade*, we should not be surprised that someone who *sells herself* might like to be called a *professional woman*' (Holder 2008, 54, emphasis in original).
2. Owing to space constraints I have focused on the most prominent studies in my discussion.
3. Empirical investigations into the impact of the German language only gained real traction from the mid-1990s onwards. Consequently, there is a substantial gap between studies at this point.
4. While this is an example of a negative influence on readers' perceptions, it also highlights the possibility of a positive change in attitudes with reverse materials.

2
Problematising the linguistic status quo
The Left Hand of Darkness and *Häutungen*

In tandem with activists and theorists, literary writers also engaged with the issue of sex/gender and language. Ursula K. Le Guin's 1969 *The Left Hand of Darkness* and Verena Stefan's 1975 *Häutungen* were two early texts to question the generic use of male nouns and pronouns in English and German. In this chapter I compare Le Guin's and Stefan's approaches to putting the spotlight on the linguistic status quo. Leibniz's *salva veritate* principle provides the frame.

Leibniz's *salva veritate* principle

Leibniz applied himself to a wide range of fields, including mathematics, philosophy and philology. While his most famous work remains within disciplinary boundaries, the occasional cross-pollination of thought led to fruitful discoveries. Leibniz's 1686 *Generales inquisitiones de analysi notionum et veritatum* (GI) is a prime example of the insights gained by interdisciplinary work. Applying mathematical principles to linguistic inquiry, Hidé Ishiguro explains in *Leibniz's Philosophy of Logic and Language*, Leibniz developed a calculus that aimed to reduce 'irregularities and unnecessary complexities in the grammar of ordinary language' (Ishiguro 1990, 122). With the help of this calculus, or *salva veritate* principle, Ishiguro adds, Leibniz 'wanted to construct a formal language with a syntax which reflected the logical relation of concepts' (Ishiguro 1990, 54). In short, Leibniz set out to make language more 'logical'. A relatively recent work in Leibniz scholarship – the text was not published until the early twentieth century – the GI, according to Franz Schupp's introduction, 'stellen die wichtigste geschlossene Arbeit von Leibniz zu Fragen der Logik dar' (Schupp 1982, VII) [constitute Leibniz's most important complete work on questions of logic]. And this work remains useful for linguistic inquiry to this day. I refer to Schupp's 1982 German translation *Allgemeine Untersuchungen über die Analyse der Begriffe und Wahrheiten* to illustrate how and why.

At the most basic level, Leibniz's *salva veritate* principle says that '*A deckt sich mit B* wenn eines an des anderen Stelle unbeschadet der Wahrheit substituiert werden kann' (Leibniz 1982, 21, emphasis in original) [*A coincides with B*, if the one can be substituted for the other without destroying its truth (O'Briant 1968, 35)]. Borrowing the notion 'sich decken' from geometry, Leibniz believes that 'A' is congruent with, or the same as, 'B' if one can be replaced by the other. However, for 'A' and 'B' to be congruent a central requirement has to be met: any replacement has to take place 'unbeschadet der Wahrheit'. But what does Leibniz mean by this? First of all, it is important to note that 'A' and 'B' are referents, not actual entities. Ishiguro interprets this as follows: 'what can be substituted for one another are names (or descriptions) of things, and what is or is not identical is the thing that the name names or the description refers to' (Ishiguro 1990, 19). Consequently, 'A' and 'B', as terms, do, or do not, refer to the same 'thing'. Secondly, the requirement 'unbeschadet der Wahrheit', rephrased as 'truth-value' (Ishiguro 1990, 31) by Ishiguro, is met 'wenn durch die Analyse beider [Begriffe] durch die Substitution der Werte (d.h. der Definitionen) an die Stelle der Begriffe an beiden Stellen dieselben Begriffe sich ergeben' (Leibniz 1982, 21) [when both are analyzed by the substitution of values (or definitions) for terms, the results are the same on both sides (O'Briant 1968, 35)]. To paraphrase, 'A' is congruent with 'B' only when each definition can take the other's place; that is, when 'definition of A' is congruent with 'B' and vice versa. In fact, Leibniz's calculus demands that this congruence extends to both definitions, so that 'definition of A' is the same as 'definition of B'.

Ultimate proof of congruence is only achieved, however, if 'für jeden der beiden [Begriffe] ihre Definition substituiert wird, und für jeden Bestandteil derselben wiederum seine Definition, bis man zu den primitiven einfachen Begriffen gelangt' (Leibniz 1982, 21) [if the definition be substituted for one as well as the other, and in turn the definition for any constituent, until one comes to simple primitives (O'Briant 1968, 35)]. To confirm then that '*A deckt sich mit B ... unbeschadet der Wahrheit*', each replacement has to be 'true' to the level of 'primitive einfache Begriffe'. As these terms are 'unzerlegbar' (Leibniz 1982,

9) [unanalyzable (O'Briant 1968, 30)], no further analysis is required or indeed possible. Consequently, the notion 'A' is congruent with 'B' is either proven or disproven, and, if confirmed, 'A' able to take the place of 'B'. The subsequent linguistic saving, as is Leibniz's intention, reduces 'irregularities and unnecessary complexities in the grammar of ordinary language'. One such presumed saving is the use of the male noun 'man' in place of 'human'; the assumption being that these terms are one and the same. But are the two terms really congruent? As Ursula K. Le Guin's *The Left Hand of Darkness* and Verena Stefan's *Häutungen* illustrate, the equation of 'man' with 'human' is problematic.

The Left Hand of Darkness and *Häutungen*

Le Guin and Stefan employ distinct approaches to problematise the linguistic status quo. While *The Left Hand of Darkness* is fictional, *Häutungen* is based on personal experiences and written from an author-narrator perspective. To provide a brief summary of each narrative: Le Guin's narrator, Genly Ai, a male representative from a planetary union, is sent to planet Gethen on a diplomatic mission. The inhabitants of Gethen, however, complicate his quest – arguably most of all because they are androgynous beings. Originating from a planet similar to Earth, Genly struggles to understand his counterparts' androgyny and classifies them according to his own sociocultural categories. This is expressed linguistically by his predominant use of male nouns and pronouns to refer to the Gethenians, who, to his mind, become female only in the specific. *Häutungen*, on the other hand, describes the experiences of the initially unnamed narrator as a woman and an activist in 1970s Berlin. Stefan/narrator is familiar with the same norms as Genly, but encounters these from the opposite position: that of the categorised 'woman'. Becoming increasingly aware of her limited position throughout the narrative, Stefan/narrator tries to shed herself of these imposed constraints. This shedding is expressed linguistically through experimentation with grammatical norms, such as capitalisation, and the questioning of male generic terms.

The excerpts that follow from the opening sections of *The Left Hand of Darkness* and *Häutungen* provide an introduction to Le Guin's and Stefan's techniques:

> I was in a parade. I walked just behind the gossiwors and just before the king. … Next come the lords and mayors and representatives, one person, or five, or forty-five, or four hundred, from each Domain

and Co-Domain of Karhide ... Next, forty men in yellow, playing gossiwors. ... Next, the royal party, guards and functionaries and dignitaries of the city and the court, deputies, senators, chancellors, ambassadors, lords of the Kingdom (Le Guin 1991, 9–10)

Der mann lehnt sich über die balustrade und starrt mich unverwandt an. Ich starre unverwandt zurück, während ich näherkomme. Etwas alarmiert mich an dieser situation mehr als sonst. Der mann gafft nicht lüsternd oder genüßlich, sondern er macht ein eindeutig empörtes gesicht. Als ich an ihm vorbeigehe, sagt er aufgebracht: Also, sag mal, mädchen, wo hast du denn deine brust hängen? (Stefan 1994a, 37)

[The man leans over the railing and stares fixedly at me as I approach. Something about this situation alarms me more than usual. The man's expression is not lustful or lewd, but instead quite righteously indignant. As I pass him he says, incensed: Hey baby, what happened to your boobs? (Stefan 1979, 3)]

While each text is narrated from the perspective of the central 'I', a key difference immediately emerges: Genly is 'in the parade' looking out, whereas Stefan/narrator is 'looked at'. The contexts both narrators find themselves in, however, have similar features. According to Genly's description, the Gethenians appear either explicitly male, as indicated by terms such as 'king', 'lords', 'men'; or male by implication, 'mayors', 'guards', 'senators', 'ambassadors'. While the latter group of nouns, in particular, might be open to debate – some would argue that 'mayor' and 'senator' are able to connote 'woman' as well as 'man' – their historic use shapes interpretation. To give an example, 'senator' is defined as '[a] member of a senate' (OD 2016, n. pag.), which seems neutral at first instance. However, originating from 'Latin *senatus*, from *senex* "old man"' (OD 2016, n. pag., emphasis in original), the term was clearly linked to 'male' in Ancient Rome. Furthermore, the term seems to retain bias. In 2018, 75 per cent of US senators were men, underscoring a predominantly male interpretation and application to this day.

While Stefan/narrator is female, her context is equally androcentric. She might claim the 'I' of the narrative akin to Genly; however, in contrast to his insider position, Stefan/narrator finds herself in opposition to her environment. In fact, she is threatened by it. 'Der mann lehnt … und starrt', Stefan/narrator states, and while she 'starr[t] unverwandt zurück', she feels 'alarmiert' by his 'Gaffen'. Furthermore, she feels alarmed that the man does not stare 'lüsternd oder genüßlich', which she seems to expect in her sociocultural context, but 'eindeutig empört'. The man expresses his 'Empörung' by stating: '[a]lso, sag mal, mädchen, wo hast du denn deine brust hängen?'. Similarly to Genly's description, men in *Häutungen* seem to be in positions of power. While 'der mann' might not be a 'lord' or 'senator', he asserts his authority nevertheless – an authority that is signified by his stance toward Stefan/narrator. He stares at her, he makes her feel alarmed, he is 'empört' or 'aufgebracht'. He addresses her and, further, addresses her as 'mädchen' and thereby disparages her. He comments on her breasts. Stefan/narrator might be able to stare 'unverwandt zurück' but this is only a reaction to his provocation, and one that is essentially without effect. He is able to put her in her place: a female body to be observed and judged by him.

Critics received the different narrative styles and perspectives of *The Left Hand of Darkness* and *Häutungen* in equally distinct ways. While both texts were highly influential, *The Left Hand of Darkness* received considerably more critical attention. This difference could be explained as follows. First, the authors differed in publishing profile: *Häutungen* was Stefan's first publication whereas Le Guin had several texts in print already. Secondly, the style of each author required different reading approaches: the personal tone of *Häutungen* might have potentially appealed less to reviewers than the (science) fictional narrative of *The Left Hand of Darkness*. Thirdly, the publishing context differed: as the women's liberation movement followed on from the civil rights movement, US critics were perhaps more ready to receive a feminist text than those in Germany. But *Häutungen* was popular among readers nevertheless. In effect, demand for the book helped to build the feminist publishing house Verlag Frauenoffensive. However, those who did critically engage with *Häutungen* remained divided.

Jürgen Serke's review 'Ein Buch, das den Markt für Frauen öffnete' reflects this ambiguity. While Serke refers to *Häutungen* as 'das Identifikationsbuch schlechthin für eine im Aufbruch befindliche neue Frauengeneration' [the identification book per se for a new generation of women ready for change], he also mentions that Stefan is 'von Beruf Krankengymnastin' (Serke 1982, 343) [a physiotherapist by profession] in the very same sentence. While some might argue that this detail simply confirms Stefan's qualification to write 'das Identifikationsbuch schlechthin', precisely because she is not an author by profession, others might counter that 'von Beruf Krankengymnastin' puts Stefan in 'her place'. She is a 'physiotherapist', not a 'writer'. This divided stance toward the text also filters down into more in-depth critical evaluations. Sophie von Behr, for example, comments in her review 'Etwas an seiner Seite' that while '"Häutungen" ist ein beunruhigendes Buch' – 'beunruhigend' here in a positive sense – the ending is 'mißlungen' (von Behr 1975, n. pag.) ['Shedding' is an unnerving book … the ending is a failure]. And while 'mißlungen' might refer to the portrayal of a lesbian relationship, in particular, the notion of failure strikes a chord with reviewers in other aspects. Stefan's problematisation of language is criticised by Brigitte Classen and Gabriele Goettle in '"Häutungen" – eine Verwechslung von Anemone und Amazone'. '[Das Buch] weist den Frauen eine Zukunft', the authors state, 'in der die Verwechslung von Worten und Begriffen als neue Erfahrung und neue (weibliche) Sprache verstanden sein will' (Classen and Goettle 1976, 46) [The book devises a future for women in which the confusion of words and terms is to be understood as a new experience and a new (female) language]. The authors consider Stefan's linguistic project ineffective as, to their minds, her problematisation of language does not lead to any fundamental revision.

On the other hand, Ricarda Schmidt applauds Stefan's engagement with the issue of sex/gender and language. As Schmidt states in her review 'Körperbewusstsein und Sprachbewusstsein: Verena Stefans "Häutungen"', 'Stefan [problematisiert] die vorgefundene Sprache als ein System, in dem patriarchalische Werte und Normen reflektiert und perpetuiert werden' (Schmidt 1982, 60) [Stefan problematises the existing language as a system, which reflects and perpetuates patriarchial values and norms]. She elaborates that '[Stefan macht] das Weibliche als das in der Sprache Abwesende sichtbar' (Schmidt 1982, 60 [Stefan renders the linguistic absence of women visible]. Jeanette Clausen agrees in 'Our Language, Our Selves: Verena Stefan's Critique of Patriarchal Language': 'her experiments with language should be seen as a serious inquiry into the oppressiveness of everyday language' (Clausen 1982, 400). To this Christa Reinig adds in 'Das weibliche Ich': '[d]ieser Autorin ist es gelungen … die Sprache der Männer aufzubrechen und ihre Vokabeln den Frauen nutzbar zu machen' (cited in Plowman 1998, 139) [this author has managed to … prise open the language of men and to render its vocabulary useful for women]. All three critics suggest that *Häutungen*'s linguistic experiments have a positive impact on readers. While reviews might be divided, *Häutungen* is understood to engage with the issue of sex/gender and language – a lack of which is a common complaint of *The Left Hand of Darkness*. In contrast, critics of Le Guin's text are concerned precisely because it seems to employ male generic terms unquestioningly.

As Elizabeth Cummins summarises in *Understanding Ursula K. Le Guin*, 'persistent criticism of the novel has been that the androgynes are not presented as menwomen. Le Guin is faulted for using the pronoun "he" to refer to them' (Cummins 1990, 78). To this Susan M. Bernardo and Graham J. Murphy add in *Ursula K. Le Guin: A Critical Companion* that 'some critics contend that Le Guin has effectively eliminated the female altogether and presented nothing but a male society. This assessment stems, in part, from Le Guin's use of language, and, more specifically, the masculinised language of "he" and "him"' (Bernardo and Murphy 2006, 33). In comparison to Stefan's critics, Le Guin's perceived failure to challenge linguistic norms is a key concern. Reviewers feel that Le Guin's persistent use of male nouns and pronouns excludes women and androgynes, which in turn cements the sociocultural premise male-as-norm. Critics are divided, however, over the origins of the author's linguistic choices. On the one hand, male-biased language use is considered an expression of Genly's androcentricity. As Pamela J. Annas states in 'New Worlds, New Words: Androgyny in Feminist Science Fiction', '[Genly Ai's] problems with the inhabitants of [Gethen/]Winter come from his inability to judge them as human beings without first defining them as men or women' (Annas 1978, 151). Bernardo and Murphy agree: '[a]s a Terran ... Genly cannot escape gendered designations' (Bernardo and Murphy 2006, 22). In short, it is Genly who is conceptually trapped by the sex/gender division of his own context and coerced to express this linguistically.

Another line of reasoning is that it is Le Guin's (unconscious) androcentricity that informs her choices. 'Perhaps ... Le Guin's imagination was limited by her own cultural conditioning' (Rhodes 1983, 117), Jewell Parker Rhodes observes in 'Ursula Le Guin's *The Left Hand of Darkness*: Androgyny and the Feminist Utopia'. Meryl Pugh concurs in '"You Canna Change the Laws of Fiction, Jim!" A Personal Account of Reading Science Fiction', and argues that 'it is the use of the masculine pronoun to describe a race of persons to whom gender is presumably irrelevant, that reveals the text's androcentricity' (Pugh 1999, 26–7). But in contrast to Rhodes, Pugh feels it is the text, rather than the author, that expresses androcentric leanings. A third possible explanation is readers' interpretations. '[T]he Catch-22 Le Guin finds herself in when attempting to create a world of androgynes', John Pennington states in 'Exorcising Gender: Resisting Readers in Ursula K. Le Guin's *The Left Hand of Darkness*', 'she is controlled by language and the gender conventions of the reader's world' (Pennington 2000, 1). He elaborates: 'male and female readers cannot escape their own gendered perspectives conditioned by society' (Pennington 2000, 2); consequently, readers seem bound to interpret male *or* female.

A particular concern arises in relation to the impact of male nouns and pronouns. Rhodes, for example, asks '[i]f as an artist she can invent a new futuristic world ... then, can't she invent new words to depict accurately her vision of the androgyne?' (Rhodes 1983, 115), thereby implying that Le Guin's use of male terms impedes the message of the novel. Pugh also feels that *The Left Hand of Darkness* fails to fulfil its potential; however, not owing to the lack of inventing new terms but by '[evading] the issue of language's gendered nature' (Pugh 1999, 27) altogether. In response, Mona Fayad argues in 'Aliens, Androgynes, and Anthropology: Le Guin's Critique of Representation in "The Left Hand of Darkness"' that this 'evasion' can also be interpreted as an attack. By consistently employing male nouns and pronouns, Le Guin can be argued to highlight the inadequacy of androcentric language to represent all human beings. In fact, Fayad believes that 'the novel can be seen as a parody of the patriarchal need for assimilation and sameness, one in which the male eye is incapable of seeing anything other than what it wishes to construct' (Fayad 1997, 4). And what the male eye is revealed to see, and to construct, is male-as-norm. '[R]eaders are invited to question' this 'parody' (Fayad 1997, 4) and thereby the linguistic status quo. Consequently, the persistent use of male terms to refer to the androgynes can also be interpreted as an effective strategy. Anna Livia agrees, in *Pronoun Envy: Literary Uses of Linguistic Gender*, that '[t]he laughter produced by the clash between the generic masculinity ... and the biological or cultural traits usually restricted to the opposite sex point to the subversiveness of Le Guin's pronoun choice' (Livia 2001, 141). What is considered Le Guin's failure by some can therefore equally be interpreted as a destabilising measure.

In the following sections I compare Stefan's and Le Guin's distinct approaches to problematising the linguistic status quo, with particular attention to the use of nouns, pronouns, names and titles. The aim is to identify how each author puts the spotlight on the issues inherent in male generic language use.

Nouns and pronouns

As shown in the introductory paragraphs, Genly predominantly employs male terms to refer to the Gethenians. Consequently, planet Gethen seems to be peopled by men, rather than women and men, or indeed androgynes. This can be observed throughout the narrative, with a particularly prominent example being Genly's description of his prime diplomatic contact, Estraven. Initially, the reader encounters Estraven from a neutral perspective. 'I ask the person on my left', Genly says in reference to his contact. As 'person' is by definition '[a] human being regarded as an individual' (OD 2016, n. pag.), the term seems open to either a female or male interpretation, and therefore also androgyny. However, Genly's subsequent depiction negates any potential neutrality. 'Wiping sweat from his dark forehead the man – *man* I must say, having said *he* and *his* – the man answers' (Le Guin 1991, 12, emphasis in original). While some might argue that 'man' and 'he' can be used inclusively, Genly's understanding of the terms, as highlighted by the association of 'he' with 'man', is clearly 'male'. This links back to the Sapir–Whorf hypothesis: language seems to influence Genly's thought. In fact, Genly feels coerced to say 'man', not 'woman', when using the male pronoun – '*man* I must say'. Furthermore, he feels coerced to say 'man', not 'person' or 'human'. This specific understanding is underscored by the following elaboration: '[Estraven] is one of the most powerful men in the country; … He is lord of a Domain and lord of the Kingdom, a mover of great events' (Le Guin 1991, 12). As the use of 'one of the most powerful men' and 'lord' underpins, Estraven is, to Genly's mind, male first and foremost.

Genly explains his conceptual struggle with androgyny as follows: 'my efforts took the form of self-consciously seeing a Gethenian first as a man, then as a woman, forcing him into those categories so irrelevant to his nature and so essential to my own' (Le Guin 1991, 18). He seems to consider it 'essential' to identify whether someone is female or male; it is his own sociocultural context that demands classification. Furthermore, the categorisation of Gethenians 'first as a man' reveals the underlying premise 'male-as-norm'. But, even though Genly acknowledges that the androgynes consider sex/gender 'irrelevant' and, furthermore, recognises that 'he' is linked to 'man', he employs the male pronoun to refer to the Gethenians. Another representative sent to Gethen, Ong Tot Oppong, gives some insight as to why this might be the case:

> Lacking the Karhidish [one of the languages spoken on Gethen] 'human pronoun' used for persons in somer [non-reproductive phase], I must say 'he', for the same reasons as we used the masculine pronoun in referring to a transcendent god: it is less defined, less specific, than the neuter or the feminine. But the very use of the pronoun in my thoughts leads me continually to forget that the Karhider I am with is not a man, but a manwoman. (Le Guin 1991, 85)

While Ong considers the male pronoun 'less defined, less specific, than the neuter or the feminine', like Genly she feels coerced to associate 'he' with 'man'. In fact, she states, 'the very use of the pronoun in my thoughts leads me continually to forget that the Karhider I am with is not a man'. As a result of male generic language use, Ong classifies the androgynes as 'male' first and foremost. Judging from their reflections, both Genly and Ong believe 'he' to be inadequate as a neutral pronoun. However, both seem unable to imagine an alternative. Conditioned by the understanding that 'it is less defined, less specific, than the neuter or the feminine', Genly and Ong seem trapped into using the male pronoun generically.

That 'he' is unable to represent both sexes/genders equally, however, is highlighted at other instances in *The Left Hand of Darkness*. For example, when Genly takes part in a foretelling led by a Gethenian, he describes the central character, Faxe, as follows: '[h]e was as tall as I, and slender, with a clear, open, and beautiful face' (Le Guin 1991, 55). While some might argue that 'he' could be interpreted neutrally; the male pronoun is, as illustrated above, to Genly's mind specific. This is confirmed when the foreteller undergoes a key change: 'in the centre of all darkness', Genly observes, 'Faxe: the Weaver: a woman, a woman dressed in light' (Le Guin 1991, 61). Along with Genly's perception of Faxe as 'a woman', his narrative undergoes a pronominal shift, '[t]he light burned sudden and intolerable, the light along her limbs, the fire, and she screamed aloud in terror' (Le Guin 1991, 61). If 'he' was inclusive, the implication of Genly's adjustment seems to be, there would have been no need to use 'she'. However, Genly clearly feels that the male pronoun is unable to represent 'Faxe, a woman'. Equally, when Faxe reverts back to his/her 'original self', Genly also resumes his use of the male pronoun. 'I knelt down beside Faxe', Genly says, '[h]e looked at me with his clear eyes' (Le Guin 1991, 62), which highlights that Genly understands 'he' as specific.

Arguably, Le Guin's problematisation of the linguistic status quo is subtle and becomes instructive only on close reading. In fact, the above shifts and reflections can easily disappear in the overwhelmingly androcentric narrative. Stefan, on the other hand, questions the use of male generic terms more directly. And this direct engagement is an integral part of the narrative; as is visible in her 1975 introduction to *Häutungen*:

> Mit dem wörtchen 'man' fängt es an. 'Man' hat, 'man' tut, 'man' fühlt…: 'Man' wird für die beschreibung allgemeiner zustände, gefühle, situationen verwendet – für die menschheit schlechthin. Entlarvend sind sätze, die mit 'als frau hat "man" ja…' beginnen.

> 'Man' hat als frau keine identität. Frau kann sie nur als frau suchen. (Stefan 1994a, 34)
>
> [It begins with the small word 'one/man'. 'One has, one does, one feels…: One is used for the description of general conditions, feelings, situations – for hu/mankind per se. Revealing are sentences that start with 'as a woman one has…'. One/man does not have an identity as a woman. One/frau can only find it as woman.]

The indefinite person pronoun 'man', according to Stefan, is equated with 'die menschheit schlechthin', and effectively excludes 'Frau'. As Stefan/narrator confirms by extending 'man' to 'mann' in the narrative, 'mann würde mich als vollwertig behandeln' (Stefan 1994a, 42) [men would find me acceptable (Stefan 1979, 7)], to her mind, both are essentially interlinked. As a result, 'Frau' is negated by male generic terms and needs to locate her own identity – and this location Stefan sets out to enable in *Häutungen*. She states in the 1994 introduction: '[w]ir wollten vorkommen, als Subjekte, nicht als die Beschriebenen aus männlicher Sicht' (Stefan 1994b, 8) [we wanted to appear as subjects, not as described from a male perspective]. However, in order to 'become' subjects, Stefan believes new terms are needed; terms that are free from androcentric preconceptions. This is tricky, as in the German language male-as-norm not only infiltrates the conceptual but also the grammatical level. This additional hurdle becomes poignant when Stefan/narrator refers to her body, '[i]rgendwie hing das alles mit meinem körper zusammen. … Er entsprach nicht den vorschriften. Er sah nicht jugendlich aus. Er hatte keine gute Figur' (Stefan 1994a, 40) [In some way it all related to my body [masc.]. … It [masc.] did not measure up to standards. It didn't look youthful. It didn't have a good figure (Stefan 1979, 5)]. Removing the first sentence containing the referent 'Körper', the subsequent three would simply read as 'er entsprach', 'er sah' and 'er hatte'; thereby shifting the male pronoun from potentially neutral to specific. 'Er hatte keine gute Figur' arguably evokes 'male' rather than 'female'. Of course, whenever a referent is removed the original meaning is lost, but it is telling to 'read' the male pronoun as it would be read in many other contexts.

Read as an anaphor for 'man', the male pronoun seems to negate Stefan/narrator's specifically female experience. However, in contrast to the indefinite pronoun 'man', she seems to employ 'er' unquestioningly. This lack of engagement with the generic use of the male pronoun is not a solitary occurrence; as Stefan/narrator states in relation to the lower half of her body: '[e]igentlich habe ich gar kein gefühl für meinen unter leib' (Stefan 1994a, 46) [I don't actually have any feeling for my abdomen]. While indicating a split relationship by visibly separating 'unter' and 'leib', Stefan/narrator does not comment on the term's grammatical gender: 'der Unterleib', as 'der Körper', is grammatically male. However, Stefan/narrator is certainly not unaware of the impact of the male pronoun. In reference to the term 'Mensch', for example, she says, '[s]o muß es gewesen sein, als der erste mensch geschaffen wurde, dachte ich. Genau so muß sie sich gefühlt haben!' (Stefan 1994a, 40) [This is how it must have been when the first human being was created, I thought. This is exactly how she must have felt! (Stefan 1979, 5)]. Here Stefan/narrator consciously adjusts the default 'er' to 'sie', and thereby reveals that 'Mensch' seems implicitly linked to 'man', not 'woman'. And this link, Stefan/narrator clearly feels, needs to be grammatically severed to allow for the concept 'female human'.

Genly similarly plays with expectations. For example, he describes his 'landlady' as 'a voluble man' (Le Guin 1991, 46), proclaims '[t]he king was pregnant' (Le Guin 1991, 89), and finds it 'difficult to imagine him [another contact on Gethen] as a young mother' (Le Guin 1991, 104). Genly thereby illustrates the specificity of language as well as highlights that the Gethenians are not men, but androgynes. However, such conscious ambiguity seems too rare an occurrence to override the dominant associations provided in the narrative. In one passage alone, Genly refers to Estraven as 'sir', the representatives of the planetary union as 'patient men' and the union overall as 'the rest of mankind' (Le Guin 1991, 21). Furthermore, siblings are referred to as 'brothers' (Le Guin 1991, 26), children as 'sons' (Le Guin 1991, 67) and the wider community as 'fellow men' (Le Guin 1991, 170). Additionally, as illustrated above, the Gethenians are consistently pronominalised with 'he', and 'she' is generally used only in the specific. In fact, if mentioned at all, female terms are used mainly in comparison, and one that is predominantly unfavourable to women. One revealing example is Genly's assessment of his diplomatic contact: 'Estraven's performance had been womanly, all charm and tact and lack of substance, specious and adroit' (Le Guin 1991, 18). Another is his explanation of his use of the term 'landlady'; 'I thought of him as my landlady, for he had fat buttocks that wagged as he walked, and a soft fat face, and a prying, spying, ignoble, kindly nature' (Le Guin 1991, 46–7). In effect, women, to Genly's mind, seem essentially inferior to men. And this understanding is reflected in his androcentric language use.

While Stefan's and Le Guin's approaches might differ, both authors clearly engage with the issues inherent in the linguistic status quo. I explore in the following section how naming practices underpin the authors' problematisations.

Names and titles

As in narrative style, *The Left Hand of Darkness* and *Häutungen* differ also in naming practices. First, Stefan uses existing names while Le Guin invents new names altogether. Secondly, Stefan refers to characters by their first names only while Le Guin creates family names as well. Starting with the main characters, the reader does not learn the name of Stefan's narrator, 'Veruschka' (Stefan 1994a, 135), a nickname for the author's first name 'Verena', until fairly late in the novel. Le Guin, on the other hand, provides the name of her narrator, 'Genly Ai', in the prelude to the narrative. And while 'Veruschka/Verena' is not of the author's choosing, 'Genly Ai' invites speculation. First of all, 'Genly' could refer to either a female or male character – the ending 'y' is used for women and men alike, with 'Tracy' and 'Andy' just two examples. Additionally, 'Genly' contains phonetic resemblance to 'gentle', allowing for ambiguity also in connotation. However, the opening paragraph already implies a certain sex/gender. As Genly predominantly employs male terms to refer to the Gethenians, this seems to signify a male point of view. While androcentric cultures train women as well as men to perceive male-as-norm, the conceptual absence of women seems to speak against a female narrator. Furthermore, Estraven's reference to 'Genly' as 'Mr Ai' (Le Guin 1991, 14) supports the assumption of Genly as male. 'Mister', defined as 'title of courtesy for a man' (Hoad 1986, 296) in T. F. Hoad's *The Concise Oxford Dictionary of English Etymology*, is linked to 'master', 'man having control or authority' (Hoad 1986, 284). The association of 'Mr' with 'man', and furthermore 'man having control or authority', negates both a female and neutral understanding. Genly's sex/gender is confirmed by Le Guin in an interview with Larry McCaffery and Sinda Gregory. 'Genly's name is *Henry*, evolved in time', she explains, '[w]hat happened to the "h" is what the Russians do, and then the "r" became "l"' (Freedman 2008, 42, emphasis in original). Equally organic was the development of the narrator's surname, '[h]e first came to me as "Genly Ao," but I thought that sounded too much like "ow"' (Freedman 2008, 42–3), Le Guin elaborates. 'You listen until you hear it', she states, 'until it sounds right. You go: Eye, I, Aye, Ai' (Freedman 2008, 43). This phonetic resemblance with 'I' and 'eye' is borne out in the narrative: 'Ai' is the narrator, the 'I' of the story, as well as the central observer, the 'eye'. 'Thus Genly Ai's name itself ... brings to the fore the relation between subjectivity ("I") and perception ("eye")' (Fayad 1997, 65). And 'Ai' is only able to perceive the androgynes in relation to himself, a self that is essentially shaped by his specifically male 'I/eye'.

In contrast, 'Cloe', the substitution for 'Veruschka/Verena' at the end of *Häutungen*, is clearly intended to be female. Curiously, the name 'Cloe', or 'Chloe', from Greek, meaning 'Beiname der Erd- und Muttergöttin Demeter' (Kohlheim and Kohlheim 2013, 92) [byname of the earth- and mother-goddess Demeter], is linked to fertility. This seems both in sync and at odds with the character's role in the narrative. On the one hand, Cloe feels at one with her specifically female body; 'sie [hatte] die brüste zu lieben begonnen' (Stefan 1994a, 153) [she had begun loving her breasts (Stefan 1979, 113)], she states. On the other, the name's inherent link to 'fertility' is restrictive, especially as it confines 'woman' to the reproductive role assigned to her culturally. In effect, Cloe's declaration '[d]er mensch meines lebens bin ich' (Stefan 1994a, 158) [I am my own woman (Stefan 1979, 118)] seems to counteract the role of 'Erd- und Muttergöttin' exactly by claiming the subject position of 'ich'. As this position is usually reserved for 'man' in androcentric cultures, 'Cloe' seems a puzzling choice. However, Stefan's selection might not have been motivated by etymology to begin with; as she indicates in her 1994 introduction, '[w]ir wollten wissen, daß Virginia Woolf schon 1928 überlegt hatte, was es für die moderne Literatur bedeutete, wenn in einem Buch zu lesen wäre: *Chloe liebte Olivia*' (Stefan 1994b, 8, emphasis in original) [we wanted to know that Virginia Woolf had already reflected in 1928 what it meant for modern literature to read in a book: *Chloe loved Olivia*]. A 'Cloe', modelled on Woolf's 'Chloe', provides a more plausible explanation – it encapsulates Stefan/narrator's 'shedding' of heterosexual norms.

The naming of 'Estraven', Genly's counterpart in *The Left Hand of Darkness*, is equally puzzling at first instance: 'Therem Harth rem ir Estraven' in full. 'Therem' refers to Estraven's 'hearth' or personal name, while 'Estraven' stands for 'the Lord of Estre' (Le Guin 1991, 109). 'Therem', which does not particularly evoke either female or male names, seems to imply that the Gethenian is an androgynous being. However, Genly's consistent reference to Estraven as 'he' and 'man' counteracts this interpretation; to Genly, Estraven is male first and foremost. But this understanding is not necessarily shared by all, as Le Guin reports in an interview with Rebecca Raas, '[i]n "Estraven" people heard "estrogen"' (Freedman 2008, 75). Whether this phonetic resemblance overrides the predominantly male imagery of Genly's narration, however, is questionable. To Genly at least, 'the Lord of Estre' is most certainly male and 'estrogen', as the narrative shows, only relevant in terms of Estraven's control over his/her female hormone levels.

While the shifting relationship between Genly and Estraven is central to *The Left Hand of Darkness*, 'Veruschka', on the other hand, engages with several other main characters throughout *Häutungen*; to begin with two of her male partners, 'Dave', short for 'David', and 'Samuel', with each name holding a key significance. For example, Stefan/narrator feels deeply connected to 'David', linked to the Hebrew 'Liebling' (Kohlheim and Kohlheim 2013, 105) [darling]; however, potentially to her detriment: '[d]u liebst Dave zu sehr' (Stefan 1994a, 62) [[y]ou love Dave too much (Stefan 1979, 27)], comments her friend. In contrast to his biblical battle against Goliath, 'die herr schaft der weißen über die schwarzen' (Stefan 1994a, 65) [the tyranny of whites over blacks (Stefan 1979, 29)], Dave does not challenge 'die herr schaft der männer über die frauen' (Stefan 1994a, 65) [the tyranny of men over women (Stefan 1979, 29)]. While Samuel might be more inclined to question androcentricity – true to his name's meaning, linked to the Hebrew 'Gott ist erhaben' (Kohlheim and Kohlheim 2013, 328) [God is sublime]; his approach seems top-down. 'Mit mir schlief er', Stefan/narrator reports, '[s]prechen denken diskutieren erforschen – das geschah mit anderen' (Stefan 1994a, 97) [I was the one who shared his bed. Speaking, thinking, discussing, researching, those things he shared with others (Stefan 1979, 59)]. Similarly to Dave, then, Samuel does not engage with Stefan/narrator as equally human.

The names of the female characters are as revealing. Ines, for example, linked to 'Agnes', Greek 'keusch' or 'rein' (Kohlheim and Kohlheim 2013, 38) [chaste or pure], is 'keusch/rein' in the sense that she does not conform to heterosexuality. 'Ines, mit der ich zu der zeit viel zusammen war, war anders', Stefan/narrator comments, '[s]ie ging mit keinem, sie ging mit sich' (Stefan 1994a, 41) [I was spending a lot of time with Ines in those days; she was different. She wasn't going with anybody, she was going with herself (Stefan 1979, 6)]. And while Ines initiates Stefan/narrator into the possibilities of same-sex relations, she feels as yet unable to engage in them. 'Ines war doch eine frau', Stefan/narrator explains, 'wie hätte sie meinem leben einen sinn geben, wie hätte sie mich erobern sollen?' (Stefan 1994a, 41) [After all, Ines was a woman, how could she give my life any meaning, how could she conquer me? (Stefan 1979, 7)]. Nadjenka, on the other hand, a nickname for 'Nadja', linked to Russian 'Nadeschda' meaning 'Hoffnung' (Varnhorn 2008, 114) [hope], breaks down these barriers. 'Eine andere frau konnte ich mir nicht vorstellen', Stefan/narrator states, '[i]ch wollte es mit einem mann so gut haben wie mit Nadjenka' (Stefan 1994a, 73–4) [I couldn't imagine myself with any other woman. I wanted a man who would treat me as well as Nadjenka (Stefan 1979, 37)]. Nevertheless, this relationship does not fully develop either, possibly because '[w]ir sind doppelgängerinnen. Treffe ich sie, treffe ich zugleich auf einen teil meiner selbst' (Stefan 1994a, 139) [[s]he is my alter ego. When I encounter her, I encounter a part of my self as well (Stefan 1979, 100)]. Nadjenka provides hope, if not fulfilment. Fenna, short for names beginning with 'Frede' or 'Friede' (Varnhorn 2008, 55) [peace], on the other hand, becomes the narrator's eventual lover. Stefan/narrator explains, '[w]ir wollten nicht nachahmen' (Stefan 1994a, 112) [[w]e didn't want to imitate (Stefan 1979, 74)], which represents their intention to meet as equals: as women and as partners. Furthermore, Fenna is the only character in Stefan's novel to name the narrator, 'Veruschka' (Stefan 1994a, 135), and by naming her to recognise her. And this recognition constitutes a central turning point in their relationship; bringing closure, 'Friede', to Stefan/narrator's shedding.

The names chosen by Le Guin and Stefan support each author's problematisation of the linguistic status quo; however, it is male generic terms that exemplify concerns around dominant language use. An etymological perspective provides further depth to Le Guin's and Stefan's literary problematisations.

The history and etymology of male generic terms

According to the *Oxford Dictionaries*' (OD) online platform, 'man' used to mean '[a] human being of either sex; a person' only. '[I]n Old English the principal sense of **man** was "a human being"', the dictionary states, 'and the words **wer** and **wif** were used to refer specifically to "a male person" and "a female person" respectively' (OD 2016, n. pag., emphasis in original). At some point, '**man** replaced **wer** as the normal term for "a male person"' (OD 2016, n. pag., emphasis in original). While 'the older sense "a human being" remained in use' (OD 2016, n. pag.), 'man' and 'male' became interlinked, which is reflected in today's primary understanding of the term as '[a]n adult human male'. Julia Penelope (Stanley) and Cynthia McGowan investigate in 'Woman and Wife: Social and Semantic Shifts in English' how the meaning of 'man' transferred from the generic, 'a human being', to the specific, 'a male person'. This shift, the authors propose, took place 'as a consequence of increased patriarchal influence' (Penelope (Stanley) and McGowan 1979, 499). '[A] male person', came to be understood as the representative 'man/human', the authors argue, and 'the semantic range of man was narrowed' to 'the male-specific use of the once-generic <u>man</u>' (Penelope (Stanley) and McGowan 1979, 500, emphasis in original). The term 'wer' was eventually dropped out of usage altogether. This new conceptual link between 'man' and 'male' was not without consequence, however. In fact, according to Dennis Baron's *Grammar and Gender*, it led in '[a]ll the Germanic languages except English' to the transference of 'the original, generic sense of *man* to a new derivative word – for example, German and Dutch *mensch*' (Baron 1986, 138, emphasis in original).

This can be traced in the German noun 'Mann', which is today defined as 'erwachsene Person männlichen Geschlechts' [adult person of male sex] only, while 'Mensch' means 'mit der Fähigkeit zu logischem Denken und zur Sprache, zur sittlichen Entscheidung und Erkenntnis von Gut und Böse ausgestattetes höchstentwickeltes Lebewesen'; 'menschliches Lebewesen, Individuum' (Duden 2016, n. pag.) [highly advanced being, equipped with the capacity for logical thought and language, moral decision and recognition of good and evil; human being, individual]. But while a new term might exist in German, 'Mensch', as 'derivative word' as Baron indicates above, is not entirely neutral either. In fact, as the online *Duden* shows, the term's etymology, 'mannisco, eigentlich = der Männliche' (Duden 2016, n. pag.) [actually = the male], essentially leads back to 'Mann'. Friedrich Kluge's 1883 *Etymologisches Wörterbuch der deutschen Sprache* seconds this interrelation and describes 'Mensch' as 'Substantivierung eines Zugehörigkeitsadjektivs zu *Mann* in der alten Bedeutung "Mensch"' (Kluge 1989, 473, emphasis in original) [noun of a related adjective to man in the old understanding 'human']. Additionally, Wilhelm Hoffmann's 1871 *Vollständiges Wörterbuch der deutschen Sprache* argues that the term is 'zusammengezogen aus Mann … und der Silbe isch' (Hoffmann 1871, 38) [contracted from man … and the syllable isch]. Consequently, the German 'Mensch' is as linked to 'male' as 'man'.

This is further illustrated by Jacob Grimm and Wilhelm Grimm in their 1878 *Deutsches Wörterbuch*. According to the authors, the Old High German 'Mensch', 'mannisko, mennisko [*ist*] *in jedem falle nur männlichen geschlechtes*' (Grimm and Grimm 1878, 2021, emphasis in original) [[is] in every case of male sex only]. And while the term underwent a shift in Middle High German from specific to generic, to 'Mensch', 'im allgemeinen Sinne' (Grimm and Grimm 1878, 2021) [in the general sense], it often remained restricted to the '*erwachsenen männlichen menschen, … wo das weib ausdrücklich durch ein anderes substantiv oder fürwort hervorgehoben wird*' (Grimm and Grimm 1878, 2022, emphasis in original) [adult human male, … where the female is explicitly referred to by another noun or pronoun]. This essential distinction remains, as Peter Braun illustrates in his 1997 *Personenbezeichnungen: Der Mensch in der deutschen Sprache*. The author entitles one of his sections 'Frauen', whereas no such counterpart exists for 'Männer'. And while '[a]llen Personenbezeichnungen gemeinsam ist das Hyperonym Mensch', he elaborates, '[f]ür alle weiteren Betrachtungen werden zusätzliche semantische Merkmale konstitutiv, z.B. das Merkmal "weiblich"' (Braun 1997, 71) [all referents share the hyperonym human … [f]or all other observations additional semantic features are constitutive, e.g. the feature 'female']. The use of 'zusätzlich' is here poignant; consequently, 'female' is essentially still considered an additional, rather than intrinsic, feature.

'Mensch' is therefore a problematic term for women, as is 'human' in fact. Now defined as 'human being', '[a] man, woman, or child of the species *Homo Sapiens*', the term originates 'from Latin *humanus*, from *homo*, 'man, human being' (OD 2016, n. pag., emphasis in original). Samuel Johnson's 1755 *A Dictionary of the English Language* seconds this connection, and defines the term as '[h]aving the qualities of a man' and '[b]elonging to man' (Johnson 1983, n. pag.). While Johnson might give 'man' the primary meaning '[h]uman being', the term is also defined as '[n]ot a woman' (Johnson 1983, n. pag.). In short, as with 'Mensch', 'female' is considered a 'zusätzliches semantisches Merkmal', rather than intrinsically 'human'. The interrelation between the two concepts is visible also in the grammatical sex/gender of 'der Menscher' and the common pronominalisation of 'human' with 'he'. The German pronoun 'er', according to *Duden*, 'steht für ein männliches Substantiv, das eine Person oder Sache bezeichnet' (Duden 2016, n. pag.) [represents a male noun that describes a person or a thing]; the Brothers Grimm define it as '*das männliche pronomen dritter person*' (Grimm and Grimm 1878, 680, emphasis in original) [the male pronoun of the third person]. While some might argue that this definition refers to grammar rather than sex/gender, the use of 'männlich' is telling. Defined as 'dem zeugenden, befruchtenden Geschlecht angehörend'; 'zum Mann als Geschlechtswesen gehörend'; and 'für den Mann typisch, charakteristisch' (Duden 2016, n. pag.) [belonging to the procreating, fertilising sex; belonging to man as a sexual being; and typical, characteristic for a man], 'männlich' implies a specific interpretation. As the Brothers Grimm state, '*von altersher pflegt unsere sprache die pronomina* er *und sie substantivisch für mann und weib … zu gebrauchen*' (Grimm and Grimm 1878, 690, emphasis in original) [from ancient times our language employs the pronouns 'he' and 'she' as nouns for man and woman].

The English pronoun 'he', primarily defined as '[u]sed to refer to a man, boy, or male animal', was '[u]sed to refer to a person or animal of unspecified sex' (OD 2016, n. pag.) but was also never inclusive to begin with. Walter W. Skeat's 1882 *A Concise Etymological Dictionary of the English Language* links 'he' to the Anglo-Saxon '*hē*' (Skeat 1984, 235, emphasis in original). And while Skeat lists the female pronoun as '*hēo*' (Skeat 1984, 235, emphasis in original), the male pronoun is not indicated to function generically. Furthermore, Johnson's definition exclusively associates 'he' with 'man' (Johnson 1983, n. pag.), and Hoad considers 'he' the '3rd s[ingular] m[asculine] pers[onal] pron[oun]' (Hoad 1986, 212). Ann Bodine investigates in 'Androcentrism in Prescriptive Grammar: Singular "They", Sex-Indefinite "He", and "He or She"' how the male pronoun came to be equated with 'person'. '[P]rior to the nineteenth century', the author states, 'singular "they" was widely used in written, therefore presumably also in spoken, English' (1975, 131–3). But 'nineteenth-century prescriptive grammarians' felt this usage was incorrect on account of 'number' (Bodine 1975, 133). Consequently, grammarians advocated using 'he', although the male pronoun also 'fails to agree with a singular, sex-indefinite antecedent by one feature – that of gender' (Bodine 1975, 133). Bodine argues that '[a] non-sexist "correction" would have been to advocate "he or she"'; however, grammarians considered this alternative '"clumsy", "pedantic" or "unnecessary"' (Bodine 1975, 133) – a premise that remains familiar to this day. In the following I apply Leibniz's *salva veritate* principle to investigate how the generic use of male terms fares on grounds of logic.

Applying the *salva veritate* principle

According to Leibniz, 'A' is congruent with 'B' if one can replace the other 'unbeschadet der Wahrheit'. But is this actually the case for the terms 'man' and 'human'? To investigate whether 'man' and 'human' are indeed interchangeable, I apply Leibniz's *salva veritate* principle. Beginning with each noun's definition, the *Oxford Dictionaries*' online platform primarily defines 'man' as '[a]n adult human male' (OD 2016, n. pag.). However, the term also holds a secondary definition, '[a] human being of either sex; a person' (OD 2016, n. pag.). While the dictionary notes that 'the [generic] use is now often regarded as sexist or at best old-fashioned' (OD 2016, n. pag.), 'man', as per definition, seems to be able to replace 'human'. 'Human', on the other hand, is defined as '[a] human being' only; with 'human being' further defined as '[a] man, woman, or child of the species *Homo Sapiens*' (OD 2016, n. pag., emphasis in original), the term represents both women and men. Moving on to the first level of analysis of Leibniz's *salva veritate* principle, 'A' should be replaceable with the 'definition of B' and 'B' with the 'definition of A' without compromising each term's truth-value. Sure enough, 'man' can be substituted with '[a] human being' on account of both its primary and secondary definition. In short, 'man' seems congruent with 'human'. A reversal, however, is more problematic: while 'human' can be substituted with the secondary definition of 'man', that is '[a] human being of either sex; a person', the term is not congruent with its primary definition. As '[a]n adult human male' does not contain 'woman', 'man' as 'male' is unable to replace 'human being'. Consequently, 'man' and 'human' are congruent when 'man' is understood as '[a] human being of either sex; a person', but not when 'man' means 'male'. However, can the *salva veritate* principle be true and false at the same time? Does this not undermine its central premise 'unbeschadet der Wahrheit'?

As Leibniz states, '[e]s gehört daher zu den ersten Prinzipien, daß die Begriffe, die wir als in ein und demselben Subjekt existierend erfassen, keinen Widerspruch enthalten' (Leibniz 1982, 61) [it is among the first principles that terms which we understand to exist in the same subject do not involve a contradiction (O'Briant 1968, 50)]. As 'man' seems at once congruent and incongruent with 'human', the dual relation of 'man' and 'human' clearly contains such a 'Widerspruch'. However, Leibniz also reserves the possibility of particular cases. For example, he divides between a 'universell affirmative Aussage "A ist B"' and a 'partikulär affirmative Aussage "Ein A ist B"', as well as a 'partikulär negative Aussage' and a 'universell negative Aussage' (Leibniz 1982, 93) [universal affirmative proposition 'A is B'; particular affirmative proposition 'Some A is B'; particular negative proposition; universal negative proposition (O'Briant 1968, 62)]. Following on, 'man' is congruent with 'human' in the particular if the secondary definition of 'man', '[a] human being of either sex; a person', is used; and incongruent in the particular if the primary definition, '[a]n adult human male', comes into play.

While this could potentially help to explain the dual function of 'man' it seems to contribute to complicating language rather than reducing its complexities as is Leibniz's aim. Additionally, an important caveat has to be introduced at this stage. As Ishiguro explains, '[i]n Leibniz's terminology, the concept of genus is included in the concept of species, or the concept of a species contains the concept of a genus, not vice versa' (Ishiguro 1990, 45). To paraphrase Ishiguro, 'man is human' is true because the notion of 'human' is included in the notion of 'man'. In turn, 'human is man' cannot be true because 'man' is a subcategory of human. The genus 'man' is essentially unable to take the position of 'species', that is be replaceable with 'human', whatever its secondary definition might be. Therefore 'man' and 'human' cannot be congruent as this violates the species/genus hierarchy.

As Ishiguro confirms, '[c]oncepts are the same if they play the same role; they play the same role if the words that express them are interchangeable without affecting the truth-value of the propositions in which they occur' (Ishiguro 1990, 17). 'Man' and 'human' cannot be congruent as they do not play the same role in language, and therefore are unable to be one and the same.

Conclusions

The Left Hand of Darkness and *Häutungen* both effectively engage with and problematise the linguistic status quo. While Le Guin's and Stefan's approaches might differ at surface level, each narrative highlights the exclusive function of male generic terms. Genly perceives 'he' as linked to 'man', and consequently feels unable to associate the male pronoun with 'woman' or 'person'. Ong agrees with this essential connection. She comments that the use of the male pronoun erases women from her imagination. In effect, both Genly and Ong express that 'he' fails women. While these instances of reflection might be rare against the dominant backdrop of male nouns and pronouns, they also show that Le Guin's characters are aware of the impact of male generic terms. *Häutungen*, on the other hand, is more direct in its problematisation of the linguistic status quo. The inadequacy of the indefinite pronoun 'man' to represent women and men equally is challenged in the introduction and confirmed in its extension to the male noun in the narrative. Additionally, Stefan/narrator shifts the male generic pronoun 'er' to 'sie' to question the underlying link between 'Mensch' and 'Mann'. She thereby exposes the premise male-as-norm and its impact on imagination.

Both *The Left Hand of Darkness* and *Häutungen* illustrate the issues inherent in the linguistic and conceptual equation of 'man' and 'human'. And this equation, when approached with the help of Leibniz's *salva veritate* principle, is problematic also in relation to the logical function of language. According to Leibniz, a genus is essentially unable to replace the species, that is 'a male person' cannot represent 'humanity'. Consequently the terms 'man' and 'human' are not congruent. As Benson Mates highlights in *The Philosophy of Leibniz: Metaphysics and Language*, '[u]nderlying Leibniz's entire logic, metaphysics, and philosophy of language is the traditional view that the essential role of language is to represent our thoughts about the extralinguistic world' (Mates 1986, 47). Male generic terms, as illustrated in *The Left Hand of Darkness* and *Häutungen*, do not communicate 'woman', nor androgyne. In fact, they predominantly convey 'man' only. While 'a male person' might have been deemed to be the representative 'human' in a previous time, 'our thoughts about the extralinguistic world', in this case 'humanity', now include 'woman'. As Le Guin and Stefan illustrate, male generic nouns and pronouns do not communicate these 'thoughts' appropriately and thereby fail 'the essential role of language'.

Language matters, as 'not only are we unable, according to Leibniz, to talk about concepts or ideas without words, we cannot even think in concepts or ideas without words' (Ishiguro 1990, 24). To think in 'concepts' such as 'woman' as equally 'human', new 'words' are needed – 'words' that are not based on male-as-norm. Stefan/narrator recognises this need in *Häutungen*: 'ich muß neue worte schaffen, begriffe aussortieren, anders schreiben, anders benutzen'; the existing terms are 'zu dürftig' (Stefan 1994a, 146–7) ['I must create new words, must be selective, write differently, use concepts in a different way'; … 'inadequate' (Stefan 1979, 105–6)]. Equally Le Guin has experimented with language; she suggested to replace 'he' with the neutral 'a' in a 1985 screenplay version of *The Left Hand of Darkness* (Livia 2001, 142). Le Guin and Stefan therefore clearly understood the limitations of the linguistic status quo, and each narrative is a pioneering text in the literary problematisation of androcentric language. Building on this, writers have tried to conceive ways to represent human beings more inclusively. June Arnold's *The Cook and the Carpenter* and Marge Piercy's *Woman on the Edge of Time* employ epicene pronouns to challenge the linguistic and conceptual male-as-norm. In Chapter 3 I compare their linguistic innovations and situate them in relation to Le Guin's and Stefan's texts. In doing so I assess the effectiveness of Arnold's and Piercy's calls for linguistic neutrality.

3
Proposing linguistic neutrality
The Cook and the Carpenter and Woman on the Edge of Time

In the 1970s, literary writers pushed the boundaries of linguistic representation, with pronouns taking centre stage. June Arnold's 1973 *The Cook and the Carpenter* and Marge Piercy's 1976 *Woman on the Edge of Time* are two key texts to reimagine anaphors. In this chapter I evaluate Arnold's and Piercy's inventions – with reference also to the German translations – as a proposal for an alternative understanding of sex/gender and language. The frame is provided by Wittgenstein's concept 'to imagine a language means to imagine a form of life'.

Wittgenstein's *Lebensform*

Ludwig Wittgenstein, like Leibniz, applied his mind to diverse fields of inquiry. It was his studies in mechanical engineering that inspired him to pursue the philosophy of mathematics and logic, and later the philosophy of language. Wittgenstein's *Philosophische Untersuchungen* (PU) are of particular interest. Published in 1953, the PU are, according to Wolfgang Kienzler, 'eines der bedeutendsten philosophischen Werke des 20. Jahrhunderts' (Kienzler 2007, 9) [one of the most significant philosophical works of the twentieth century]. This standing relates to Wittgenstein's exploration of the social function of language, which had a profound impact on later thought. First of all, Wittgenstein believes that language-learning is highly regimented. He explains that '[d]as Lehren der Sprache ist hier kein Erklären, sondern ein Abrichten' (Wittgenstein 1998, 4) [the teaching of language is not explanation, but training (Wittgenstein 1998, 4e). Language-learners are taught to follow rules, not question them. Wittgenstein elaborates, '[d]ie Kinder werden dazu erzogen, *diese* Tätigkeiten zu verrichten, *diese* Wörter dabei zu gebrauchen, und *so* auf die Worte des Anderen zu reagieren' (Wittgenstein 1998, 4, emphasis in original) [[t]he children are brought up to perform *these* actions, to use *these* words as they do so, and to react in *this* way to the words of others (Wittgenstein 1998, 4e)]. And as children are trained, that is 'abgerichtet', to perform certain tasks, to use certain terms and respond to others in a certain way, they are trained to function within certain sociocultural boundaries.

This concept of language-learning reminds of Stefan/narrator's evaluation of the overall socialisation process. 'Wir sind *abgerichtet*', she states, '[d]ieses kümmerliche wort sozialisation! Dieser beschönigende begriff konditionierung!' (Stefan 1994a, 111, emphasis in original) [They have *broken our spirits*. This inadequate term, socialisation! This prettifying concept, conditioning (Stefan 1979, 72)]. It is the social training of human beings, Stefan implies, that results in a particular behavioural performance. Language plays a central part in the practice of 'Abrichten', as Wittgenstein confirms. However, neither language nor behaviour is fixed. He explains, '[m]an kann sich leicht eine Sprache vorstellen, die nur aus Befehlen und Meldungen in der Schlacht besteht. – Oder eine Sprache, die nur aus Fragen besteht und einem Ausdruck der Bejahung und der Verneinung' (Wittgenstein 1998, 8) [[i]t is easy to imagine a language consisting only of orders and reports in battle. – Or a language consisting only of questions and expressions for answering yes and no (Wittgenstein 1953, 8e)]. Such languages are tied to particular 'Tätigkeiten'. For example, a language 'der Schlacht' [battle] requires a certain environment to operate effectively; a language of giving and receiving orders is particular to the context of war. And as a language is inextricably linked to a particular context, Wittgenstein concludes, 'eine Sprache vorstellen heißt, sich eine Lebensform vorstellen' (Wittgenstein 1998, 8) [to imagine a language means to imagine a form of life (Wittgenstein 1998, 8e)]. However, while Wittgenstein illustrates his understanding of 'imagining a language', his use of 'Lebensform' is obscure. What does he actually mean by it? Marie McGinn gives one explanation in *The Routledge Guidebook to Wittgenstein's Philosophical Investigations*. '[T]he term "form of life"', she states, 'is intended to evoke the idea that speaking a language is a way of conducting oneself with words in a life with others' (McGinn 2013, 55). Understood as such, 'Lebensform' refers to the social function of language – speakers employ language to communicate with others. This communication takes place in the context of 'life', and as this 'life' is shared with others, a speaker has to be able to communicate in an accepted way to be able to effectively 'conduct oneself with words'.

Wittgenstein elaborates that 'in der *Sprache* stimmen die Menschen überein. Dies ist keine Übereinstimmung der Meinungen, sondern der Lebensform' (Wittgenstein 1998, 88, emphasis in original) [they agree in the *language* they use. That is not agreement in opinions but in form of life (Wittgenstein 1998, 88e)]. In short, the particular context, a particular 'Lebensform', is agreed upon and reflected in the collective language. Consequently, 'Lebensform', as Karl Brose coins it in *Sprachspiel und Kindersprache: Studien zu Wittgensteins 'Philosophischen Untersuchungen'*, signifies 'den "gesellschaftlichen" Handlungs-Spiel-Raum ..., in dem sich Sprechen und Sprache abspielen' (Brose 1985, 31) [the 'social' context ..., in which talking and language take place]. As mentioned above, 'Sprache' and 'Lebensform' are flexible. 'The idea of a form of life', McGinn states, 'applies ... to historical groups of individuals who are bound together into a community by a shared set of complex, language-involving practices' (McGinn 2013, 55). These groups, the author highlights, are shaped by a particular set of circumstances. As circumstances are 'historical', that is bound to a certain context, any shift is therefore accompanied by an adaptation of the 'language-involving practices'. Equally, '[t]he techniques that constitute a language take their point from what lies around them, in the lives of those who use the language ... New techniques arise and others fall away ... in response to the needs and purposes of those who employ them' (McGinn 2013, 54). As a result, Wittgenstein explains, 'neue Typen der Sprache ... entstehen und andre veralten und werden vergessen' (Wittgenstein 1998, 11) [new types of language ... come into existence, and others become obsolete and get forgotten (Wittgenstein 1998, 11e)]. Linguistic change is therefore not only a possibility but a necessity in some instances. As language is a tool to communicate it has to be fit for purpose – and this purpose is determined by the requirements of the speech community.

June Arnold's *The Cook and the Carpenter* and Marge Piercy's *Woman on the Edge of Time* imagine a radically different 'language' and 'form of life' to the status quo. Following on from Stefan's and Le Guin's problematisation of male generic terms, Arnold and Piercy experiment with the linguistic representation of women and men, and, in particular, with epicene terms. Before I evaluate the authors' innovations in relation to Wittgenstein's proposal, I present their literary approaches. The aim is to assess how a neutral 'form of life' is imagined in language, and what the consequences of such an imagination might be.

The Cook and the Carpenter and *Woman on the Edge of Time*

June Arnold's *The Cook and the Carpenter* and Marge Piercy's *Woman on the Edge of Time* were written in the same decade, 1973 and 1976 respectively, and both experiment with the linguistic representation of women and men. However, the texts differ in narrative perspective. *The Cook and the Carpenter*, narrated by 'the carpenter', tells the story of a commune in Texas. Against the backdrop of dominant social and linguistic practices the group tries to create an egalitarian alternative. The attempt to establish cohabitation unmarred by biological markers is communicated by the group's use of the epicene pronoun 'na', as well as names that aim to obscure the sex/gender of the referent, such as 'cook', 'Stubby' and 'Chris'. Those on the outside of the commune, on the other hand, remain predominantly specific in the carpenter's narrative – this linguistic separation signifies the central conflict between the status quo and neutrality. Connie, the narrator of *Woman on the Edge of Time*, also belongs to a separate community; however, this group is not of her making or choosing. Deemed 'not normal', Connie is interned in a psychiatric hospital. The narrative follows her experiences in the confined environment as well as in a future society, which Connie accesses through contact with Luciente, one of its inhabitants. Luciente lives in a reality where sex/gender no longer matter and this irrelevance is expressed through the neutral pronoun 'person'. In contrast, Connie employs traditional pronouns, thereby highlighting her role as insider/outsider to both the dominant norms and the egalitarian society.

The following excerpts from *The Cook and the Carpenter* and *Woman on the Edge of Time* illustrate this central difference in perspective:

> The carpenter walked around to the east side of the porch and started the sander up again. ... The sander screeched across the worn boards, pulling up the patches of thick deck paint in gluey streaks, melting it, mixing the smell of burning lead and color into the air already thick with grit and dampness. The carpenter's breathing was protectively shallow. Na wore a strip of diaper around nan forehead to catch the sweat and prevent it from streaking nan glasses. (Arnold 1973, 4)

> 'Magdalena is unusual. Person does not switch jobs but is permanent head of this house of children. It is per calling. Sometimes a gift expresses itself so strongly, like Jackrabbit's need to create

color and form, like Magdalena's need to work with children, that it shapes a life. ... person must do what person has to do.' A small figure with velvety black skin – she had to be a woman from the delicacy of her bones – a long neck, hair cut to her scalp in an austere tracery of curls, descended toward them, smiling slightly. (Piercy 1989, 136)

Both passages are narrated in the third person; the pronoun 'na', replacing 'she' or 'he', is used to refer to the 'carpenter'. Equally the use of 'them' in Piercy's narrative, rather than 'us', confirms a third person narrator. However, the use of the third person perspective also marks a key difference between the texts. While 'na' is an integral part of the narrative of *The Cook and the Carpenter*, the epicene pronoun 'person' is only employed in reported speech. Connie's pronoun usage remains specific: 'she had to be a woman', 'her bones' and 'her scalp' highlight that the narrator of *Woman on the Edge of Time* continues to employ the traditional pronominal system. However, the names and actions given in each neutral description also seem to guide interpretation: the 'carpenter', 'start[ing] the sander up' and '[wearing] a strip of diaper around nan forehead', arguably evokes one particular sex/gender, while 'Magdalena', 'permanent head of this house of children' that is 'per calling', evokes another. This seems to defy conceptual neutrality; however, the conflict between 'na'/'person' and interpretation might also be what each narrative aims to achieve. As Arnold states in the preface to *The Cook and the Carpenter*, '[s]ince the differences between men and women are so obvious to all ... I have therefore used one pronoun for both, trusting the reader to know which is which' (Arnold 1973, n. pag.). While withholding sex/gender on the pronominal level, Arnold's narrative also expects readers to 'identify' it.

The need to identify whether a character is female or male reflects the norms of the wider sociocultural context. If sex/gender is culturally and linguistically significant, neutrality can only be an alien concept. Genly poignantly comments on this dilemma of seeing a Gethenian first as male and then as female, in line with the categories he is familiar with. Equally, Connie feels coerced to ascertain sex/gender: 'she had to be a woman', Connie observes in relation to Magdalena, despite Magdalena's neutral context. And as Genly finds 'clues' to aid categorisation, Connie classifies on the basis of names, 'Magdalena', and physicality, 'the delicacy of her bones'. Even though sex/gender might be pronominally absent, neutrality is bound to fail against the weight of Connie's own sociocultural environment. She seems to have to identify 'which is which', as Arnold terms it.

Connie's role as an indirect commentator on the neutral pronoun marks another key difference between the two passages. While Connie interprets Luciente's use of 'person' from within her own context, the carpenter provides no such filter: the epicene 'na' is presented without qualification. Jan Hokenson argues in 'The Pronouns of Gomorrha: A Lesbian Prose Tradition' that it is this immediate replacement that makes the text 'profoundly unsettl[ing]' (Hokenson 1988, 67): '[w]ith ciphers instead of common subject pronouns, we are unable to imagine the body. Unable to imagine the body, we are unable to relate to the "self"' (Hokenson 1988, 67). However, this failure to link pronoun and body highlights norms that often remain unnoticed. In effect, it shows how interconnected 'she' and 'he' are with a certain understanding. By constantly asking 'is it female? is it male?', Hokenson states, '[readers come] face to face with every shred of our own sexism' (Hokenson 1988, 67). The direct encounter with neutral pronouns therefore unsettles any easy assumptions linked to anaphors. Julia M. Allen and Lester Faigley agree in 'Discursive Strategies for Social Change: An Alternative Rhetoric of Argument'. 'This lack of gender definition [in Arnold's text]', the authors argue, 'forces readers to guess at the gender of each character – and to reflect upon their need to know' (Allen and Faigley 1995, 148). This 'need to know', to identify 'which is which', reveals specific expectations that the epicene 'na' both highlights and disturbs: 'because pronouns are the most direct representation of the subject, a change in pronoun will necessarily affect the cultural construction and expectations of the subject' (Allen and Faigley 1995, 147). A neutral pronoun then demands a reassessment of the significance of the biological markers 'female' and 'male', as well as the social behaviours associated with them.

Pamela J. Annas confirms this disruption in 'New Worlds, New Words: Androgyny in Feminist Science Fiction' also in relation to Piercy's text. '[N]eutral terms, "person" and "per" tend not to carry with them a whole set of assumptions and expectations, based on sex, about what is possible for a given character' (Annas 1978, 154), she says. The subsequent lack of 'assumptions' and 'expectations' connected to neutral pronouns is therefore, as in *The Cook and the Carpenter*, a clear illustration of the importance of sex/gender. As Annas argues, '[i]n a society that defines people by sex, sex is a social and political issue' (Annas 1978, 155); and the adjustment of 'she/he' to 'person', Sarah Lefanu adds in *In the Chinks of the World Machine: Feminism and Science Fiction*, is an expression of 'the interconnection of language and politics' (Lefanu 1988, 63). The linguistic presence or absence of sex/gender is consequently linked to a particular world view. Anna Livia agrees in *Pronoun Envy: Literary Uses of Linguistic Gender* that '[g]endered pronouns are clearly established as the status quo, while the epicene forms are an egalitarian development' (Livia 2001, 152). And this contrast brings fruitful insights.

Arnold's and Piercy's narratives both highlight the essential link between sex/gender and language, according to critics, and *The Cook and the Carpenter* and *Woman on the Edge of Time* generally received reviews regarding their linguistic innovations. This might have several reasons, such as the particular publishing context as well as their readership. Arnold's narrative was published by Daughters Inc., a publisher Arnold founded with Parke Bowman. As Kayann Short describes the focus of Daughters Inc. in 'Do-It-Yourself Feminism', '[it] published nineteen of the most experimental novels found in the feminist lesbian movement' (Short 1996, 21). Readers of *The Cook and the Carpenter* might have been familiar with experimentation. This is illustrated in Sam Stockwell, S. S., Carol Anne Douglas and Margie Crow's review: while '[o]ne of the criticisms ... is that the carpenter gets too didactic, rather than experiential', the authors add, '[t]rue, the politics are expressed didactically, but they are the setting, not the focus' (Stockwell et al. 1974, 20). The authors therefore focused on the novel's merits, despite the narrative's limitations.

Woman on the Edge of Time was equally well received. Initially published by Alfred A. Knopf in the United States, the novel was soon taken on by The Women's Press in the UK, a feminist publisher. Reviewers were able to compare Piercy's novel with the work of authors who had first problematised the linguistic status quo, such as Le Guin's *The Left Hand of Darkness*. As Annas argues, '*Woman on the Edge of Time* ... [is] more immediately threatening to the reader than Ursula Le Guin precisely because ... [it is] describing the present more explicitly than Le Guin is' (Annas 1978, 155). To this Meryl Pugh adds in '"You Canna Change the Laws of Fiction, Jim!" A Personal Account of Reading Science Fiction': '[i]n contrast to *The Left Hand of Darkness*, ... it tackles the issue of language's gendered nature' (Pugh 1999, 27). The groundwork provided by authors such as Le Guin therefore might have contributed to the particular reception of Arnold's and Piercy's texts.

The longevity of each author's pronominal choice, on the other hand, is contested. Livia, for example, feels that the pronouns fundamentally diverge in potential uptake: '[w]hile Piercy's pronouns *per* and *person* are clearly related to the epicene noun *person*, ... Arnold's *naself* stands out, not readily assimilated' (Livia 2001, 147, emphasis in original). In the following sections I evaluate the use of nouns and pronouns, and names and titles in more depth. I thereby assess the effectiveness of *The Cook and the Carpenter* and *Woman on the Edge of Time* in relation to proposing linguistic neutrality.

Nouns and pronouns

As quoted above, each text employs a slightly different perspective. *The Cook and the Carpenter* is narrated from within the context of an egalitarian commune, while *Woman on the Edge of Time* provides access to a future society through Connie's perceptions. This difference can already be seen in the opening sections. '"You know Texas. Do you think it's true?" the cook had asked an hour ago. The carpenter's answer was forgotten now in nan pursuit of truth: do I know Texas? Na surrounded this fact in the usual way' (Arnold 1973, 3). In contrast, *Woman on the Edge of Time* opens as follows: 'Connie got up from her kitchen table and walked slowly to the door. Either I saw him or I didn't and I'm crazy for real this time, she thought' (Piercy 1989, 9). In accordance with their positions as insiders or outsiders to the neutral community, the carpenter is referred to by the epicene 'na' and Connie by the traditional 'she'. However, neither usage is fixed: the carpenter employs specific pronouns at the end of *The Cook and the Carpenter*, and while Connie might not use 'person' to refer to her counterparts in the future society, her assignment of 'female' and 'male' is fluid. This fluidity is most obvious in her interactions with Luciente – as the opening line quoted above indicates, Connie initially identifies Luciente as male: '[e]ither I saw *him* or I didn't'. This classification is further established by subsequent references to Luciente: 'Dolly had heard her talking with Luciente: therefore he existed' (Piercy 1989, 10); 'she had been hallucinating with increasing sharpness a strange man' (Piercy 1989, 31) and '[y]oung man of middling height with sleek black hair to his shoulders' (Piercy 1989, 33) are just three examples of the linguistic identification of Luciente's sex/gender. Taking the cue from the androcentric premise male-as-norm, Luciente's physicality, Luciente's behaviour or all three, Connie categorises Luciente as one sex/gender rather than the other. This is expressed linguistically through the use of 'man' and 'he'.

However, this identification is less stable than it might initially seem, and Connie soon begins to waver in her assessment: '[h]e lacked the macho presence of men in her own family' (Piercy 1989, 36). Furthermore, Luciente's voice seems to her mind '[h]igh-pitched, almost effeminate' (Piercy 1989, 36). This destabilisation continues throughout her encounters with Luciente, but Connie does not adjust her pronoun usage until she has physical evidence:

> Pressed reluctantly, nervously against Luciente, she felt the coarse fabric of his shirt and … breasts! She jumped back. 'You're a woman!' '… Of course I'm female.' Luciente looked a little disgusted. She stared at Luciente. Now she could begin to see him/her as a woman. (Piercy 1989, 66–7)

Connie seems to require bodily proof to shift away from male nouns and pronouns. Nevertheless, her decision is far from final even at this stage. Despite confirmation of Luciente's 'breasts!', Connie continues to be puzzled by Luciente's behaviour. 'Luciente spoke, she moved with that air of brisk unselfconscious authority Connie associated with men. Luciente sat down, taking up more space than women ever did' (Piercy 1989, 67) and 'Luciente's face and voice and body now seemed female if not at all feminine' (Piercy 1989, 99) are just two examples of the perceived conflict between social gender and biological sex. However, it is sex that ultimately determines the terms of reference: from the moment of Connie's identification, Luciente remains 'she' and 'woman'. 'Although she could sense in Luciente a bridled impatience, the woman held her gently … A woman who liked her: she felt that too' (Piercy 1989, 68), Connie confirms. In fact, just as Luciente remained 'male' until proven otherwise, it is the physical categorisation of Luciente as 'female' that overrides social expectations.

Like Genly, who shifts from 'he' to 'she' in his encounter with Faxe, Connie's pronominal shift highlights the significance of sex/gender in her sociocultural context. She has to identify Luciente as either 'male' or 'female', and this need is expressed through the pronouns 'she' or 'he'. This linguistic separation stands in direct opposition to Luciente's pronoun usage: in her future society human beings are not categorised as one or the other, and this egalitarian understanding is represented by the neutral pronoun 'person'. In contrast to Connie, Luciente consistently employs 'person', and as 'person' encompasses the whole of humanity, her classification does not get compromised or swayed. To give just one example, 'I was also mother to Neruda, who is waiting to study shelf farming. Person will start in the fall' (Piercy 1989, 74), Luciente says. But despite being a consistent linguistic feature, the epicene pronoun is certainly not without history. In fact, it marks a shift from the traditional system used by Connie: 'we've reformed pronouns' (Piercy 1989, 42), Luciente explains. 'It was part of women's long revolution. When we were breaking all the old hierarchies' (Piercy 1989, 105). Luciente is here referring to 'breaking the hierarchies' of reproduction, in particular – all parents identify as 'mothers' in her society – but her statement is also transferrable to linguistic changes. The replacement of the specific pronouns 'she' and 'he' by the neutral 'person' is nothing if not 'revolutionary'.

A similar linguistic revolution took place in the Texan commune in *The Cook and the Carpenter*. The narrative is set in the present rather than a possible future, and therefore directly at odds with the traditional pronoun system: members employ 'na' to obscure sex/gender. This opposition is visible in the following: '[t]hey were planning to come Saturday, the woman said' (Arnold 1973, 4), the carpenter recounts, '[t]here was no doubt in the cook's mind, one knew from the way na told the story, that na not only believed the woman but admired na tremendously' (Arnold 1973, 6). On the basis of 'na', the 'cook' could be either 'female' or 'male' whereas 'woman' cannot. However, the pronoun does not exist in isolation. As the name 'Magdalena' in *Woman on the Edge of Time* potentially contributes to one particular interpretation, so does 'cook' come with certain connotations – the German term 'Koch', owing to its default grammatical gender, arguably even more so. Nouns, such as 'cook', are intertwined with names in Arnold's novel and I address these in more detail in the next section. Nevertheless, it is important to acknowledge that pronouns are necessarily interpreted as part of the wider narrative; consequently, 'na', like 'person', inevitably struggles to erase sex/gender completely. Just as Connie is forced to linguistically categorise 'she' or 'he', so are readers of *The Cook and the Carpenter* effectively bound by their sociocultural contexts.

The essential significance of sex/gender is highlighted in Arnold's novel. For example, by referring to the outsider as 'the woman', 'she' is specifically categorised as 'female', which points out the importance of this biological marker beyond the commune. At the same time, however, 'the woman' is referred to as 'na' just like the group's members; the cook 'admired na tremendously', the carpenter states. This pronominalisation seems to imply a hybrid status; 'the woman' seems at once part of the group and outside it. While sex/gender might matter in her sociocultural context, the text implies, she is identified as open to transition. This position is rare; most characters are presented in direct opposition to the commune's neutrality. A key part of the narrative is the threat of violence, and male violence in particular. '[T]he men were talking and laughing and carrying on about what they would do' (Arnold 1973, 5), the woman explains. The cook's question, '[b]ut what were ... are the men planning to do' (Arnold 1973, 6), might not be answered in the specific; however, the woman's response implies some form of confrontation: '[w]hatever it was last night, they're liable to think up eight different things by Saturday' (Arnold 1973, 6). As to the root cause of the threat of violence – 'we should find out why these men feel threatened and explain to them that they're wrong to feel threatened' (Arnold 1973, 16) – group members understand that it stems from their alternative existence. But while this alternative is established peacefully, 'the men' and 'these men' feel the need to respond with violence.

Violence is also a key component of Luciente's egalitarian society; the inhabitants of her community are forced to defend the gains of 'women's long revolution'. In fact, this struggle results in death for many of them, including Luciente's lover Jackrabbit. Nevertheless, giving in to the opposition might result in succumbing to an extreme version of the status quo. As Connie learns in her encounter with Gildina, who exists in a parallel reality to that of Luciente, the sex/gender division Connie is familiar with can also be revised in other ways. In Gildina's society, the 'female', '[c]osmetically fixed for sex use' (Piercy 1989, 299) and 'ashed' when no longer needed (Piercy 1989, 290), exists only to service the 'male', who, like a machine, 'turns off fear and pain and fatigue and sleep' (Piercy 1989, 297). This essential difference is embodied in the pronouns 'she' and 'he', which represent two extreme ends of the sex/gender hierarchy. Establishing, and defending, neutrality, *Woman on the Edge of Time* seems to say, might prevent this ultimate division and denigration of human beings. *The Cook and the Carpenter* makes a similar case; however, in Arnold's narrative the status quo is shown to succeed. As a result, the commune reverts to a 'group of women' (Arnold 1973, 139), and as 'women' they are linked to the specific 'she'. 'The accusation sent the carpenter's mind back into a reinterpretation of her past; her imagination offered up a flood of faults' (Arnold 1973, 151), which marks the end of consistent neutral pronominalisation. In a context that categorises people according to their sex/gender, the narrative seems to indicate, human beings can only be divided into either 'female' or 'male'.

Pronouns such as 'na' and 'person' are only one way of expressing neutrality in language; nouns are another. To give a few examples: 'permanent head of this house of children' (Piercy 1989, 136), which is Magdalena's role in *Woman on the Edge of Time*, has neutral connotations at first instance. This is confirmed by its definition: 'head' is '[a] person in charge of something; a director or leader' (OD 2016, n. pag.). Furthermore, 'person', defined as '[a] human being regarded as an individual' (OD 2016,

n. pag.), refers to either sex/gender. However, the historical connotations of 'director', '[a] person who is in charge of an activity, department, or organization' (OD 2016, n. pag.); 'leader', '[t]he person who leads or commands a group, organization, or country' (OD 2016, n. pag.), and indeed 'head', seem to sway interpretation. While Connie's observation that 'Magdalena' is a 'woman' might override any male-specific interpretation, Magdalena is introduced as the 'head' in a field that is considered female-specific to begin with: she is 'head of this house of children'. In short, the term remains unchallenged in its dominant associations; it corresponds with the norms of Connie's context, that is 'woman' in charge of children only. The German translation, 'Leitungsperson' (Piercy 2000, 163), causes a similar dilemma. While neutral at surface level – 'Person' is defined as 'Mensch als Individuum' (Duden 2016, n. pag.) – 'Leitung' has certain historical connotations; 'Tätigkeit, Funktion, Amt des Leitens' and 'leitende Personen, Führungsgruppe' (Duden 2016, n. pag.) are traditionally associated with 'Mann' rather than 'Frau'. Interestingly, however, both 'Person' and 'Leitung' are grammatically female, which counteracts the dominant connotations. Nevertheless, 'dieses Kinderhauses', as in the English version, confines both to a female-specific context. Therefore the German term is equally unable to function neutrally.

Another example is Luciente's use of 'healer' (Piercy 1989, 159). While the term again appears neutral at surface level, defined as '[a] person who claims to be able to cure a disease or injury using special powers' (OD 2016, n. pag.), it seems to imply 'female' rather than 'male'. In contrast to a medical doctor, a 'healer' merely 'claims to cure disease or injury'. As Connie's identification highlights, '[w]hat does she do in the hospital?' (Piercy 1989, 159), the healer is indeed a 'woman'. Equally, the German translation's 'eine Heilperson' (Piercy 2000, 192) seems to evoke 'Frau' first and foremost, arguably more so owing to the term's grammatical gender. Connie's equation with the role as 'Hexendoktor' briefly disrupts this association; however, the context of 'Handauflegen, Schmerzlindern, Knochenflicken' (Piercy 2000, 192) [witch doctor... Manipulating, pain easing, bone knitting (Piercy 1989, 159)] seems to reassert a female-specific interpretation: 'Handauflegen' and 'Schmerzlindern' are arguably practices predominantly associated with women. A neutral understanding, despite the use of 'Person', is therefore hard to conceive. However, this far from reflects any inherent meaning but exposes Connie's, and the reader's, associations. In fact, any specific interpretation seems to be driven by the need to identify sex/gender by any means necessary. The nouns employed in *The Cook and the Carpenter* are a similar case in point. As terms such as 'cook' and 'carpenter' are employed as personal names in the main, I evaluate them in relation to this additional layer of meaning. In the following section I assess names and titles in light of their support for or disruption of linguistic neutrality.

Names and titles

Titles are only employed in the narration of the dominant context: 'Mr. Jack' (Arnold 1973, 5) is used in reference to one of the potential aggressors in *The Cook and the Carpenter*, for example, and 'Miss Ferguson' (Piercy 1989, 25) – the German version also employs 'Miss' rather than 'Fräulein' (Piercy 2000, 26) – is mentioned by Connie in relation to her caseworker. In the carpenter's community and Luciente's society, on the other hand, titles have been omitted. Just as the lack of titles makes an important point about linguistic neutrality – sex/gender is irrelevant for both groups and so is status – names are also significant. However, in line with their distinct narrative perspectives, Arnold and Piercy employ names differently. While Arnold's narrative uses job titles, 'carpenter' and 'cook', to refer to the novel's main characters, Piercy employs recognisable first names instead, such as 'Connie' and 'Luciente'. To begin with Arnold's choices, 'cook' and 'carpenter' obscure sex/gender in line with the epicene pronoun; and at first sight both job titles seem linguistically neutral. 'Carpenter', defined as '[a] person who makes and repairs wooden objects and structures' (OD 2016, n. pag.), seems as open to interpretation as 'cook', '[a] person who prepares and cooks food, especially as a job or in a specified way' (OD 2016, n. pag.). However, both also have specific connotations in the reader's sociocultural context. 'Carpenter' is traditionally considered a 'male' occupation – Jesus was a 'carpenter', not Mary. And 'cook', although less weighted, seems possibly more 'female' as the male prestige term is generally 'chef'. In fact, these understandings appear to be supported by the narrative. For example, the carpenter is described as '[w]hat you say is important to people ... People have learned to value your mind because it is clearer than most of ours, and usually fair (Arnold 1973, 46)'. The cook, on the other hand, is perceived as follows: '[n]a is too sensitive; na has spent nan life feeling what other people – the other person – feel(s); it is the instinct of the short and the method of the timid. Na never creates a situation of nan own' (Arnold 1973, 42). The carpenter's 'clear mind', 'valued by others', is opposed by the cook's 'feelings' and 'timidity'. As these character traits have been historically associated with one particular sex/gender, they sway interpretation. A German translation might challenge the association of 'cook' in particular – 'der Koch' and 'der Tischler' are both grammatically and conceptually male.[1] However, it would equally inhibit a neutral understanding. In fact, because of grammar, linguistic neutrality is even more difficult to achieve in the German language. While an epicene pronoun potentially opens up the possibility of a neutral understanding in English, a more profound revision of German would need to take place to evoke a neutral referent. 'Der Tischler, na', for example, remains more firmly linked to 'male' than its English equivalent – to convey that the term is neutral its grammatical structure would need to be adapted as well. Nevertheless, even if this was achievable, German, just like English, remains subject to sociocultural norms. And as long as a binary understanding of human beings shapes interpretation, linguistic neutrality continues to be a challenge.

Arnold is aware of the preconceptions evoked by language and the narrative consciously plays with interpretation, 'trusting the reader to know which is which'. The need to identify one particular sex/gender from any clues given is subverted at the end of the novel: while many English readers might have been reassured to learn that the cook was indeed 'female', some might have been surprised at the carpenter's sex/gender. 'She was no longer the carpenter. Since jail, she had used the name her mother had given her at birth ... Henrietta' (Arnold 1973, 159), the narrator states. Like Connie's shifting response to Luciente, dominant practices require categorisation, and the status quo eventually defeats the carpenter's attempts at neutrality. Just as 'na' is replaced by 'she', the 'carpenter' becomes 'Henrietta'. The name is poignant for the carpenter, 'the "hen" which had humiliated her childhood with its connotation of silly maternity, the "etta" which pursued her adolescence like a weak rime for "get her"' (Arnold 1973, 159). In contrast to the chosen 'carpenter', '[a] person who makes and repairs wooden objects and structures', 'Henrietta' seems to epitomise 'female' in an androcentric culture. She is mother and sexual object, classified not according to her abilities but her sex/gender. The carpenter challenges this categorisation first through renaming and then, reassociation, 'Henrietta – sometimes shortened to Rietta – had taken on a new sound ... she was getting used to it like a face in a love affair' (Arnold 1973, 159–60). While 'Henrietta' might not be able to self-identify completely in her sociocultural environment, she is able to redefine the name's connotations. By reclaiming 'Henrietta', the novel can be seen to imply, she is also able to redefine what it means to be 'woman' in a context biased against her.

While *The Cook and the Carpenter* portrays the significance of personal names in the carpenter's shift, *Woman on the Edge of Time* makes this case through the opposition of naming practices. First of all, the inhabitants of the egalitarian future only have a first name, while Connie has a family name as well. Secondly, in Luciente's society people change names on the basis of experience and aspiration, whereas names in Connie's context are fixed. 'Luciente' and 'Connie' represent these essential differences. When introduced to Luciente, Connie reflects, 'luciente: shining, brilliant, full of light' (Piercy 1989, 36), which stands in contrast to Connie, short for 'Consuelo'. Originating from Spanish, Consuelo means 'consoler' or 'comforter' (Shane 2015, 105); 'Consuelo' has a particular place assigned to her. 'Consuelo's a Mexican woman', Connie explains, 'a servant of servants, silent as clay. The woman who suffers. Who bears and endures' (Piercy 1989, 122). But Connie refuses to be defined by her given name, '[t]hen I'm Connie, who managed to get two years of college', she explains, 'till Consuelo got pregnant. Connie got decent jobs from time to time and fought welfare for a little extra money for Angie' (Piercy 1989, 122). However, despite getting 'two years of college' and 'decent jobs from time to time', Connie is never entirely free of 'Consuelo'. As 'until Consuelo got pregnant' implies, Connie is restricted by her sex/gender; and this constraint is difficult to overcome. Connie might be able to go to college; however, when Consuelo 'gets pregnant', Connie's time at college comes to an abrupt end. In short, in her sociocultural context she is restricted to being a 'consoler', 'mother', 'woman'.

Connie's restriction is also implied by her family name(s): 'Ramos is my last name', she says, '[w]hen I was born I was called Consuelo Camacho. Ramos is the name of my second husband: therefore I am Consuelo Camacho Ramos' (Piercy 1989, 76). Additionally, Connie is called 'Álvarez, the name of her first husband, Martín' (Piercy 1989, 76), and therefore fully referred to as 'Consuelo Camacho Álvarez Ramos'. These three family names all indicate male ownership; 'Camacho' is her father's name, while 'Álvarez' and 'Ramos' are her husbands'. From birth Connie has been linguistically claimed and passed on through marriage, and she continues to be linguistically owned despite living independently. The inhabitants of Luciente's society, in contrast, 'have no equivalent' (Piercy 1989, 77). In fact, their naming practices are founded on entirely different principles, as Jackrabbit explains:

> When I was born, I was named Peony by my mothers … When I came to naming, I took my own name. Never mind what that was. But when Luciente brought me down to earth after my highflying, I became Jackrabbit. You see. For my long legs and my big hunger and my big penis and my jumps through the grass of our common

life. When Luciente and Bee have quite reformed me, I will change my name again, to Cat in the Sun. (Piercy 1989, 77)

While Jackrabbit was named at birth as Connie was, he changed his name in light of key experiences. For example, meeting Luciente resulted in a shift from 'my own name' to 'Jackrabbit'; the next period in his life will be reflected by 'Cat in the Sun'. And this is by no means the last time Jackrabbit would be able to make an adjustment; Jackrabbit is free to choose as 'person' pleases. Connie, on the other hand, is only able to self-identify by shortening her first name; her full name is permanent and binding.

And as each narrative highlights, in contexts based on a sex/gender division names are necessarily interpreted as specific. Connie, for example, 'reads' Luciente as 'male' despite the name's linguistic neutrality, reminding of both female names such as Lucía and male names such as Vicente. Similarly, readers might understand 'carpenter', essentially a neutral term in itself, as linked to one sex/gender in particular. To further illustrate the challenges and opportunities presented by neutral language, I will provide an etymological perspective.

The history and etymology of neutral terms

Beyond Arnold's and Piercy's fictional narratives, the invention of neutral pronouns has a long history in the English language. According to Dennis Baron's 'The Epicene Pronouns: A Chronology of the Word that Failed', suggestions for an alternative to generic 'he' were made as early as 1850 – the same year a United Kingdom Act of Parliament declared the male pronoun as inclusive. As *The Cook and the Carpenter* and *Woman on the Edge of Time* highlight, epicenes have continued to occupy speakers ever since, and in fact continue to do so to this day. To give a few examples, the 1850 'ne', with the possessives 'nis' and 'nim' (cited in Baron n.d., n. pag.) is one proposal and seems neutral at first instance. However, neutrality is not easy to achieve as a closer look reveals – 'ne/nis/nim' are just one letter removed from 'he/his/him'. Equally, 'hiser' (cited in Baron n.d., n. pag.), suggested at around the same time, indicates a connection to male terms of reference – its components 'his-her' continue to privilege 'male' in line with dominant norms and understanding. However, not all epicene pronouns are tied to male-as-norm. Charles Crozat Converse, for example, recommends 'thon' in 1884, and Emma Carleton proposes 'ip' the same year (cited in Baron n.d., n. pag.); both of which seem entirely unrelated to 'he' and remind of Arnold's epicene.

Other recommendations take their cue from neutral nouns in existence, examples being Piercy's 'person' and Dorothy Bryant's 1969 'kin' (cited in Baron n.d., n. pag.). Others still use the female pronoun as a blueprint; Gregory Hynes, for example, recommends 'se, sim, sis' in 1938, while Dana Densmore proposes generic 'she' in 1970 (cited in Baron n.d., n. pag.). The sheer range of proposals is overwhelming: throughout the 1970s alone, Baron records over 40 different suggestions. However, as all of these have yet to be accepted into everyday usage, Baron is right to refer to these neologisms as 'the word that failed'.

On the other hand, some speakers also recommend existing epicenes. 'It', for example, is mentioned as one alternative to generic 'he', as are 'one' and 'they'. In his essay 'The Epicene Pronoun: The Word That Failed', Baron provides some further insight into the debates on using these alternatives. According to Lindley Murray, for example, 'it' is suitable 'when we speak of an infant or child' (cited in Baron 1981, 84); however, '[w]e hardly consider little children as persons' (cited in Baron 1981, 83). This controversial restriction limits the anaphor's potential to function as a neutral pronoun in the wider sense. 'One' is equally contested. While Wolstan Dixey, for example, suggests 'the expansion of the already existing *one*', G. L. Trager condemns the pronoun as 'pedantic' (cited in Baron, 1981, 85–6, emphasis in original). And while 'they' might be considered 'expressive' by William D. Armes, he also deems its usage 'incorrect' (cited in Baron 1981, 85). This grammatical understanding of 'they' is often given as a core reason for employing 'he' generically, as Bodine illustrates. Nevertheless, 'they' continues to be employed by English speakers to this day – a brief etymological study of the anaphor provides further insight into whether 'they' is able to represent human beings equally.

Nathan Bailey's 1721 *An Universal Etymological English Dictionary* lists 'they' as of Saxon and Latin origin, 'pı' and 'Hi' respectively. The author defines the pronoun as referring to 'thoſe Perſons' (Bailey 1776, n. pag.). Samuel Johnson agrees in his 1755 *A Dictionary of the English Language* and adds the definition 'the plural of *he* or *ſhe*'; '[t]he men; the women; the perſons' (Johnson 1983, n. pag., emphasis in original). Furthermore, Johnson states that the pronoun is 'uſed indefinitely; as the French *on dit*' (Johnson 1983, n. pag., emphasis in original) – 'they' represents 'persons' in the plural and functions also as a singular generic term akin to the French 'on'. The *Oxford Dictionaries'* online platform confirms this understanding: '**they** ... as a singular pronoun to refer to a person of unspecified sex has been used since at least the 16th century' (OD 2016, n. pag., emphasis in original). The definitions quoted link 'they' to 'person'; 'thoſe Perſons', Bailey states; 'the perſons', Johnson says. Of Latin origin, 'person' is defined by Bailey as 'individually applied to every Man or Woman' as well as 'the outward Form and Shape of the Body' (Bailey 1721, n. pag.), to which Johnson adds, '[i]ndividual or particular man or woman'; '[a] general looſe term for a human being; one; a man' and '[e]xteriour appearance' (Johnson 1755, n. pag.). The use of 'outward Form and Shape of the Body' and '[e]xteriour appearance' are problematic, especially in light of Johnson's definition of 'person' as linked to 'human being; one; *a man*'. In a sociocultural context informed by a sex/gender divide, the 'body' is considered to be either 'male' or 'female'. Based on the etymological link between 'human being' and 'man', as explored in Chapter 2, might this particular 'body' not be exclusive? The final description provided by *Oxford Dictionaries* confirms this suspicion. While 'person' is today understood as 'human being regarded as an individual', the term was previously '([e]specially in legal contexts) used euphemistically to refer to a man's genitals' (OD 2016, n. pag.). 'Person' therefore implied a particular 'body' and seems compromised, at least from a historical perspective. However, the very plurality of 'they' seems to defy the link to one sex/gender only – and thereby also the singularity of 'person'. So while 'person' might be lacking, 'they' seems to be able to encompass all of humanity.

The examples discussed in this chapter predominantly focus on the English context, but the German language equally struggles with neutral terms of reference. Moreover, it has the dual burden of grammar and culture to contend with. For example, terms such as 'der Tischler' and 'der Koch' carry not only social connotations but also are grammatically weighted – with 'er' the default pronoun, the dominant association seems to be 'male'. Therefore, could 'der Tischler, sie' potentially avert a specific interpretation, such as 'the carpenter, they' might achieve? This seems a tricky solution. First of all, plural 'sie' is, besides representing 'in M[ehrheit] … alle drei Geſchlechter', also 'das perſönliche F[ürwort] der dritten weiblichen Perſon in der E[inheit]' (Hoffmann 1871, 229) [in the plural … all three sexes/genders; the personal pronoun of the female third person singular], as Wilhelm Hoffmann states in his 1871 *Vollständiges Wörterbuch der deutschen Sprache*. This latter understanding is dominant, according to Rothermund's study. Investigating the impact of plural terms, he found that participants mainly associated 'female' with plural 'sie'. Therefore, the German plural pronoun seems less effective at conveying neutrality.

Other alternatives have been proposed akin to English epicenes – and while neutral pronouns might be much better documented for the English language, they equally occupy German speakers. In 'Die SYLVAIN-Konventionen – Versuch einer "geschlechtergerechten" Grammatik-Transformation der deutschen Sprache', Cabala de Sylvain and Carsten Balzer suggest 'nin' as a neutral alternative to 'er' and 'sie'. As the authors state, this epicene aims to create a linguistic space for 'alle geschlechtlich unbestimmten, uneindeutigen, zwei- oder mehrdeutigen und anderen Formen geschlechtlicher Liminalität' (de Sylvain and Balzer 2008, 42) [all undefined, ambiguous, plurivalent and other forms of sex/gender liminality]; however, it can also be used 'wenn das Geschlecht einer Person oder Personengruppe nicht bekannt oder nicht eindeutig bestimmbar ist' (de Sylvain and Balzer 2008, 42) [if the sex/gender of a person or group of people is not known or not definitely determinable]. 'Nin' effectively functions like Arnold's 'na' and Piercy's 'person'. However, as grammatical gender is a key feature of the German language, an adjustment of pronouns alone is not sufficient to communicate neutrality. Sylvain and Balzer therefore recommend that definite articles incorporate 'din' in addition to 'der', 'die' and 'das', and indefinite 'einin'. Akin to English language proposals, usage is yet to be widely accepted and, in the current context, is bound to 'fail'.

Suggestions closer to current linguistic practices are Luise Pusch's proposal to neutralise grammar altogether. Pusch recommends '[d]as *Professor*', for example, 'wo Präjudizierung eines der beiden Geschlechter diskriminierend wäre' (Pusch 1980, 71, emphasis in original) [where the predetermination of one of the sexes/genders would be discriminatory]. The neutral article is considered a potential way forward. A related suggestion is to use the article 'de', which, as Anatol Stefanowitsch points out, is employed in Low German to refer to both sexes/genders (Oltermann 2014, n. pag). However, neither suggestion addresses pronouns, which are an integral part of the sex/gender and language debate. Moreover, dominant German-language practices remain androcentric. In light of grammatical structure and epicene availability, the English language seems therefore more open to adaptation at this stage. A return to Wittgenstein's premise 'to imagine a language means to imagine a form of life' enables an in-depth assessment of the opportunities and challenges of neutral language.

New pronouns, new *Lebensform*?

The use of 'na' and 'person' is effectively tied to a new 'form of life' in Arnold's and Piercy's novels. The commune in *The Cook and the Carpenter* does not differentiate according to sex/gender, and this is reflected in the epicene pronoun. Equally, the inhabitants of the future society in *Woman on the Edge of Time* replace 'she' and 'he' with 'person' as sex/gender is no longer considered relevant. Both communities live together peacefully in a non-binary collective; however, they are under attack from outside forces. The carpenter's group faces male violence in response to their alternative to the status quo, while Luciente's community is at war to defend the gains of 'women's long revolution'. And while the outcome of Luciente's struggle is left open, the carpenter's neutral language and 'Lebensform' are defeated: the group reverts back to specific pronouns at the end of the narrative. Each community imagines a new language and therefore a new 'form of life'; however, both are contested, and violently so. The consequences of this contest are twofold: in the future society it leads to loss of life and in the carpenter's case to the de-establishment of the epicene.

The struggle portrayed in *The Cook and the Carpenter* and *Woman on the Edge of Time* highlights a central caveat of Wittgenstein's proposal – the imagination of a 'language' and a 'Lebensform' does not take place in isolation. As Lynne Rudder Baker explains in 'III. On the Very Idea of a Form of Life', 'forms of life are communal property; there is no private practice' (Baker 1984, 278). Furthermore, 'they are in a certain sense conventional … [and] rest on *agreement*' (Baker 1984, 278, emphasis in original). Baker elaborates that 'all human practices depend upon agreement in the sense that anyone claiming to participate in a practice can be checked by others in the community' (Baker 1984, 279). In short, language is communal property. The understanding of human beings as sexed/gendered is a key principle of the status quo, as represented by Connie's and the wider Texan community. As such, the neutral 'practices' of the carpenter's group and the inhabitants of Luciente's society are at odds with the dominant 'menschlichen Gepflogenheiten und Institutionen' (Wittgenstein 1998, 108) [human customs and institutions (Wittgenstein 1998, 108e)], as Wittgenstein terms it. Their practice is 'checked by others', which takes the form of threat, attack and ultimately defeat. Steven Shaviro reflects in 'From Language to "Forms of Life": Theory and Practice in Wittgenstein' why 'na', in particular, might have been bound to fail. He states that 'a rule that forms part of a given social institution or practice can no more be altered by individual fiat than it can be followed privately' (Shaviro 1986, 225). The 'social practice' of deeming sex/gender a central marker needs to be reconsidered more widely before epicenes can succeed. It follows that, as long as pronouns are proposed in isolation, 'na' and 'person' will remain ineffective.

This shift is not impossible, however, Shaviro believes: '[s]ocial practice consists in a multiplicity of possible contexts and types of relations' (Shaviro 1986, 224). Therefore, neutrality, as one 'type of relation', is certainly imaginable. Joyce Davidson and Mick Smith agree in 'Wittgenstein and Irigaray: Gender and Philosophy in a Language (Game) of Difference', that 'social relations are not fixed or predetermined, … the world contains many possible kinds of social practices and therefore many possible forms of life' (Davidson and Smith 1999, 93). McGinn suggests that 'Lebensformen' evolve in tandem with new understandings, as 'our human form of life is fundamentally cultural' (McGinn 2013, 55). Equally, languages adapt, Brose explains. 'Wenn die Regel … schlecht [funktioniert]', he states, 'so stört sie das Sprachspiel und andere und genauere Regeln müssen an ihre Stelle treten' (Brose 1985, 49) [If the rule … functions badly, it disturbs the language game and has to be replaced with other and more precise rules]. For example, if linguistic classification of sex/gender is no longer considered relevant, the pronouns 'she' and 'he' will eventually be replaced by epicenes. Davidson and Smith concur that 'languages evolve constantly, and different language-games can and do develop in conjunction with different forms of life' (Davidson and Smith 1999, 88). In fact, 'eine Sprache vorstellen heißt, sich eine Lebensform vorstellen' is not a one-way interaction: 'the relationship between a form of life and a language-game is co-constitutive' (Davidson and Smith 1999, 93). That is, they jointly shape social practices and understanding.

The central role of language is not to be underestimated, however, as Wittgenstein points out. In fact, he considers language a key tool to influence others and their perceptions. '[D]as Lernen der deutschen Sprache betrachte ich nun als ein Einstellen des Mechanismus auf eine gewisse Art der Beeinflussung' (Wittgenstein 1953, 138) [For here I am looking at learning German as adjusting a mechanism to respond to a certain kind of influence (Wittgenstein 1953, 138e)]. In particular: 'Begriffe leiten uns zu Untersuchungen. Sind der Ausdruck unseres Interesses, und lenken unser Interesse' (Wittgenstein 1953, 151) [Concepts lead us to make investigations; are the expression of our interests, and direct our interests (Wittgenstein 1953, 151e). As specific pronouns lead speakers to consider 'sex/gender' a key marker, epicenes such as 'na' and 'person' present an alternative understanding. The linguistic expression of each understanding consequently leads 'unser Interesse' in distinct ways. These two different conceptions of human beings are represented in Arnold's and Piercy's narratives: Connie's need to sex/gender the inhabitants of the future society stands in stark contrast to Luciente's use of 'person';

equally, readers of the carpenter's narrative might feel coerced to identify 'na' as either 'male' or 'female'. Confronted with the opposition between the two 'languages', readers might reflect on the related 'Lebensformen', that is, why sex/gender might, or might not, be considered relevant. This reflection reveals the binaries inherent in the linguistic and social norms, as well as illustrates potential alternatives. In short, as Wittgenstein argues, it is language that allows speakers to reflect on a 'form of life', whether already in existence or a potential alternative. And it is language that can be adapted if our conceptions of our 'Lebensform' change.

Conclusions

In proposing linguistic neutrality, *The Cook and the Carpenter* and *Woman on the Edge of Time* enable a different representation and thereby understanding of human beings. Rather than being classified according to sex/gender, as women and men continue to be according to the linguistic status quo, the epicenes 'na' and 'person' suggest people could be referred to in terms of their shared humanity. This egalitarian language use clashes fundamentally with dominant norms – and as Arnold and Piercy explore in their novels, this clash has violent consequences. Both the inhabitants of the future society and the carpenter's group are under attack. This struggle results in an uncertain future for Luciente's community and the abandonment of the neutral pronoun at the end of the carpenter's narrative. But while the use of 'na' and 'person' is presented as fraught with tension, it also illuminates the status quo's limitations. Connie's need to identify sex/gender, for example, seems crude in contrast to Luciente's neutral understanding. Equally, the threat of 'male' violence in response to the carpenter's peaceful use of 'na' highlights to whom neutrality might be a threat.

As Wittgenstein argues, language and social practices are interlinked, and the 'Lebensform' imagined by Arnold and Piercy is essentially at odds with the dominant context. Before both language and 'form of life' are able to transition into the mainstream, they need to first become accepted by the wider community. Still, as Wittgenstein states, '[w]ir benennen die Dinge und können nun über sie reden: Uns in der Rede auf sie beziehen' (Wittgenstein 1953, 13) [[w]e name things and then we can talk about them: can refer to them in talk (Wittgenstein 1953, 13e)]; that is, by giving a 'name' to a neutral understanding, speakers have the means to talk about it. In effect, by being able to speak about neutrality, language users are able to contemplate its possibility. Wittgenstein elaborates, 'das Hören des Namens [ruft] uns das Bild des Benannten vor die Seele' (Wittgenstein 1953, 18) [hearing the name calls before our mind the picture of what is named (Wittgenstein 1953, 18e)]; that is, language helps speakers to imagine a referent, whether new or customary. Nevertheless, this imagination takes place in the context of 'menschlichen Gepflogenheiten und Institutionen' [human customs and institutions] and if these 'Gepflogenheiten' are essentially opposed to neutrality, any alternate vision is necessarily limited.

'[L]anguage is vitally connected to our value system and social and cultural background' (Tanner 1987, 419), Laura E. Tanner states in 'Self-Conscious Representation in the Slave Narrative', and as such it reflects how speakers understand themselves and their reality. However, this understanding shifts and evolves with new insights and perspectives – as illustrated in Arnold's and Piercy's narratives. While neutral pronouns are yet to be commonly accepted, they certainly illustrate the status quo's constraints. A third approach highlighting the underlying premise of the prevailing 'value system' is linguistic reversal. As Gerd Brantenberg's *Egalias døtre*, and its translations, show, male-as-norm is never more surprising than when confronted with the opposite ideology. In Chapter 4 I assess the English and German versions of Brantenberg's novel with particular focus on the author's use of language. As my discussion shows, what seems peculiar in reversal can hold up a compelling mirror to what is deemed ordinary. I evaluate the translators' problematisations from a linguistic and philosophical perspective, and assess the effectiveness of both versions in relation to the other texts.

Note

1. A German translation of *The Cook and the Carpenter* is yet to be published; all translations are my own.

4
Reversing the linguistic status quo
Egalias døtre

As well as problematising the linguistic status quo and proposing linguistic neutrality, literary writers have employed the technique of reversal to highlight the issues inherent in the dominant representation of women and men in language. Gerd Brantenberg's 1977 *Egalias døtre* is a key example. In the following I evaluate the text's translations to explore the effectiveness of Brantenberg's approach in relation to English and German. Freud's thought on humour provides the frame.

Freud's liberating laughter

Sigmund Freud is probably best known for his work on psychoanalysis and the interpretation of dreams, rather than humour. As Kai Rugenstein confirms in *Humor: Die Verflüssigung des Subjekts bei Hippokrates, Jean Paul, Kierkegaard und Freud*, 'das Thema [Humor nimmt] in der Interpretation seines Werks … traditionell eine eher marginale Position ein' (Rugenstein 2014, 241) [The topic [humour has] in the interpretation of his works … traditionally a rather marginal position]. However, Susanne Riester believes that Freud's thought is 'ungerechterweise vernachlässigt' (Riester 2006, 90). She argues in '"Der Witz und seine Beziehung zum Unbewussten" von Sigmund Freud' that jokes '[lieferten] interessantes und wichtiges Material für sein theoretisches Gebäude der Psychoanalyse' (Riester 2006, 90) [[provided] interesting and valuable material for his theoretical construct of psychoanalysis]. In fact, Freud considered 'Humor "eine der höchsten psychischen Leistungen" des Menschen' (Rugenstein 2014, 241) [humour 'one of the greatest mental achievements' of human beings], according to Rugenstein. So instead of being marginal to Freud's understanding of the human psyche, humour plays a central role. Written in 1905, *Der Witz und seine Beziehung zum Unbewussten* explores the individual and social impact of humour; the notion of its liberating potential is of particular interest.

'Der Witz wird uns gestatten, Lächerliches am Feind zu verwerten, das wir entgegenstehender Hindernisse wegen nicht laut oder nicht bewußt vorbringen durften' (Freud 1948, 113) [A joke will allow us to exploit something ridiculous in our enemy which we could not, on account of obstacles in the way, bring forward openly or consciously (Freud 1975, 103)]. A 'Feind' might be a figure of authority, for example, whom speakers are prevented from openly challenging owing to social norms. Such 'Hindernisse' might be caused by 'innerliche Hemmungen oder äußerliche Umstände' (Freud 1948, 115) [internal inhibitions and external circumstances (Freud 1975, 105)], and thereby maintain the dominant order. Humour, however, and the joke in particular, allow a release from this hierarchy. As Freud explains, '[d]er Witz stellt dann eine Auflehnung gegen solche Autorität [dar]', and thereby enables 'eine Befreiung von dem Drucke derselben' (Freud 1948, 115) [[t]he joke then represents a rebellion against that authority, a liberation from its pressure (Freud 1975, 105)]. This 'Befreiung' stems from the subversion of the usual power-positions, which is both funny and pleasurable. '[Die] Beseitigung von Hemmungen', '[erlaubt es] Lust frei zumachen' (Freud 1948, 151) [liberating pleasure by getting rid of inhibitions (Freud 1975, 134)]. As compliance with social norms requires 'psychische[n] Aufwand' (Freud 1948, 133) [psychical expenditure (Freud 1975, 118)], the elimination of these norms also reduces the psychological effort. Consequently, humour has desirable side effects.

This pleasure is particularly linked to 'Quellen des Spielens mit Worten' (Freud 1948, 151) [sources of play upon words (Freud 1975, 134)], as Freud terms it. '[T]echniques such as displacement, condensation with or without substitutive formation, modification, formation of mixed words, ambiguity, representation through the opposite, double meaning', Mary Eloise Ragland elaborates in 'The Language of Laughter', 'deflect word and thought expectations' (Ragland 1976, 94). By playing with the norms of association and expression, language becomes the site of 'Lust', with puns an effective tool to subvert linguistic constraints. As Walter Redfern argues in *Puns*, wordplay is 'an agent of disorder … [as it] breaks the conventions of orthodox speech or writing' (Redfern 1984, 14). In doing so, 'as well as pointing outwards', he adds, 'wordplay always points inwards and refers to the duplicity of language' (Redfern 1984, 10). By turning language in on itself, puns essentially reveal its normative function. Alan Partington agrees in *The Linguistics of Laughter:*

A Corpus-Assisted Study of Laughter-Talk. '[Puns] can be a highly effective rhetorical weapon' (Partington 2006, 113), he states; 'the disruptive nature of wordplay is explained by its abruptly switching attention away from the subject matter in hand ... to language' (Partington 2006, 118). Through wordplay, then, language can be revealed for what it is: a key tool to both communicate and uphold 'normality'.

The response to such humour is what Zvi Lothane terms the 'laughter of recognition' (Lothane 2008, 233). He argues in 'The Uses of Humor in Life, Neurosis and in Psychotherapy: Part 2' that this type of laughter occurs 'when something not consciously thought, something previously repressed, rises to consciousness' (Lothane 2008, 233). So when made aware of 'the duplicity of language', as Redfern calls it, speakers experience pleasure. And this pleasure stems from recognising the normative role of language as well as its liberating potential. The generic use of 'he' and 'man' is one example of 'repressed' or 'unconscious' usage; and one means to highlight the underlying premise is through reversal. As Gerd Brantenberg, and her translators, show in *Egalias døtre*, employing female generic terms has humorous potential precisely because speakers recognise the familiar male-as-norm. Before I assess the impact of Brantenberg's approach in relation to Freud's conception of laughter as 'liberation', I present how *Egalias døtre*, and specifically its English and German translations, turn dominant linguistic practices upside down. I thereby evaluate the effectiveness of Brantenberg's reversal as well as situate it in relation to the previously presented approaches.

Egalias døtre in translation

Published in 1977, Gerd Brantenberg's *Egalias døtre* was a key text of the Norwegian second wave feminist movement. Brantenberg took a unique approach to illustrating the disparity between the sexes/genders, which in turn contributed to the success of her novel: in Egalia women, not men, are considered the norm. The reversal of the familiar world view is presented through the experiences of the text's central character. Petronius, a male in a gynocentric context, encounters sexism in every environment, be it at home, school or in wider society. Following him through his teenage years to young adulthood, the narrative explores the restrictions imposed on Petronius. And these restrictions are also communicated in language: generic terms are female and positive connotations associated with women only. By reversing the premise male-as-norm, *Egalias døtre* effectively highlights the androcentricity of the Norwegian language. To provide one example, by rendering the indefinite pronoun 'man' as 'dam' (Brantenberg 1977, 11), the author brings linguistic bias to the fore.

Translations into several languages, including English and German, followed, with Louis Mackay's 1985 English version *The Daughters of Egalia* and Elke Radicke and Wilfried Sczepan's 1987 German translation *Die Töchter Egalias* at the centre of my discussion. Both versions provide a valuable insight into the workings of each language; like Brantenberg's original they effectively highlight the extent and impact of an androcentric status quo. However, as English and German differ in structure, so do the translations of *Egalias døtre*. While sex/gender is predominantly assigned according to social expectations in English, German is additionally grammatically gendered. Furthermore, key terms have distinct etymologies in each language that consequently lead to different interpretations. The below examples from the opening sections of each text illustrate the distinct approaches:

> 'But I want to be a seawom! I'll just take the baby with me', said Petronius ingeniously. ... His sister laughed derisively. She was a year and a half younger and she teased him constantly. 'Ha, ha! And a manwom can't be a seawom either, a mafele seawom! Ho ho! Or perhaps you're going to be a cabin *boy* or a sea*manwom*, or a helms-*manwom*? I'll die laughing, I will.... ' (Brantenberg 1985, 9–10, emphasis in original)

> 'Aber ich will Seefrau werden! Ich nehme die Kinder einfach mit', sagte Petronius erfinderisch. ... Seine Schwester lachte gemein. Sie war anderthalb Jahre jünger als er und ärgerte ihn immer. 'Haha! Ein Mann soll Seefrau werden? Denkste!' Neunmalklug fügte sie noch hinzu, daß der Widersinn doch schon in den Wörtern liege. 'Eine männliche Seefrau! Der blödeste Ausdruck seit Wibschengedenken. Ho, ho! Vielleicht solltest du Schiffs*junge* werden? Oder Zimmer*mann*? oder Steuer*mann*?! Ich lach' mich tot. ...' (Brantenberg 1987, 7–8, emphasis in original)

Petronius's exclamation in either language, 'I want to be a seawom!' and 'ich will Seefrau werden!', respectively highlights a key difference. Mackay creates a neologism to express Petronius's career aspiration, 'seawom', whereas the German translation reverses existing terminology, 'Seefrau'. 'Seawom' is striking on two levels: first of all, it is based on 'seaman', which is less familiar than the more commonly used 'sailor'. And secondly, in reversing 'man', 'woman' is condensed to 'wom'. Opting for the reversal of 'seaman', rather than 'sailor', makes sense on two accounts. On the one hand, 'seawom(an)' is a direct translation of the Norwegian 'sjøkvinne' (Brantenberg 1977, 11); on the other, it preserves the visible bias of the noun. While 'sailor' and 'seaman' have similar definitions, '[a] person whose job it is to work as a member of the crew of a commercial or naval ship' and '[a] person who works as a sailor' (OD 2016, n. pag.) respectively, 'sea-man' additionally highlights the terms' specificity. 'Sailor', like 'seaman', is an occupation traditionally reserved for men; in turn, 'seawom' conveys female-as-norm. Additionally, 'sailor', while more familiar to most readers, would have been more challenging to reverse. The suffix 'a', commonly employed in female names, might have been one potential option; however, 'saila', for example, is potentially too obscure for readers to understand. Furthermore, the term 'wom' plays a central role in the reversal, and introducing it at this stage alerts readers and also prepares them for the Egalian norm.

The use of 'wom', rather than 'woman', highlights a gynocentric understanding. In contrast to 'woman', which contains 'man' and implies that 'woman' might be a particular type of 'man', 'wom', and its derivative 'manwom', convey that the female half of 'huwomity' (Brantenberg 1985, 137) is the norm. The link between terms and associations is brought to the fore: a 'manwom' is considered a lesser kind of 'wom' and therefore perceived unable to perform any of the roles associated with female Egalians. Consequently, for Petronius, a 'manwom', to take on a profession such as 'seawom' requires a linguistic and conceptual shift that seems unsurmountable. In fact, as his sister's response shows, the extension of the female term to include the male seems laughable. '[A] mafele seawom' and 'seamanwom' imply an essential deviation from a gynocentric point of view, with the use of 'mafele' underscoring the specificity of the female terms. Based on 'fele', 'mafele', like 'manwom', is linked to the notion that 'wom' is the linguistic and conceptual norm. Its English equivalents 'male' and 'female' are considered etymologically unrelated, since 'female' originates from the Latin *'femella'* (OD 2016, n. pag., emphasis in original). Nonetheless, the *Oxford Dictionaries*' online platform confirms that '[t]he change in the ending was due to association with male' (OD 2016, n. pag). Consequently, 'fele', assuming the role of blueprint, relegates 'mafele' to the secondary sex/gender once more. The need for double specification of 'mafele' as a type of 'fele' and 'manwom' as a type of 'wom' aptly underscores the ridiculousness of Petronius's proposal in the sociocultural context of Egalia.

As the German version explains, 'der Widersinn [liegt] doch schon in den Wörtern'; that is, it is nonsensical for Petronius to desire what he is linguistically and therefore conceptually excluded from. A 'mafele seawom' is literally 'unheard of' and consequently inconceivable – a point that is also made in the German translation. While 'Seefrau' is a more direct reversal of the familiar 'Seemann' – 'Frau' and 'Mann' are etymologically unrelated – it equally highlights the term's specificity. Consequently, '[e]in Mann soll Seefrau werden' and '[e]ine männliche Seefrau' are, according to Petronius's sister, as ludicrous as their English equivalents. In fact, she believes that Petronius's ambition is '[d]er blödeste Ausdruck seit Wibschengedenken' [the most stupid expression since the beginning of time]. While Radicke and Sczepan might not have chosen a neologism to communicate female-as-norm in the reversal of 'Seemann', the use of 'Wibsche' shows that invented terms are not restricted to the English translation. 'Mensch' is etymologically linked to 'Mann', as explored in Chapter 2; consequently, the term 'Menschengedenken' results in the implication that male thought is the norm. To reverse the noun according to Egalian ideology, it needs to be associated with 'woman': 'Wibsche', based on 'Weib', allows for the conception of 'Frau' as the default 'hu-wom'. With the help of terms such as 'Wibschengedenken', the artificiality of the premise male-as-norm is underlined. Consequently, 'this is how it has always been' seems no longer to be an adequate explanation for the binary division of human beings. It was 'Menschengedenken', the implication seems, that resulted in linguistic and conceptual othering, and it is human thought also that can alter the hierarchy of the sexes/genders.

Androcentric bias is deeply engrained in the English and German language as the following examples illustrate: 'cabin *boy*', 'Schiffs*junge*' and 'Steuer*mann*' exist also in the reader's context and are therefore distinctly recognisable. And while the italicisation of 'boy', 'Junge' and 'Mann' implies that their Egalian usage is a novelty, the very familiarity of the terms seems to override the translators' intention. 'Cabin boys' and 'Steuermänner' might not be everyday terms; however, their specificity is. As a result, the associated Egalian nouns 'cabin girls' and 'Steuerfrauen' might be lost as the male terms are essentially unexceptional to readers. On the other hand, the recognisability of 'cabin boy' and 'Steuermann' can also be argued to direct the reader's attention. Rather than being dismissed as a fictional world with no impact on the readers' context, the use of familiar terms in conjunction with neologisms accentuates the linguistic status quo. The specificity of 'cabin boy' and 'Steuermann' might usually remain unnoticed; however, in juxtaposition with the female terms, their linguistic and conceptual limitation is illuminated. Consequently, the translations create a dialogue with their respective languages, playfully revealing bias where it might not usually be perceived. This reminds of Iser's conception of literary texts as a form of communication – one that is rooted in the experience of existing norms but also opens up new perspectives on them.

Grammar is a key site of this communication, as the heading of the first chapter indicates. 'Bram, the director, and her family', and 'Direktorin Bram und ihre Familie: Kristoffer, Petronius und Ba' underscore the extent to which each language functions on the premise male-as-norm. The use of 'director' in conjunction with the male pronoun, as in 'Bram, the director, and his family', would be as unremarkable as 'Direktor' and 'seine Familie'. The reversed version, however, was, and still is, decidedly less familiar. This is visible in the default grammatical gender of the German term: the suffix '-in' implies a deviation. Additionally, 'director' and 'Direktor' are biased conceptually. As men continue to dominate positions of power, English and German speakers are more likely to associate the terms with 'man' and 'Mann' rather than 'woman' and 'Frau'. This link is reflected pronominally in the familiar 'director, he' and 'Direktor, er'. Turning this norm upside down has a poignant effect: 'director, she' and 'Direktorin, sie' disrupt the linguistic and conceptual status quo. Naming practices further enshrine the social standing of the sexes/genders; while 'Direktorin Bram' is referred to by her last name, her husband is listed as part of the family group and addressed by his first name, Kristoffer, only. Consequently, Bram is presented as a public person commanding respect whereas Kristoffer is restricted to the private sphere of domesticity and familiarity.

Critics have commented on the pertinence of Brantenberg's text, and its translations, and especially their use of subversion to uncover the dominant norms. Denise Kulp, for example, understands the narrative as 'a satire, and one with a bite' (Kulp 1986, 19), in her review of the English version. Luise F. Pusch agrees in her review; she deems the German translation 'witzig', 'bissig' and 'scharfsinnig' (Pusch 1984, 69) ['funny', 'biting' and 'perceptive']; its engagement with language is considered particularly effective. '[D]ie Regeln der Männersprache', she explains, 'werden listig und sinnig auf den Kopf gestellt, uns spiegelverkehrt vorgeführt, mit dem einzigen Ziel, die Sprache des Patriarchats … als solche erkennbar zu machen' (Pusch 1984, 70) [[T]he rules of male language are artfully and purposefully turned upside down, shown mirror-inverted, with the one goal to render the language of patriarchy … recognisable as such]. Karin Richter-Schröder concurs in *Frauenliteratur und weibliche Identität: Theoretische Ansätze zu einer weiblichen Ästhetik und zur Entwicklung der neuen deutschen Frauenliteratur.*

The linguistic reversal is 'provokant', according to Richter-Schröder, as the text shows that 'weder die Strukturen unserer Sprache noch unser Sprachgebrauch als geschlechtsneutral aufgefaßt werden können' (Richter-Schröder 1986, 38) [provocative ... neither the structures of our language nor our language use can be understood as neutral]. The German translation clearly illustrates the issues inherent in the linguistic status quo. Through reversal, 'die Sprache des Patriarchats' is revealed as anything but 'geschlechtsneutral' – by showing the status quo in a new light, Brantenberg's text, and its translations, enable readers to question its androcentric rules and conventions.

Not all reviews were as favourable, however, as this reference to the Swedish reception highlights. Verne Moberg illustrates in 'A Norwegian Women's Fantasy: Gerd Brantenberg's "Egalias Døtre" as "Kvinneskelig Utopia"' that some consider the Swedish version lacking. Lars Olof Franzén and Bernt Eklundh, for example, 'found the novel worthwhile and entertaining *up to a point*', but overall they deem the narrative to be 'tiresome', 'dragged out' and 'mechanical' (Moberg 1985, 329, emphasis in original). Another unnamed (male) reviewer takes this judgement one step further, describing the translation as 'vulgar', 'superficial', 'sterile' and 'sadistic' (Moberg 1985, 329). While these responses could be dismissed as simply antagonistic, they also point to certain concerns readers may have. Jan Relf's argument in 'Women in Retreat: The Politics of Separatism in Women's Literary Utopias' illustrates why this might be the case. Brantenberg's text might not be a 'separatist utopia' per se; however, it shares similarities to some degree. For one, by turning the dominant norms on their head rather than altering their core premise, *Egalias døtre* could be perceived as separatist. As such, the novel, to follow Relf, might cause 'inverted sexism and a perpetuation of the unproductive binary opposition game' (Relf 1991, 141). By presenting one sex/gender as superior, the other is perceived as lacking. At the same time, however, the reversal of the hierarchy can also be seen to uncover that such a classification exists. Many readers might not be aware of the extent and impact of the status quo. As it is effectively integrated into everyday language, the persistent use of male nouns and pronouns might often remain unnoticed. Through reversal this suddenly becomes obvious. Considered from this angle, Brantenberg's novel, and its translations, do not perpetuate 'the binary opposition game' but expose its very mechanisms. And by exposing them, it enables speakers to challenge and disrupt the underlying premise male-as-norm.

'Der von *Brantenberg* angestrebte und erzielte Lerneffekt', Pusch confirms, 'ist der, daß uns **unsere** Bedingungen, die des Frauseins im

Patriarchat, allmählich oder auch schlagartig genauso fremd, absurd, unerhört und ungeheuerlich vorkommen' (Pusch 1984, 72, emphasis in original) [The aspired and achieved learning effect of *Brantenberg* is that our conditions, of being female under patriarchy, gradually or even abruptly appear just as strange, absurd, shocking and outrageous]. In effect, by holding up a mirror to the dominant norms, the translations of *Egalias døtre* help to illuminate them. But how does this 'spiegelverkehrte' illumination take place? And how does it differ in English and German? In the following sections I assess Mackay's and Radicke/Sczepan's versions with particular focus on nouns and pronouns, names and titles. The aim is to evaluate the breadth of Brantenberg's translators' linguistic revision and explore its consequences. This ties in with my previous evaluations and will illustrate the effectiveness of this particular literary approach.

Nouns and pronouns

As shown above, both versions work with neologisms and direct reversals to communicate the premise female-as-norm. And the choice for either tactic depends on a term's connotation and/or etymology. Examples of word creations are 'manwom', which plays on the link between the nouns 'woman' and 'man', while 'Wibsche' comments on the etymological connection between 'Mensch' and 'Mann'. Where no such link is perceived male terms are reversed, that is, replaced by their female counterparts, such as 'Frau' being used instead of 'Mann'. However, all terms remain recognisable. The neologisms 'manwom' and 'Wibsche' are visibly tied to existing English and German nouns, 'woman' and 'Weib' respectively. This ensures intelligibility as well as the ability to reflect on the status quo of each language. The German indefinite pronoun is here a good example. 'Es ist viel grauer und trister, nicht werden zu dürfen, was dam will' (Brantenberg 1987, 7) [It's more dreary and depressing not being able to be what one wants (Brantenberg 1985, 9)], Petronius responds when told that his ambition to become a 'Seefrau' was ludicrous. Instead of the familiar 'man' the reader encounters 'dam'. And while this term is new to German speakers, it is nevertheless recognisable. First of all, 'dam' and 'man' seem visibly similar, and secondly, the neologism contains a link to the German noun 'Dame'. This link, in particular, aims to prompt readers to question the generic use of 'man'. As 'dam' is related to 'Dame', the connection between 'man' and 'Mann' is highlighted in turn. Consequently, through reversal, the German indefinite pronoun is exposed as far from generic.

However, 'dam' is also a puzzling choice. First of all, its root 'Dame' is a rather formal term. Secondly, in contrast to 'Mann'/'man', the noun is not part of everyday language. And thirdly, the pronoun 'frau', which has been in existence since the late 1970s, is a more direct equivalent. The translators' preference can nevertheless be justified: on the one hand, it is a replication of the Norwegian original, 'dam' (Brantenberg 1977, 11), and on the other, it performs a similar function to 'man'. Like 'man', 'dam' could potentially pass unnoticed. As the indefinite pronoun is used frequently, and without much consideration or comment in the German language, the more subtle 'dam' mirrors its linguistic form and function. And while 'dam' is of course more noticeable than 'man', it equally requires closer investigation. Additionally, unlike 'man' and 'dam', 'frau' is openly specific and might therefore be more easily dismissed as an inadequate comment on the German language. This issue is easily circumvented in the English translation. The existing pronoun 'one' (Brantenberg 1985, 9) is able to represent 'man'/'dam' without obvious connotations. Nevertheless, in a sociocultural setting founded on the division of the sexes/genders, what does 'one' stand for? The subsequent use of '[n]owom' (Brantenberg 1985, 15) and 'anywom' (Brantenberg 1985, 44), instead of 'no one' and 'anyone', proposes that even 'one' might not be as neutral as it initially seems. In effect, the English indefinite pronoun is considered similarly problematic. As 'one' shifts to 'wom', male-as-norm is once more subtly revealed in reversal.

Not all are conscious problematisations. Occasionally, both translations simply slip in consistency – however, these slippages often provide a poignant commentary in themselves. The German version struggles with gynocentric terms, in particular. For example, Petronius's sister's justification, '[e]s gibt ja gar keine Taucheranzüge für Männer' (Brantenberg 1987, 8) [[t]here are no diving suits (masc.) for men], is contradictory. First of all, 'Taucher' is a male generic term, with 'Taucherin' its appropriate reversal. Secondly, as the noun is 'male' by default the explanation, 'für Männer', is unnecessary. For the translation to reflect the Egalian context, either 'Taucher' would have to be italicised akin to 'Schiffs*junge*' and 'Steuer*mann*', or it should read 'Taucherinnenanzüge für Männer' to indicate the deviation from female-as-norm. The English version's 'frogwom suits for menwim' (Brantenberg 1985, 10) is a good example of the second tactic; it replaces 'man' with 'wom' while highlighting the incompatibility of the female term and 'menwim' through specification. As such, it is more successful than its German equivalent in conveying the Egalian status quo. Another slippage of the German translation is the use of 'Vaterschaftspatronat' (Brantenberg 1987, 9) [fatherhood patronage] to indicate the legal arrangement between 'wim' and 'menwim' in relation to children.[1] Again, 'Patronat' is a male term, stemming from 'Patron', 'lateinisch patronus, zu: pater = Vater' (Duden 2016, n. pag.). Consequently, 'Vaterschaftsmatronat' would have been a more suitable term to express 'female patronage'. As it stands, the term is confusing. The English version is again more successful by circumventing the issue altogether: it employs the more neutral 'fatherhood protection' (Brantenberg 1985, 11) to convey that it is menwim who are in a legally precarious position. A third example of a difference in effectiveness between the German and English versions is the expression 'hysterische Mannspersonen' (Brantenberg 1987, 65) [hysterical men] in contrast to 'testerical menwim' (Brantenberg 1985, 70). While the English translation reverses the underlying premise of 'hysterical', 'from *hustera* "womb" (hysteria being thought to be specific to women and associated with the womb)' (OD 2016, n. pag., emphasis in original), and associates the condition with testes, the German reproduces its inherent prejudice. According to the Egalian norm, the womb has distinctly positive connotations; therefore 'hysterical' is inconceivable to begin with. 'Testerical', on the other hand, underscores female-as-norm and male-as-deviation.

However, not all instances of slippage into the linguistic status quo are as obvious. Male-as-norm sometimes creeps into the German translation even less noticeably, which aptly comments on the extent and opaqueness of male generic terms. For example, the term 'Schüler' (Brantenberg 1987, 14) [pupils (Brantenberg 1985, 17)] is used in at least six instances and 'Arbeiter' (Brantenberg 1987, 42) [workers (Brantenberg 1985, 47)] in at least two across the novel. Additionally, the translation refers to 'Vertreter' (Brantenberg 1987, 40) [member (Brantenberg 1985, 45) and 'Egaliataner' (Brantenberg 1987, 27) [Egalians (Brantenberg 1985, 32)]. These examples highlight how challenging it is to maintain consistency in reversing the status quo. As the translators' context and language are shaped by one particular world view, communicating the opposite is tricky. Furthermore, the default grammatical gender of the German language, in particular, is challenging to reverse at all times. However, when translated consistently, the German version is more effective in conveying gynocentricity. As the following examples show, grammar can be a distinct advantage when communicating the Egalian world view:

> The Narcisseum Club for Gentlewim was situated halfway up the Moonhill ... In principle, anywom who wanted to could become a member; in practice, the club's membership consisted almost exclusively of company directors, senior civil servants, chief divers, school

principals, members of Parliament and scientists. (Brantenberg 1985, 44)

Der Frauenklub 'Freiheit' lag auf halber Höhe des Plattenbergs ... Im Prinzip konnte jede Mitglied werden. Praktisch jedoch waren die Mitglieder vor allem die Direktorinnen und Unterdirektorinnen der staatlichen Kooperative, Cheftaucherinnen, Taucherinnen, Rektorinnen, Volksvertreterinnen, Forscherinnen, Künstlerinnen und die Leiterinnen der Handelsorganisationen. (Brantenberg 1987, 39)

Both translations state that the club is reserved for women; the English version uses 'Club for Gentlewim' and the German 'Frauenklub' to highlight its specificity. Additionally, the quantifiers 'anywom' and 'jede' underscore gynocentricity. Linguistically and conceptually, women are the norm. However, the subsequent listing of club members in the English version seems to contradict a female-specific interpretation. '[C]ompany directors, senior civil servants, chief divers, school principals, members of Parliament and scientists' all carry particular connotations in the reader's sociocultural context. Despite appearing neutral at surface level, similarly to Genly's opening description in *The Left Hand of Darkness*, the terms predominantly imply male-as-norm.

To give one example, a 'Member of Parliament' (MP), defined as '[a] person formally elected to the UK national legislative body' (OD 2016, n. pag), seems neutral to begin with. A 'person', '[a] human being regarded as an individual' (OD 2016, n. pag.) according to its definition, could be a 'man' or a 'woman', after all. However, historically the role of MP was reserved for men – as women were not allowed to vote until 1918,[2] the first female MP was not elected until that year. While the noun has opened up conceptually over the past 100 years, in 2017 only 32 per cent of 650 seats were taken up by women despite almost a century of access to the UK Parliament. And as less than a third of MPs are female, the noun continues to connote 'male' first and foremost. The German 'Volksvertreterinnen', on the other hand, clearly communicates 'female'. By employing the suffix 'in' it overrides the dominant associations present also in the German-speaking context. In 2017, 31 per cent of 'Volksvertreter' in the Bundestag were female, resulting in preconceptions akin to the English version. 'Volksvertreterinnen', on the other hand, implies female-as-norm; the term is consequently much more effective in conveying the Egalian understanding. This effectiveness is underscored by the long list of female-specific nouns: 'Direktorinnen und Unterdirektorinnen der staatliche Kooperative, die Cheftaucherinnen, Taucherinnen, Rektorinnen, Forscherinnen, Künstlerinnen und die Leiterinnen der Handelsorganisationen'. In contrast to 'company directors' and 'scientists', the German version specifies 'Direktorinnen' and 'Forscherinnen' – terms that are linguistically and conceptually associated with 'female'. As a result, the German translation prompts readers to imagine a gynocentric environment, one that is not compromised by male-as-norm.

Despite occasional differences, both versions comment on the linguistic status quo of each language. The German reversal of male-as-norm highlights that generic terms associated with one sex/gender are not inclusive of the other – just as 'Volksvertreterinnen' does not imply 'male', the male generic 'Volksvertreter' struggles to evoke female. In a similar vein, the English translation shows that terms that might be linguistically neutral do not necessarily represent women and men equally. In line with dominant associations, terms such as 'members of Parliament' are interpreted as one particular sex/gender if they are linked to this sex/gender in reality and/or imagination. In fact, the noun 'member' is telling in itself; while the term is mainly defined as '[a] person, animal, or plant belonging to a particular group', it has previously been '[u]sed euphemistically to refer to the penis' (OD 2016 n. pag.). The German term 'Mitglied', while linguistically neutral, as highlighted by the pronoun 'es', carries similar connotations – 'Mit-glied', 'with-member' in translation, is equally biased. 'Glied', a term also for 'äußeres männliches Geschlechtsorgan; Penis', shares the same Latin origin as the specific understanding of 'member': 'membrum (verile)' (Duden 2016, n. pag.). Consequently, even seemingly inclusive terms can at times be shown to contain an etymological link to sex/gender. As these connotations lie beneath the surface level, reversing them is challenging. However, as 'testerical' and 'dam' show, closer inspection and wordplay can provide surprising insights.

Names and titles are another central tool to communicate linguistic and sociocultural norms; surnames, for example, also often imply a male norm. In the following section I assess Mackay's and Radicke/Sczepan's approaches to naming practices to explore how they support Brantenberg's approach in presenting a gynocentric world view.

Names and titles

As in *The Left Hand of Darkness*, *Häutungen*, *The Cook and the Carpenter* and *Woman on the Edge of Time*, names and titles play an important role in the English and German translations of *Egalias døtre*. The reversal of naming practices provides an additional perspective on the linguistic status quo, and further illustrates the differences between English and German. Mackay and Radicke/Sczepan employ distinct techniques to highlight the issues inherent in each language. The following translation is here a good example: the English form of address 'ladies and gentlemen' is reversed to 'lordies and gentlewim' (Brantenberg 1985, 11), while the familiar German 'Damen und Herren' [ladies and gentlemen] is rendered as 'Herren und Damen' (Brantenberg 1987, 9). Both approaches put the spotlight on dominant linguistic practices; however, their tactics clearly differ – a difference that is informed by the language's grammar and etymology. 'Gentlewim', for example, subverts the linguistic link between 'wo-man' and the male term, and 'lordies' is a humorous play on 'ladies'. The phonetic and structural similarity in each case ensures that the nouns remain recognisable to readers while providing a poignant commentary. 'Herren und Damen', on the other hand, remain the same; their shift in meaning is indicated only through a change in position. While less complex, the switching of terms equally ensures that readers are made aware of the difference in world view. In the Egalian context, the social hierarchy is clearly turned upside down.

'Herr' is also the male title in German and its altered understanding is consistently stressed throughout the narrative. In Egalia it is men, not women, who are categorised according to their marital status; the use of 'Herrlein' (Brantenberg 1987, 13) and 'Herr Cheftaucherin Ödeschär' (Brantenberg 1987, 33) signify the complete reversal of norms. 'Herrlein' mirrors the role of 'Fräulein', '(veraltet) kinderlose, ledige [junge] Frau' (Duden 2016, n. pag.) [(archaic) childless, single [young] woman]. Similarly, 'Herr' indicates a shift from 'unmarried' to 'married man'. And while 'Fräulein' might no longer be in everyday usage, the concept of marriage as a key event for women remains. This is confirmed by the definition of 'Frau' as 'Ehefrau' (Duden 2016, n. pag.) [wife], whereas the title 'Herr' holds no such equivalent meaning. 'Frau' of course functions both as title and noun, while 'Herr' does not; however, this dual role highlights an ingrained link between 'female' and 'married'. This connection is further supported by the superseding of her family name by his, aptly illustrated in reversal. The form of address 'Herr Cheftaucherin Ödeschär' implies that while the identity of 'Cheftaucherin Ödeschär' remains unchanged on marriage, her husband becomes an appendage to his wife. He loses his 'damename' (Brantenberg 1985, 56), as the English version terms it, and acquires a new title, 'Herr'. Consequently, 'Herrlein' is linguistically and conceptually passed from mother to wife, just as Connie is passed from father to husband in *Woman on the Edge of Time*.

Petronius explores this linguistic dependency in a reversal of the reversal. Writing a satire akin to Brantenberg's, he invents the title 'Frau Direktor Berg' (Brantenberg 1987, 227). And while this usage might seem ludicrous to Egalians, to German readers it did, and still does, appear fairly commonplace. This dual problematisation effectively highlights the extent of women's secondary standing in language.

The English version illustrates the issue with titles in a similar vein; moreover, it emphasises the social undesirability of 'mafele' singledom. As the use of '[s]pinnerman' (Brantenberg 1985, 15) shows, unmarried 'menwim' are subject to judgement. Modelled on 'spinster', which 'used to mean simply "unmarried woman"; it is now always a derogatory term, referring or alluding to a stereotype of an older woman who is unmarried, childless, prissy, and repressed' (OD 2016, n. pag.). 'Spinnerman' has equivalent connotations: a single 'manwom' is considered an aberration in the Egalian context. In contrast, the title 'Msass' implies a mafele's rightful place. Functioning as 'Mr' and 'Mrs' respectively, the titles 'Ms and Msass Bram' (Brantenberg 1985, 41) represent the norm. 'Ms', akin to its English equivalent, is 'used before the surname or full name of any woman regardless of her marital status' (OD 2016, n. pag.), while 'Msass' signifies 'husband', or 'housebound' (Brantenberg 1985, 17) as the English version terms it, of 'Ms Bram'. A 'Msass' is the approved position for 'menwim', and the title an interesting choice, albeit a problematic one. First of all, it is phonetically similar to 'Mrs', ensuring recognisability. Secondly, its components 'Ms' and 'ass' indicate linguistic and conceptual dependency. Additionally, the use of 'ass' is humorous – 'Msass' is 'made an ass of' by becoming the housebound of 'Ms'. And while this is a telling comment on the subjugation of 'Mrs', it misrepresents the relationship between the English titles at least linguistically. 'Mrs', an 'abbreviation of mistress' (OD 2016, n. pag.), is not as dependent a term as it might initially seem. In fact, 'Mr', according to Walter W. Skeat's 1882 *A Concise Etymological Dictionary of the English Language*, is '[a] corruption of *master*, due to the influence of *mistress*' (Skeat 1984, 330, emphasis in original). Being 'an older word than *mister*' (Skeat 1984, 330, emphasis in original), 'Mrs' was therefore far from always secondary. Nevertheless 'Mrs' is not understood as it once was; 'Msass' consequently underlines that 'Mrs' is no longer her 'own mistress'.

Titles are just one tool to reveal bias; first names and family names equally communicate the positions assigned to the sexes/genders. This becomes particularly visible in the following: while male characters carry names such as 'Lillerio Moondaughter' (Brantenberg 1985, 22) and 'Baldrian Bareskerry' (Brantenberg 1985, 22), their female counterparts are called 'Vita Strong' (Brantenberg 1985, 22) and 'Gro Maydaughter' (Brantenberg 1985, 29). These are prominent examples and more moderate versions certainly exist; however, they provide a useful perspective on the social status of 'wim' and 'menwim'. To evaluate two names in more depth, 'Vita', from 'Latin, literally "life"' (OD 2016, n. pag.), especially in combination with the family name 'Strong', seems to represent one end of the social hierarchy, while 'Lillerio Moondaughter' is positioned at the other. In name she is 'solid', 'robust', the giver of 'life' and in effect 'life' itself, while he seems 'frilly', without substance. Furthermore, his last name underlines this effaced role: 'Moondaughter' leaves no linguistic or conceptual room for a 'son'. Akin to androcentric names, such as 'Jefferson' and 'Zimmermann', 'Moondaughter' is modelled on the premise female-as-norm. Consequently, 'Lillerio Moondaughter' seems to exist only in dependency, and moreover enshrines the Egalian notion that 'their [menwim's] only purpose is decorative and ornamental' (Brantenberg 1985, 97). Brantenberg employs names consciously to communicate this division, as Moberg confirms. 'Petronius', in particular, Moberg argues, highlights a deeper commentary. 'The Petronius in *Egalias døtre*', she states, 'had a fitting namesake in Caius Petronius … considered to be the author of a fragment of a preserved humorous adventure novel, *Satirae*' (Moberg 1985, 331, emphasis in original). The use of 'Petronius' then is not only decorative but also implies the ability to subvert. And in his satirical reversal of the Egalian norms, he puts the spotlight on the extent and implications of the linguistic status quo.

To extend Brantenberg's linguistic experiment, I will present the history and etymology of female terms. This further underscores the sociocultural origins of language and thereby Brantenberg's effectiveness in problematising the linguistic status quo.

The history and etymology of female terms

A conversation between two of the novel's characters, Fandango and Baldrian, highlights the central concern around key terms in the English and German language. As Fandango argues in English, 'take the word "manwom" … it suggests that a manwom is just a certain sort of wom, though a wom isn't any sort of manwom. Why don't they just say "man"?' (Brantenberg 1985, 145). And in German he states, '[d]as Wort "Wibsche" hört sich an, als ob alle Wibschen Weiber sind. Warum könnte es nicht genausogut "Mannschen" heißen? Oder "Menschen"?', equally 'das Wort "dam" … Warum könnte es nicht genausogut "herr" heißen?

Oder "mann"?' (Brantenberg 1987, 129). Egalian nouns and pronouns are founded on the premise female-as-norm; their English and German counterparts are linked to the opposite world view. 'Man', 'human' and 'Mensch' are far from neutral terms, as explored in Chapter 2. However, to reverse Fandango's argument, is 'woman' really 'just a certain sort of man'?

To begin with 'woman', Nathan Bailey's 1721 *An Universal Etymological English Dictionary* and Samuel Johnson's 1755 *A Dictionary of the English Language* both define the term as 'the Female of the Human Race', linking it to the Saxon 'Wıman' (Bailey 1776, n. pag.) and 'pımman' (Johnson 1983, n. pag.) respectively. Bailey elaborates the origin of the noun as follows, 'Dr *Th. H.* derives it of Wıp, *Sax.* Wife and Man, but others of Wumb, *Sax.* and Man, *Sax.*' (Bailey 1776, n. pag., emphasis in original), which introduces two notions akin to Fandango's problematisation. First of all, 'woman' seems indeed a 'sort of man', and secondly, the term seems associated with 'womb' – the reproductive organ signifying the essential difference between women and men. Walter W. Skeat's 1882 *A Concise Etymological Dictionary of the English Language* confirms a link to 'man'; as he explains, 'woman' is '[a] phonetic alteration of A.S. *wīfman*, lit. wife-man' (Skeat 1984, 614, emphasis in original). But as Skeat adds, 'the word *man* ... [was] formerly applied to both sexes' (Skeat 1984, 614, emphasis in original), and thereby complicates the notion that 'woman' is 'just a certain sort of man'. While 'man' is now predominantly used in the specific sense, it was once a generic term. At some point, however, as illustrated previously, its meaning shifted and 'wo-man' became considered the specific counterpart to the generic/specific 'man'. But where does the prefix 'wo' originate from? Skeat relates it to 'wife' which comes from 'A.S. *wīf*, a woman'; however, he believes its '[r]oot [is] obscure; certainly not allied to *weave* (A.S. *wefan*) as the fable runs' (Skeat 1984, 610, emphasis in original). Bailey is also unsure as to its origin and links it to 'Wip, *Sax.* Wife' as well as 'Wumb'. This uncertainty carries over into T. F. Hoad's 1986 *The Concise Oxford Dictionary of English Etymology*, which deems 'woman', 'a formation peculiar to Eng.' (Hoad 1986, 541), and '*wīf*', 'of unkn[own] orig[in]' (Hoad 1986, 544, emphasis in original).

Julia Penelope (Stanley) and Cynthia McGowan explore the origin of both terms in 'Woman and Wife: Social and Semantic Shifts in English'. 'The OE [Old English] word wīf', the authors explain, 'retained its original meaning, "female human being," well into the OE period' (Penelope (Stanley) and McGowan 1979, 499, emphasis in original). So the shift to 'wo-man' is a relatively new development. However, '[a]t the same time, the term was becoming narrower in its semantic range'; that is, 'wife' was increasingly understood as 'female attached to a male' (Penelope (Stanley) and McGowan 1979, 499). And '[p]erhaps as a consequence of the narrower semantic range', Penelope (Stanley) and McGowan elaborate, 'the compound wīfman came to be used more and more frequently' (Penelope (Stanley) and McGowan 1979, 499, emphasis in original). The authors believe that this shift from 'wife' to 'woman' was due to 'increased patriarchal influence'; in line with the narrowing of 'the semantic range of man ... the range of reference of the word wīf' also narrowed (Penelope (Stanley) and McGowan 1979, 499–500, emphasis in original). The merging of 'wife' and 'man' signified that 'a female person' was now understood as essentially linked to 'a male human'. However, this linguistic and social dependency is an invention of the Old English period; it seems 'wife' once used to be her own 'woman'. But 'like other English words referring to women, [wif] might have undergone some degree of pejoration' (Baron 1986, 154), Dennis Baron argues in *Grammar and Gender*, which explains its demotion to prefix of 'man'. While this establishes the linguistic and conceptual standing of 'woman', could this past, and now obscure, understanding of 'wife' point to a different world view of 'woman'?

Skeat and Hoad both list the German noun 'Weib' as a direct relation, which is a good place to begin to answer the above. According to the online *Duden*, the term has four distinct meanings: '(veraltend) Frau als Geschlechtswesen im Unterschied zum Mann'; '(umgangssprachlich) [junge] Frau als Gegenstand sexueller Begierde, als [potenzielle] Geschlechtspartnerin'; '(abwertend) unangenehme weibliche Person, Frau' and '(veraltet) Ehefrau' (Duden 2016, n. pag.) [(archaic) woman as sexual being in contrast to man; (colloquial) [young] woman as an object of sexual desire, as [potential] sexual partner; (derogatory) unpleasant female person, woman; (archaic) wife]. Like 'wife' then, 'Weib' means 'Frau' in general as well as 'Ehefrau'; however, in contrast to the English noun, both definitions are confined to history. What remains are the connotations of 'Frau als Gegenstand sexueller Begierde' and 'unangenehme weibliche Person'. 'Weib' seems to have undergone a semantic derogation akin to 'wife', but in contrast to its English equivalent the noun has been banished from everyday language. Jacob Grimm and Wilhelm Grimm provide an insight into the shift to 'sexuelle' and/or 'unangenehme' understandings. They state in the 1878 *Deutsches Wörterbuch* that 'Weib' is understood as *'die niedrige'* and 'Frau' as *'die hochgestellte'* (Grimm and Grimm 1878, 353, emphasis in original) [the base ... the superior]. This change in meaning has a similar origin to the one proposed by Penelope

(Stanley) and McGowan for 'wife'. '[A]*ls gefahr für den mann wird das weib schon vom mittelalter beredt nach allen seiten dargestellt*' (Grimm and Grimm 1878, 367, emphasis in original) [woman has been represented as dangerous to the man from the Middle Ages], the Brothers Grimm explain. This particular conception of the sexes/genders potentially marks a change from a pre-Middle-Age understanding, and might have influenced the shift from 'wife' to 'wo-man'.

It is of course challenging if not impossible to locate evidence; just as the etymology of the term is opaque, so is its previous standing. While one could speculate either way – an Egalian perspective would hold a decidedly different position to an androcentric one – '*sicherheit ist bisher nicht gewonnen*' (Grimm and Grimm 1878, 329, emphasis in original) [certainty has not been gained so far]. Consequently, 'Weib' remains 'etymologisch ganz unklar' (Kluge 1989, 781), as Friedrich Kluge confirms in his 1883 *Etymologisches Wörterbuch der deutschen Sprache*, and continues to be so to this day: 'Herkunft ungeklärt' (Duden 2016, n. pag.) [origin unclear], the online *Duden* asserts. The origin of its substitute 'Frau', on the other hand, is well documented. According to the Brothers Grimm, 'Frau', from '*goth*. fraujô … *ist moviert aus* frauja' (Grimm and Grimm 1878, 71, emphasis in original) [goth. fraujô … derives from frauja]. The authors elaborate its origin as follows: 'frauja [*war*] *der waltende herr und gebieter, die* frau *seine genoszin*' (1878, 73, emphasis in original) [frauja [was] the ruling lord and master, the woman his companion]. And while the Grimms portray 'Frau' as 'mitherrschend' (Grimm and Grimm 1878, 73) [codominant], it is 'man' who is considered 'der waltende herr und gebieter'. 'Frau' is therefore deemed as dependent as 'wo-man'. Equally, the term has a long history, for '[s]chon im Beginn des 13. Jahrh. war der Gebrauch Frau für Weib gebräuchlich, um einen vornehmen Stand zu bezeichnen' (Hoffmann 1871, 610) [already at the beginning of the thirteenth century, Frau was used instead of Weib to describe a noble status], according to Wilhelm Hoffmann's 1871 *Vollständiges Wörterbuch der deutschen Sprache*. The linguistic and conceptual demotion of 'Weib'/'wife' therefore seems to symbolise the onset of a new androcentric norm: 'Frau' as Mann's 'companion', 'Weib' as 'dangerous', 'wife' as 'married to a man' and 'wo-man' as 'womb-man'.

But what about 'she': is the female pronoun also tied to male-as-norm? According to Skeat, its Anglo-Saxon origin 'hēo' is linked to 'hē', the root of the male pronoun, 'he' (Skeat 1984, 235). And while the two are distinct they share a close relationship. In fact, this seems to have become problematic as 'hēo' 'caused confusion with the masc. *he*' (Skeat 1984, 479, emphasis in original) – this confusion must have complicated male-as-norm and must have therefore inspired the later adaptation of the female pronoun 'hēo', via 'sēo' and 'scho', to 'she' (Skeat 1984, 479, emphasis in original). The distinction between the two sexes/genders was clearly significant prior to the pronominal shift, as the difference between 'hēo' and 'hē' indicates. However, it seems to have become more important since. '[T]he English pronominal system underwent a veritable grammatical upheaval during the Middle English period' (Stanley and Robbins 1978, 71), Julia P. Stanley and Susan W. Robbins explain in 'Going through the Changes: The Pronoun *She* in Middle English'. Around the same time as 'wife' was transformed into 'woman', 'hēo' was adapted to 'she'. '[T]he apparently persistent need for a pronoun which uniquely specifies the female gender', the authors argue, 'must spring from the same conception of the identities and roles assigned to females and males in a male-dominated culture' (Stanley and Robbins 1978, 81). To maintain the sociocultural boundaries between the sexes/genders, firm linguistic borders were needed. And as 'hēo' permeated these borders by 'causing confusion', the pronoun 'she' eventually came into being.

The German female pronoun, 'sie', has a similar history to 'she' to a large extent. Like Skeat, the Brothers Grimm list its etymology under the male pronoun, again implying a close connection. Furthermore, it seems to have also undergone a shift, albeit a little earlier. The Gothic roots 'is' and 'si', 'er' and 'sie' respectively show a linguistic link; however, the Old High German 'ir, ër' and 'siu' (Grimm and Grimm 1878, 680) already begin to segregate into the distinct pronouns used today. The reasons for this alteration are presumably similar to those provided by Stanley and Robbins – the need to distinguish clearly between the sexes/genders.

Can laughter be liberating?

When reading Petronius's satirical reversal of the Egalian status quo, his father, Christopher, experiences what Lothane terms 'laughter of recognition'. In contrast to his mother's 'bad-tempered' response, 'Christopher went on laughing until he fell over' (Brantenberg 1985, 267). In fact, '[h]e felt invigorated' by Petronius's writing; so much so that he demanded to be taken seriously and 'slammed his fist on the table' (Brantenberg 1985, 267). The 'mafele Egalian reader', it seems, is liberated by the humorous text. However, is Brantenberg's text likely to have a similar impact on the female English and German reader? In '"Laughing in a Liberating Defiance": *Egalia's Daughters* and Feminist Tendentious Humor', Marleen S. Barr takes the position that laughter can indeed be liberating. She states, 'laughing at patriarchy breaks the rules', and by breaking the rules it is 'a feminist achievement' (Barr 1989, 90–1). Like Christopher and Petronius, women are meant to comply with the dominant social order, one that considers them secondary on the basis of their sex/gender. By provoking a gleeful reaction to the reversal of norms, the novel, according to Barr, acts as 'a social corrective – a weapon' (Barr 1989, 93). Barr considers humour a powerful social tool; Freud agrees, '[der Witz] schafft dem Feind ein Heer von Gegnern, wo erst nur ein einziger war' (Freud 1948, 149) [creates for the enemy a host of opponents where at first there was only one (Freud 1975, 133)]. By uniting people, humour has liberating potential.

However, the longevity of this liberation is contested. Ragland, for example, believes that shared laughter at an opponent is simply 'a safety valve' (Ragland 1976, 93). And like a safety valve it 'rebels against norms, aiming not to destroy, but to restore harmony and freedom through fusion, through momentary wholeness' (Ragland 1976, 102); that is, it only provides momentary release. This view seems to negate Barr's notion of Brantenberg's text as 'a social corrective'. As any response is temporary, the novel can be argued to be without long-term consequence. Michael Billig supports this position; in *Laughter and Ridicule: Towards a Social Critique of Humour*, he argues that while '[a]uthority is challenged and the guardians of rules are mocked … [by] rebellious humour', the impact is little more than 'momentary freedom' and 'a brief escape' (Billig 2005, 208). Moreover, Billig believes that humour can consolidate prevalent norms. 'The more we laugh and the more we imagine ourselves to be daringly free in the moments of our laughter', he explains, 'the more we are complying with the demands of the so-called free market' (Billig 2005, 212). In effect, precisely because it allows the imagination of freedom without demanding a struggle for it, humour essentially keeps everyone in their place.

Lisa Merrill disagrees with Ragland and Billig. In 'Feminist Humor: Rebellious and Self-Affirming' she states that 'humor empowers women to examine how we have been objectified and fetishized' (Merrill 1988, 279). According to the author, feminist humour, in particular, provides women with an understanding of their position within the social hierarchy and thereby the tools to dismantle it. Helga Kotthoff seconds this. 'By violating norms and creating unconventional perspectives, humor certainly influences norms' (Kotthoff 2006, 5), she argues in 'Gender and Humor: The State of the Art'. In fact, '[humour] … communicates sovereignty, creative power, and the freedom to intervene in the world' (Kotthoff 2006, 5), according to the author. Consequently, the 'unconventional perspectives' provided in Brantenberg's novel have the potential to act as 'a weapon', as Barr believes. In 'Between Women: A Cross-Class Analysis of Status and Anarchic Humor', Regenia Gagnier argues that this potential can be explained by sex/gender. In her evaluation of 'working women's autobiographies' (Gagnier 1988, 140), Gagnier found that 'women's humor tends toward anarchy rather than the status quo, to prolonged disruption rather than, in Freudian theory, momentary release' (Gagnier 1988, 145). It is women's marginal position that results in accessing laughter's liberating potential. As Barr believes, Brantenberg's novel, in particular, 'acts as a catalyst to encourage the untapped and unpredictable power of women's shared laughter' (Barr 1989, 97).

While the long-term impact of humour remains contested, Freud nevertheless affirms its revelatory potential. The tactic of 'Entlarvung' [unmasking], of which *Egalias døtre*, and its translations, can be seen as a prime example, especially reveals that '[d]ieser und jener gleich einem Halbgott Bewunderte ist doch auch nur ein Mensch wie ich und du' (Freud 1948, 231) [such and such a person, who is admired as a demigod, is after all only human like you and me (Freud 1975, 202)]. Through the humorous reversal of the status quo, readers are able to perceive its artificiality. And this new understanding, facilitated by 'Entlarvung', allows them to challenge the privileges and limitations assigned on the basis of sex/gender. These norms, as the English and German translations of Brantenberg's novel show, are engrained in language. Employing gynocentric terms effectively highlights androcentric bias, and responses shift between amusement and recognition. This dual response might not automatically be liberating, but it certainly prompts reflection. And creating awareness by sensitising readers, as Koeser, Kuhn and Sczesny (2015) found in relation to inclusive language, is often a first step to facilitating change.

Conclusions

Like problematising the linguistic status quo and proposing linguistic neutrality, reversing the linguistic status quo is an effective tool to highlight the issues inherent in the linguistic representation of women and men. *Egalias døtre* and its English and German translations, in particular, aptly illustrate the extent and impact of male terms by reversing their underlying logic to female-as-norm. What is frequently perceived as insignificant, that is language use, is revealed to be a powerful reiteration of a world view that privileges one sex/gender over the other. As the generic use of 'wom' and 'Frau' highlights in each version, 'manwom'/'Mann' are linguistically and conceptually absent. Moreover, if visible, he is presented as a specific, and often specifically sexual, addition to the female norm. While she is able to inhabit a variety of social positions, such as 'seawom' and 'Direktorin', he is defined only in relation to her, a 'spinnerman'/'Herrlein' or 'housebound'. The translators' inventiveness often has a humorous effect – 'Herrlein', for example, is a comical counterpart to the familiar 'Herr' – however, reversals go deeper than simply producing mirth. If 'Herrlein' seems ludicrous, readers are prompted to ask, then why would its equivalent 'Fräulein' be deemed acceptable? As a result, via the means of humour, the novel invites a contemplation of the linguistic status quo, and this contemplation intends to lead to questioning and eventual change.

Freud's notion of the liberating potential of laughter is relevant in this context. The long-term impact of humour might be contested – Ragland, for example, simply considers it a 'safety valve' whereas Barr deems it a 'social corrective'. The technique of 'Entlarvung', however, which Brantenberg, and her translators, employ in *Egalias døtre*, certainly highlights that male-as-norm is a sociocultural product. As Brantenberg and her translators show, the linguistic and conceptual understanding of the sexes/genders could equally be reversed; humour allows readers to be both entertained and unnerved by this discovery. And this humorous insight, Kotthoff argues, enables readers to realise that they are able to challenge and revise what is often presented as fixed and 'natural'. Moreover, it is through the means of entertainment that readers are able to take in this insight in the first place.

As I proposed in the introduction, literary texts allow the presentation of alternative viewpoints precisely because they are considered to be 'mere' entertainment. In Chapter 5 I return to this proposal and investigate the impact of the three literary approaches with the help of a focus group study. The research questions guiding my study are whether literary texts can help to raise awareness of the impact of biased terms and whether they can sensitise readers to the importance of inclusive language use.

Notes

1. Pusch terms this usage 'sinnwidrig' and suggests 'Vaterschaftsmatronat' (Pusch 1980, 75).
2. The 1918 Representation of the People Act granted suffrage to women over the age of 30 who met certain criteria. It took another ten years until all women over 21 years of age were able to vote.

5
'It's good to make people realise ... double standards'
Evaluating the impact of literary texts thematising sex/gender and language

To test how other readers perceive the effectiveness of the three literary approaches, I conducted a focus group study. I asked participants to respond to an excerpt from Ursula K. Le Guin's *The Left Hand of Darkness*, June Arnold's *The Cook and the Carpenter* and Gerd Brantenberg's *Egalias døtre* in either English or German. The resulting data allows me to gauge the texts' impact, and explore whether and how they might be a useful tool to sensitise readers to the importance of inclusive language.

Methodology

Focus groups as a dialogic tool

As Sue Wilkinson explains in 'Focus Groups: A Feminist Method', '[f]ocus groups ... draw on people's normal, everyday experiences of talking and arguing' and thereby '[tap into] this ordinary social process' (Wilkinson 1999a, 225). While the context remains created by the researcher, 'the interactions that take place within focus groups are closer to everyday social processes than those afforded by most other research methods' (Wilkinson 1999a, 227). However, the very communality of focus groups can create complications. Martha Ann Carey, for example, warns in 'The Group Effect in Focus Groups: Planning, Implementing, and Interpreting Focus Group Research' that 'a person [might] elect ... to tailor his or her contributions to be in line with perceptions of the group members' (Carey 1994, 236). Further, as Sue Wilkinson highlights in 'Focus Groups in Feminist Research: Power, Interaction, and the Co-construction of Meaning', in addition to individuals silencing themselves, they might also be silenced by others. She argues that 'group participants can collaborate and collude effectively to intimidate and/or silence a particular member' (Wilkinson 1998, 116). A third type of silencing, or censoring, can occur when group members 'create a silence around a particular topic or issue' (Wilkinson 1998, 116); a fourth is conformity with the presumed views of the researcher. As Terrance L. Albrecht, Gerianne M. Johnson and Joseph B. Walther confirm in 'Understanding Communication Processes in Focus Groups', 'responses may reflect what it is they [participants] think the facilitator wants to hear' (Albrecht et al. 1993, 55). These need to be considered to ensure a fruitful discussion.

Two additional factors to consider are status and diversity. As Kitzinger and Barbour argue in 'Introduction: The Challenge and Promise of Focus Groups', 'hierarchies within groups and in broader society may inhibit the contributions of members' (Kitzinger and Barbour 1999, 9). And while Michael Bloor, Jane Frankland, Michelle Thomas and Kate Robson reflect in *Focus Groups in Social Research* that '[t]here has to be sufficient diversity to encourage discussion', if a group is too diverse 'conflict and the repression of views of certain individuals' may arise (Bloor et al. 2001, 20). Participants' sex/gender can be a particularly salient factor for this. As Richard A. Krueger states in *Focus Groups: A Practical Guide for Applied Research*, '[a]t times, it is unwise to mix gender in focus groups, particularly if the topic of discussion is experienced differently by each sex' (Krueger 1994, 78). The author elaborates: '[m]en may have a tendency to speak more frequently and with more authority when in groups with women – sometimes called the "peacock effect"' (Krueger 1994, 78). This can silence female group members as well as be 'an irritant' to them (Krueger 1994, 78). On the other hand, mixed groups 'better reflect the structure of the society and thus allow ... the participants and researcher to learn about social differences and social relationships' (Goss and Leinbach 1996, 119), Jon D. Goss and Thomas R. Leinbach highlight in 'Focus Groups as Alternative Research Practice: Experience with Transmigrants in Indonesia'. Mixed groups in terms of sex/gender, in particular, the authors reflect, 'work ... to reveal to participants the gender-differentiated nature of social knowledge and the distinctive experiences and perspectives of men and women' (Goss and Leinbach 1996, 119). That is, mixed groups can provide new insights to both sexes/genders.

Sex/gender comes into play not only between participants but also between the researcher and respondents. As Karen Taylor comments in 'Keeping Mum: The Paradoxes of Gendered Power Relations in

Interviewing', women interviewing men can equally cause complications. 'As a dominant group the men resist traditional research power dynamics of the researcher/researched' (Taylor 1996, 116), she states. Disruptions to the research process might consist of relatively 'harmless' non-compliance, but might also include defiance and aggression. Additionally, the position of a female researcher will have an impact on the group dynamic. As Maria Mies reflects in 'Towards a Methodology for Feminist Research', 'their own existence as *women* and *scholars* is a contradictory one. As women, they are affected by sexist oppression together with other women, and as scholars they share the privileges of the (male) academic elite' (Mies 1983, 120, emphasis in original). So while female facilitators and participants might be able to co-operate on the basis of sex/gender, it does not necessarily prevent misunderstanding. As Catherine Kohler Riessman found in 'When Gender is Not Enough: Women Interviewing Women', 'the lack of shared cultural and class assumptions' (Riessman 1987, 190) can also impede the research process.

A key benefit of focus groups is that they help to level the usual research hierarchy to a large degree. '[They] are a relatively *non-hierarchical* method', Wilkinson explains in 'How Useful Are Focus Groups in Feminist Research?', 'they shift the balance of power away from the researcher towards the research participants' (Wilkinson 1999b, 64, emphasis in original). Esther Madriz agrees, and elaborates in 'Focus Groups in Feminist Research' that 'more weight [is given] to the participants' opinions, decreasing the influence the researcher has over the interview process' due to 'the interaction among group participants' (Madriz 2000, 836–7). Goss and Leinbach also propose that 'both the researcher *and* the research subjects may simultaneously obtain insights and understanding of [a] particular social situation *during* the process of research' (Goss and Leinbach 1996, 116–17, emphasis in original). This allows both parties to benefit. Focus groups are *'dialogic'*, as the authors term it, not just in terms of participants' interaction but also the facilitator's understanding (Goss and Leinbach 1996, 118, emphasis in original). This dialogic aspect of focus groups can be enhanced further by encouraging participants to develop their own viewpoints as much as possible. One way to do so is by 'beginning [the focus group] with participants writing, rather than saying, their ideas' (Albrecht et al. 1993, 57). This allows the researcher to access 'internalized opinions' (Albrecht et al. 1993, 57), which limits conformity both with what the researcher 'wants to hear' and the opinions of other group members.

In effect, the introduction of reflective tasks can circumvent many of the concerns around focus groups from the beginning. As my study was focused on the impact of literary texts on readers' perceptions of the importance of inclusive language, participants were provided with excerpts from three of the literary texts I evaluated and asked to take notes prior to our discussion. This helped to maximise the dialogic potential of the focus groups.

Grounded theory as reflective methodology

Developed by Barney G. Glaser and Anselm L. Strauss and first published in *The Discovery of Grounded Theory: Strategies for Qualitative Research*, 'grounded theory is derived from data and then illustrated by characteristic examples of data' (Glaser and Strauss 1968, 5). Additionally, according to the authors, '[o]ur strategy of comparative analysis for generating theory puts a high emphasis on *theory as process*; that is, theory as an ever-developing entity, not as a perfected product' (Glaser and Strauss 1968, 32, emphasis in original). This means data is not only constantly compared but also any theory emerging from this comparison is subject to alteration. This puts participants' responses at the heart of the analysis – what matters most to them also matters most in the analytic process. Linking in with the dialogic potential of the focus group method, grounded theory was highly suited to assess reader responses.

While Glaser and Strauss developed the original methodology, I chose to work with Kathy Charmaz's *Constructing Grounded Theory*. Glaser and Strauss's thinking originated in the late 1960s, a time perhaps when qualitative research was measured even more strongly against the standards of positivist science. In consequence, the authors did not reflect in-depth on the researcher as a central participant in the research process. By proposing a 'constructivist approach perspective' that 'shreds notions of a neutral observer and value-free expert' (Charmaz 2014, 13), Charmaz proposes the (re)integration of the researcher who 'must examine rather than erase how their privileges and preconceptions may shape the analysis' (Charmaz 2014, 13). This approach takes concerns around the status of the researcher into account, which is also a central feature of a considered focus group study. As a result, grounded theory, and Charmaz's reflective approach in particular, complements the creation of a non-hierarchical research environment. As Charmaz elaborates in '"Discovering" Chronic Illness: Using Grounded Theory', '[t]he "groundedness" of this approach fundamentally results from these researchers' commitment to analyze what they actually observe in the field or in their data' instead of 'limit[ing] themselves to preconceived hypotheses … [or] follow[ing] the prescribed canons of traditional random sampling' (Charmaz 1990, 1162). Analysts are guided by the data and the findings that emerge from it, which means that 'rather than focusing time and energy on investigating a preconceived, researcher-driven problem or process that is of little concern to the participants, this openness enables the researcher to be more responsive to the participants' problem' (Cutcliffe 2005, 423), John R. Cutcliffe adds in 'Adapt or Adopt: Developing and Transgressing the Methodological Boundaries of Grounded Theory'.

To get to the core of 'the participants' problem', as Cutcliffe terms it, grounded theory employs a variety of methods. The first step of analysis is the coding of data, which has an 'initial' and a 'focused' stage, according to Charmaz. She explains that '[d]uring initial coding, the goal is to remain open to all possible theoretical directions' (Charmaz 2014, 114) while '[f]ocused codes advance the theoretical direction of your work' (Charmaz 2014, 138). In the beginning, then, researchers consider all possible interpretations. This openness allows them to listen to what participants are actually saying, which interlinks with the explorative aims of my focus group study. The subsequent move from initial codes to focused codes is supported by the 'constant comparative methods' (Charmaz 2014, 132), and focused coding enables 'concentrating on what your initial codes say and the comparisons you make with and between them' (Charmaz 2014, 140). By comparing 'data and data, data and codes, codes and codes' and the emergent 'categories and categories' (Charmaz 2014, 171), researchers slowly arrive at the beginnings of a theory. This is tested against further data: 'theoretical sampling', as this part of the process is called, 'means seeking and collecting pertinent data to elaborate and refine categories in your emerging theory' (Charmaz 2014, 192). It essentially allows the analyst to test categories and with them the theory. And rather than traditional demographic sampling, 'theoretical sampling pertains only to conceptual and theoretical development of your analysis; it is *not* about representing a population' (Charmaz 2014, 198, emphasis in original). Its function is therefore to progress the emerging theory.

Coding and theoretical sampling are not the only core components of grounded theory. Memo-writing is arguably the practice that allows codes to evolve and a theory to emerge in the first place. As Charmaz explains, '[m]emos catch your thoughts, capture the comparisons and connections you make, and crystallize questions and directions for you to pursue' (Charmaz 2014, 162). In short, memo-writing 'provides a space to become actively engaged in your materials, to develop your ideas, to fine-tune your subsequent data-gathering, and to engage in critical reflexivity' (Charmaz 2014, 162–3). But in order to be effective, reflexivity must incorporate several components, as Virginia L. Olesen highlights in 'Feminist Qualitative Research and Grounded Theory: Complexities, Criticisms, and Opportunities'. These are: '(1) Full explanation of how analytic and practical issues were handled; (2) Examination of the researcher's own background and its influences on the research; and (3) Reflections on the researcher's own emotions, worries, feelings' (Olesen 2010, 423).[1] Some might argue that this level of personal involvement impedes the research process; however, working under the assumption, or even pretence, of objectivity seems much more damaging. One way of looking at the integration of reflexivity is as 'provid[ing] a way for readers to assess the researcher in action and accord trustworthiness and credibility' (Olesen 2010, 428). In fact, reflexivity enables the reader to consider the researcher, along with the participants, as an agent in the research process. And this understanding encourages the levelling of any findings from 'the' truth to 'a' truth, which helps to deflate the hierarchy of researcher and researched in the analytic process. Grounded theory therefore goes hand in hand with the dialogic potential of the focus group method.

Research design

The design of my topic guide was heavily influenced by Richard A. Krueger's *Focus Groups: A Practical Guide for Applied Research* and Lia Litosseliti's *Using Focus Groups in Research*. Both authors give valuable advice on how to conduct focus groups, including how to make participants feel at ease, how to structure the discussion and what type of questions to ask. After deciding whom to approach to take part, choosing the ideal group size was the next step in enabling a fruitful discussion. As Litosseliti states, '[f]ocus groups typically consist of between six and ten participants, but the size can range from as few as four … to as many as twelve' (Litosseliti 2007, 3). While '[l]arger groups are difficult to manage, moderate and analyse', she explains, they 'can be useful for brainstorming' (Litosseliti 2007, 3). 'Smaller groups', on the other hand, 'are more appropriate if the aim is to explore complex, controversial, emotional topics, or to encourage detailed accounts' (Litosseliti 2007, 3). According to Litosseliti, smaller groups 'offer more opportunity for people to talk and are more practical to set up and manage' (Litosseliti 2007, 3). Krueger agrees: '[s]mall groups of 4 or 5 participants', he adds, 'afford more opportunity to share ideas' (Krueger 1994, 17). Such *'mini-focus groups'* (Krueger 1994, 17, emphasis in original), as Krueger terms them, were most appropriate for the purposes of my study. As respondents were asked to share their opinions and ideas on three literary excerpts, I wanted to ensure there was sufficient opportunity for everyone to fully participate. Furthermore, the issue of sex/gender and language is potentially considered a sensitive or controversial topic, making smaller groups more suitable to discuss it. Another factor to consider was the number of focus groups. As Litosseliti comments, '[i]t is too risky to build a research project around a single focus group' as this 'could hinder both comparative and in-depth exploration of the topic' (Litosseliti 2007, 4). In order to access rich and comparable data, I followed Litosseliti's advice that '[a] typical number is between four and six groups' (Litosseliti 2007, 4). I conducted a pilot focus group to test my guide and materials, as well as two native English- and two native German-speaking groups. In sum, I conducted five groups.

Based on Krueger's recommendations I developed the following structure for my topic guide. This remained the same throughout my study, bar one or two adjustments after the pilot focus group meeting. As a preamble to the discussion, I welcomed the participants, stated why the focus group was taking place and clarified how the data would be used. I explained that all responses would be equally valid and that participants were not meant to reach a consensus. I then asked the respondents to introduce themselves and say briefly why they were interested in taking part. Following this introduction, I handed out reading packs – in either English or German – which contained the introductory pages of three of the literary texts I evaluated[2]. These were *The Left Hand of Darkness* (Le Guin 1991, 1–4), *The Cook and the Carpenter* (Arnold 1973, 3–6), and *The Daughters of Egalia* (Brantenberg 1985, 9–12) for the English groups, and *Winterplanet* (Le Guin 1981, 5–9), my own translation of *The Cook and the Carpenter* (Arnold 1973, 3–6) and *Die Töchter Egalias* (Brantenberg 1987, 7–10) for the German groups. I instructed participants to underline anything they noticed about the language employed in the excerpts and to write a few bullet points or sentences on their impressions on a separate piece of paper. I asked respondents to pay particular attention to the use of nouns, for example job titles such as 'doctor', and pronouns, such as 'she' or 'he'. Participants were given about 25 minutes to complete the task; I extended the reading and writing time in each group as and when required.

Respondents' perceptions of the three excerpts were elicited with the help of general explorative questions. First, we discussed the excerpt from *The Left Hand of Darkness* by sharing what each participant noticed about the language used in the text. I wrote down key points and used these to prompt a more in-depth discussion. This remained the same throughout the study; for example, I asked respondents to reflect on whom they imagined when reading the text and to elaborate on why this was the case. After all opinions had been exhausted, I moved the group on to the second excerpt, *The Cook and the Carpenter*, and asked participants to share what they noticed. I also instructed them to consider the similarities and differences between the two texts. In the German groups, I additionally referred to the outcomes of previous groups whenever useful to further probe certain comments. Finally, we explored respondents' thoughts in relation to *The Daughters of Egalia*. I asked participants to put their bullet points on the text's language use onto a whiteboard and read what the others had written. We then reconvened to explore what respondents had noticed and discussed how all three excerpts compared. I was particularly interested in what participants considered the goal of each excerpt and how effective the texts were in meeting it. I also asked which of the three excerpts participants found most effective in highlighting the issue of linguistic representation.

The discussion was concluded by a brief summary during which I listed the key points of our exploration. I asked the participants if this was a fair reflection and provided space to make any other comments. I then formally concluded by thanking them for their participation, reiterated how the data would be used and confirmed that their contributions were anonymous. I handed out an information sheet with my details and contacted them by email a few days later to offer another opportunity for comments and feedback. Following on, I transcribed the responses and analysed the data with grounded theory.

Focus group analysis

In this section I assess the data resulting from the focus group discussions. I explore how codes and categories emerged from participants' responses, and how grounded theory evolved in consequence.

Emerging codes and categories – pilot

The aim of the pilot focus group was to test my topic guide and materials. I recruited participants by approaching other students, and three respondents agreed to take part in this initial meeting. All participants, Claudia,[3] Janine and Martina, were of white European ethnicity, female, on average 32 years old and non-native English speakers. Two participants I knew well and the third I had met several times before. The same two participants were also familiar with one another; the third was relatively new to the group. All, however, had previously encountered each other in a conference setting. Motivations to take part therefore reflected this pre-existing connection. While one respondent commented that 'I am here because of my interest, I suppose, in language and gender', the other two reflected, 'I'm here because you asked me to come' and 'I'm here because you need some help for your focus group.'

After transcribing the pilot focus group, I evaluated the data by reading closely and coding line by line. I selected line-by-line coding as, according to Charmaz, '[it] encourages you to see otherwise undetected patterns' (Charmaz 2014, 125) and 'frees you from becoming so immersed in your research participants' world-views that you accept them without question' (Charmaz 2014, 127). Charmaz advises, 'to remain open to all possible theoretical directions' (Charmaz 2014, 114), I therefore chose '*in vivo* codes' – using a word or phrase from the data – at this stage as they allow 'to preserve participants' meanings of their views and actions in the coding' (Charmaz 2014, 134, emphasis in original). This ensured that I stayed close to what was said. While coding, I also wrote memos to reflect on emerging patterns, and as the following example shows these were mainly summaries to begin with. A line-by-line evaluation of the first comment on *The Left Hand of Darkness* looks as follows: first, Janine began by saying that '[o]kay, so I don't know if it's what you wanted or not', which I coded as 'unsure if "got" the task'. She then stated, 'so yeah, the narrator usually uses "I"', which was coded as 'focus on "I" in first comment'. Janine continued by explaining, 'so you don't, he or she doesn't really, like, specify if we're talking about a male or a female', coded as '"I" female or male?' The final two lines, 'so I came to the conclusion that with the rest of the text because it's only talking about men and kings and everything' and 'that we're talking only about men here', were coded as 'only men referred to, so only men'. The corresponding memo states, 'the participant mentions the use of "I" by the narrator – but is unsure if that is what I was looking for; she at first can't tell whether the narrator is male or female. However, the respondent assumed that the narrator has to be male as the text only talks about men.'

As is visible from my response to these five lines my initial analysis stayed very close to the transcript. Further, as is equally clear, I struggled with what is one of the key recommendations by Charmaz: '[c]oding for actions' (Charmaz 2014, 116) or 'coding with gerunds' (Charmaz 2014, 121). Charmaz instructs, '[a]ttempt to code with words that reflect action ... [as it] reduces tendencies to code for types of people' (Charmaz

2014, 116). '[C]oding for actions', she adds, 'curbs our tendencies to make conceptual leaps and to adopt extant theories *before* we have done the necessary analytic work' (Charmaz 2014, 117, emphasis in original). This proved easier said than done, as my default was to summarise in statements rather than in actions and perceptions. But as codes began to condense into themes, I began to apply gerund-coding – with verbs ending in 'ing' – more thoroughly.

Theme codes that emerged from the first half of the transcript included 'imagining men only', 'feeling frustrated/confused' and 'seeing women only in the specific'. A few examples help to illustrate how these codes came into being. For example, 'imagining men only' and 'seeing women only in the specific' stemmed from comments on the impact of language on the ability to imagine characters. In relation to *The Left Hand of Darkness*, Claudia reflected as follows: 'the only time when a woman is specified is to illustrate a metaphor about beauty.' The use of 'only time' and 'specified' highlight that, to the mind of the respondent, women are linguistically and conceptually excluded from the text, except 'to illustrate … beauty'. She continued, 'if you follow conventions you picture just men', supporting her previous statement that women are visible only in the 'specific'. Claudia's reference to 'conventions' is striking in this instance. For example, what type of conventions led her to picture only men? Are these linguistically or contextually informed, or perhaps both? Her subsequent comment gives some explanation: 'I think people will have to consciously make themselves picture a female ambassador because that's just not [inaudible] how it is.' Subsequently, the two theme codes emerged from the data, and further, they were linked. The linguistic and/or conceptual exclusion of women creates the impression that the text is portraying 'just men'.

The third code, 'feeling frustrated/confused', arose from another key theme in participants' responses, and was mainly, but not exclusively, connected to *The Cook and the Carpenter*. As Martina reflected on her reaction to the text, 'the second text really frustrated me' and 'I just got so confused'. The audible emphasis on 'really' and 'so' highlights the force of her response – an experience connected to the neutral pronoun 'na'. She stated, 'as much as I want to believe in the fact that we can actually use a gender-neutral pronoun to refer to people and etc. etc. I got so confused at some point that I stopped reading it.' This perception proved central also for the other participants and therefore resulted in the code above.

Additional codes that emerged from the data were: 'making people think', 'considering feasibility of changes' and 'linking language and imagination'. Already, connections between these initial theme codes became visible, which supported the formation of categories later on. 'Linking language and imagination' can be employed as an overarching category for 'imagining men only' and 'seeing women only in the specific', therefore combining three codes into one. 'Making people think' and 'considering feasibility of changes', however, were unrelated to previous findings. A few examples help to illustrate their formation. In relation to *The Daughters of Egalia*, for example, Martina stated, 'it's useful in as far as it kind of makes people realise stereotypes about women and men in our society by reversing them', which, along with similar comments made by other respondents, led to the emergence of 'making people think'. The second, 'considering feasibility of changes', stemmed from reflections such as, 'but are we ready to get rid of pronouns completely, I'm not sure in language use.' All of the above are of course not exhaustive and only marked the first step of moving away from *in vivo* coding to more analytic perspectives. It took a second close reading of my initially coded material to test these initial findings and see patterns emerge. Structural codes aside, which describe the respondents and their environment, eight theme codes crystallised from the data. These evolved from the above emerging codes and developed into 1. 'linking language and imagination', 2. 'linking language and reality', 3. 'reflecting on the relation between texts', 4. 'reflecting on the effectiveness of texts', 5. 'reflecting on the feasibility of changes/proposals', 6. 'commenting on the status quo', 7. 'misunderstandings' and 8. 'getting it'.

Again, a few examples help to illustrate how I arrived at one of these theme codes in particular. To return to the first response to *The Left Hand of Darkness*, even though Janine was uncertain about the sex/gender of the narrator, she felt led to assume her/him to be male. She stated that 'the rest of the text' was to her understanding 'only talking about men and kings', which seemed to imply 'that we're talking only about men here'. The predominantly male language of the excerpt then, according to the participant, created a link between 'the rest of the text' and the sex/gender of the narrator. This perceived connection formed the basis for 'linking language and imagination' – a code that proved relevant also for other responses. In fact, I applied this code 25 times as either a main or subcode throughout the second close reading.

The next step in my analysis was to refine these eight codes, with comparing and sorting data an essential component. I created a diagram that provided an overview of all the coded data and allowed me to construct links between them. It also enabled me to understand which codes had little supporting evidence and might be better off submerged under an umbrella code, and which were fairly comprehensive and therefore of key importance for the analysis. From the eight emerging codes above, 'language' and 'effectiveness' were major themes. Of course, my research design specifically asked participants to consider the language employed in each excerpt as well as its effectiveness in highlighting the linguistic representation of women and men. This is a concern in terms of grounded theory and needs to be addressed at this stage. A key question might be: were these indeed of most interest to respondents, or was their emergence simply preconditioned by my instructions? One could argue either way; however, issues such as these are hard to circumvent for most researchers. As Cutcliffe states, '[l]ack of precision in the research question can also cause considerable difficulty for ethics committees' (Cutcliffe 2005, 424). A completely open exploration is therefore difficult to achieve. Based on the data available, language and effectiveness emerged as key concerns, and adequate categories were therefore required to reflect their centrality, even if their emergence was potentially compromised. Consequently, 'reflecting on language' and 'reflecting on the effectiveness of texts' emerged as two new cores, with 'reflecting on language' now including 'linking language and imagination', 'linking language and reality' and 'reflecting on the feasibility of changes/proposals' as subcategories. A fourth separate subcategory emerged from comments on the use of 'I' in *The Left Hand of Darkness* and the neutral pronoun 'na' in *The Cook and the Carpenter*. This was termed 'considering the ambiguous subject'. 'Reflecting on the effectiveness of texts', on the other hand, acted as an umbrella for 'commenting on the status quo', 'misunderstandings' and 'getting it'. I re-included the theme of 'frustration/confusion' under 'effectiveness' as it proved to be of central concern – this now incorporated comments on 'intentionality' and 'writing style'. As became clear from the diagram, the code 'reflecting on the relation between texts' did not integrate into the core codes. And with only two relevant pieces of data it was eventually discarded.

The categories emerging from the diagram initially complicate the above codes as much as they merge codes into useful categories. However, seeing links between data and codes as well as considering their differences allowed me to progress to the final stage of coding. For example, it enabled me to see a connection between respondents' comments coded as 'linking language and imagination' and 'frustration/confusion'. Reflections on *The Cook and the Carpenter*, in particular, highlighted participants' inability to imagine characters. As Janine reflected, 'I agree with you with the frustrating thing … it's just because you get lost in all the characters. I couldn't follow the story, like, who is "Will"? And who is the "cook"? And who is the "carpenter"? And the stranger, is the stranger the woman?' Not being able to imagine 'who is who' resulted in frustration for respondents and therefore signposted an important connection. The linguistic status quo enables speakers to differentiate between 'female' and 'male' – a differentiation that the novel fundamentally challenges.

Another example of a link emerging from the diagram is the following comment: 'I don't think it's because they're using "nan" or "na" or whatever, it's because all those characters get mixed up in the way that the story is told', Janine stated, 'so yeah, the story is really frustrating because you can't actually understand it.' The 'way that the story is told' signals a reflection on the 'writing style' of the text, while the latter half of the statement implies 'frustration/confusion'. There are many more examples of how links became visible in the diagram; these connections fundamentally shaped my final categories.

The core that emerged from the initial coding of data, the comparison of data and codes, and the collation of codes into categories is 'reflecting on (sex/gender and) language'. This core category originally included eight subcategories: 1. 'considering feasibility/reality', 2. 'considering the impact of pronouns', 3. 'perceiving female-specific images', 4. 'perceiving male-specific images', 5. 'struggling with the ambiguous subject', 6. '(not) getting it', 7. 'reflecting on effectiveness' and 8. 'noticing the highlighting of issues'. Focused coding established clearer links, resulting in the condensing to four subcategories: 1. 'perceiving specific images', combining 'perceiving female-specific images' and 'perceiving male-specific images'; 2. 'considering the impact of pronouns', which includes 'struggling with the ambiguous subject'; 3. 'reflecting on effectiveness', which incorporates 'noticing the highlighting of issues' and '(not) getting it'; and 4. 'considering feasibility/reality'. In the following I analyse the data from the native English-speaking focus groups in relation to these subcategories and the data that emerged from the pilot focus group. The aim is to evaluate whether these subcategories remain the most suitable or whether the native English focus group data provides new insights. I thereby put the emerging categories to the test.

Testing emerging categories – native English responses

Respondents were recruited by approaching members of two pre-existing groups: one was a postgraduate discussion group and the other a feminist writing group. I was a member of both groups, which, similar to the pilot focus group, resulted in a pre-connection with participants. Four members of the postgraduate group took part, Sam, Jennie, Rich and Sarah, all of whom knew one another from previous discussion group encounters. Two members were newer to the group; the third I had known for over a year and the fourth I knew well. Of the four respondents from the feminist writing group, Jo, Alice, Mandy and Jessica, I knew two relatively well, and the third I knew well. All three had been part of this and another writing group for some time. The fourth participant was new to the group, but a close friend of one of the other members. I chose to work with these networks for two reasons: first, I wanted to be able to access an 'ordinary social process', as Wilkinson terms it; and secondly, I intended to level any hierarchy between the researcher and the researched as far as possible. This enabled a dialogic focus group study, while my awareness of the impact of this setting allowed for a reflective analytic practice.

All participants were native English speakers and identified as either white British or white European. The postgraduate group consisted of three female and one male participant with an average age of 26 years, while all respondents from the feminist writing group were female and the average age was 31 years. Prior to the focus group discussions I asked participants to complete a questionnaire, which aimed to assess attitudes toward the issue of sex/gender and language. I decided on 'The Inventory of Attitudes toward Sexist/Nonsexist Language – General (IASNL-G)', developed by Janet B. Parks and Mary Ann Roberton (2000, Appendix), to access participants' responses. The inventory has been thoroughly tested and revised by Parks and Roberton (2000/2001) and also employed by other researchers. Oriane Sarrasin, Ute Gabriel, and Pascal Gygax, for example, used part of the questionnaire in their 2012 study 'Sexism and Attitudes Toward Gender-Neutral Language: The Case of English, French, and German'. As Sarrasin et al. describe the inventory, it is 'divided into subscales for beliefs about sexist language, recognition of sexist language, and willingness to use nonsexist language' (Sarrasin et al. 2012, 117), all of which were useful for the purposes of my study. Further, the IASNL-G is open-access and provided 'for use by any interested researcher' (Parks and Roberton 2000, 433). The authors recommend the tool 'should be used *exactly* as it appears …, including the presentation of the operational definition of sexist language' (Parks and Roberton 2000, 433, emphasis in original). I reproduced the questionnaire as advised with the following results.

The respondents from the postgraduate discussion group shared a supportive attitude toward non-sexist language, with an average score of 86. Results were similar for participants from the feminist writing group, who also had a supportive attitude, but, perhaps predictably, with an even higher average score of 95. According to Parks and Roberton's inventory, 'total scores between 73.6 and 105 reflect a supportive attitude' (Parks and Roberton 2000, 433–4); respondents from both groups therefore scored solidly within that range. Consequently, it could be expected that all participants would have similar viewpoints on the issue of sex/gender and language. In the following section I explore how responses from each group overlap and where they differ. Further, I evaluate how the data from the two native English-speaking focus groups supports or challenges the categories emerging from the pilot focus group. To test the four developing themes, 'perceiving specific images', 'considering the impact of pronouns', 'reflecting on effectiveness' and 'considering feasibility/reality', the analysis is given in separate sections. This is not to say that the categories are fixed or self-contained with no potential for crossovers or linkages; but to investigate their validity it was most useful to keep them distinct at this stage.

Perceiving specific images: How language evokes a particular sex/gender

One key category emerging from the pilot focus group was the perception of specific images. Respondents from the pilot as well as the two native English-speaking groups all commented on the understanding of certain terms, and therefore certain characters, as either male or female. This illustrates the relevance of the hypothesis that language influences thought, and more specifically, of Tohidian's interpretation that language influences perception. However, this association was shaped by the language used in the literary excerpts as much as the context imagined or given. The introductory pages from *The Left Hand of Darkness* stimulated most reflection and debate, which centred on the assumption that nouns and pronouns with predominantly male associations also predominantly evoke men. In reference to Le Guin's text, respondents saw a clear link between sex/gender and language, even if sex/gender was not openly given. In fact, several participants initially commented that most terms, in themselves, were not necessarily specific. '[T]here are lots of lists of job titles and I thought only one was gender-specific which was "lords"', Sam from the postgraduate discussion group stated. This was supported by Jennie, who said, 'yeah professions aren't gendered.' However, 'even though the professions aren't gendered', Jennie continued, 'they're like traditionally gendered professions.' This highlights that even when terms are not specific on the surface, their historical usage and meaning impact on readers' understanding.

'Convention' was central to evoking specificity, according to Claudia from the pilot group, a point that was picked up also by native English-speaking respondents. The interpretation of terms such as 'guards', 'functionaries' and 'dignitaries' is inevitably shaped by history and context, leading Sam to reflect, '[q]uite honestly with the procession I pictured a medieval procession with this processional order ... so in that context everyone would have to be male.' The impact of convention was also explored in the feminist writing group, where Jessica commented, 'although a lot of the professions or job titles [inaudible] were non-gender-specific, the context of the piece, which you could see as sort of medieval, sort of defined it.' She explained, 'the fact that, you know, the procession of those, were only those who were in the public life and of high rank and in trade', and added 'that historical standing would eliminate them [women] from masonry or being a student or an ambassador.' Jessica continued, 'I thought it's kind of because of our knowledge of historical norms that gave us the only, for a while, the only indication of gender.' Jennie from the postgraduate group explored this further: 'I think we're all people that sort of think about gender academically as well so obviously, like, we don't want to just automatically think of like a "mason" as a man or something but actually you still find I have to make a conscious effort.' As the respondent remarked, even those who share an interest in sex/gender and language have to make 'a conscious effort' to override historical associations. Jennie therefore concluded, 'I think for most people probably the instant response to the professions and names would be masculine.'

These reflections built on the explorations in the pilot group, where the discussion developed as follows among two participants:

Martina: I was alerted by the fact that we got a 'king', we got 'lords'
Janine: hm
Martina: and then come on, we all know that when people say 'mayors' and you know
Janine: yeah and 'masons'
Martina: 'guards' and 'functionaries'
Janine: yeah
Martina: etc. believe it or not they're mostly men ... no matter what you say

While male images seemed to be readily available in the excerpt from *The Left Hand of Darkness,* women came to mind rarely, if at all. As Sarah from the postgraduate group commented, 'even things like "deputies", "senators", "mayors", though we shouldn't associate them with just men, and you can have obviously … female "senators", but I think, yeah we do associate them more with men.' Linguistically neutral terms are therefore not necessarily perceived as such, leaving the association 'female' confined to the specific. '[T]he only time when a woman is specified is to illustrate a metaphor about beauty', Claudia from the pilot group confirmed. This was also commented on by Jo from the feminist writing group: 'the only time a woman is even referred to is right at the beginning where they talk about the women wearing a jewel … and that was like metaphorically, wasn't it, not like literally a woman wearing a jewel.' Rich from the postgraduate group added, 'as far as I can see there's no mention, there's no explicit mention of women'; a similar perception led Claudia to conclude that 'for me it [the excerpt] was devoid of women.' Returning to my application of the *salva veritate* principle: this highlights that 'man', and in extension, terms associated with 'male', are unable to evoke 'a human being of either sex', and therefore 'woman'.

But despite the overwhelming understanding of the nouns employed in *The Left Hand of Darkness* as male, one term in particular remained open to interpretation. 'Jugglers' was potentially more ambiguous, several participants commented. '[I]n that context [of a medieval procession] everyone would have to be male pretty much apart from the "jugglers"', Sam from the postgraduate discussion group stated. Alice from the feminist writing group seconded this: 'when it got to the "jugglers" I thought perhaps that in my mind's eye I saw it as a group of mainly men but possibly gender-diverse', which was picked up on by Mandy: 'you're right as well, I saw the "jugglers" as oddly male and female I don't know why.' But not all participants agreed on this potential ambiguity: 'I'm not very visual so I didn't see the "jugglers" as women as well so I don't read in that way', Jo added. A potential conclusion given by Claudia from the pilot group was therefore: 'if you want to set the picture and talk about women as well then you have to feature [them] somewhere.' In short, to counteract the predominantly male associations imposed by either language and/or convention, a text needs to explicitly 'talk about women' to stop 'talking only about men'. As the respondent summarises, in line with the Sapir–Whorf hypothesis, language influences thought; linguistic change is consequently paramount to effect a change in perception.

Specific images were not only perceived in *The Left Hand of Darkness*; the excerpt from *The Cook and the Carpenter* equally sparked debate. The terms 'cook' and 'carpenter' are on a linguistic level as neutral as 'guards' and 'functionaries' but, to the participants, they also carried specific associations. Two postgraduate group respondents assigned sex/gender as follows: Jennie stated that 'they're like defined by their professions and I think it was the way you'd expect that the man was the "carpenter" and the woman was the "cook"', while Sarah added, 'we're never told who is the woman, who is the man there and we, I think yeah, we just obviously assume the "cook" is going to be a woman and the "carpenter" is going to be a man.' This 'traditional' interpretation was seconded by Mandy from the feminist group: 'you automatically go "the cook" is a woman, "the carpenter" is a man and it's sort [of] how much those two professions obviously come with their own sort [of] preconceived gender.' Again, sex/gender was interpreted even if not linguistically present. Nevertheless, not all participants made the same associations; Sam reflected during the postgraduate discussion group: 'I thought the cook was a man I don't really know why' and 'I thought the carpenter was a man.' Jessica from the feminist writing group, on the other hand, commented, 'I saw them both as female.' She explained, 'just because of this story and the pronouns and it just made me think, you know, there's a possibility in that world that they are both female.'

What becomes clear from the above is that the identification of sex/gender mattered greatly to all respondents. Whether characters are 'read' as female or male, participants understood them as either 'one' or the 'other', never as neutral or in between. As Jennie from the postgraduate group stated, 'the assumption is that as we picture a character we'd have to pick a gender for them between these two choices.' She continued: 'I don't know if anyone else pictured like just a completely androgynous person …, I think probably most people don't get to that as an option. But there's nothing to say that any of these worlds needed to [be] underst[ood] as binary, sexist.' Respondents felt conditioned to 'pick a sex/gender' even when a 'binary' understanding is not inherent in the language. If terms were potentially neutral, such as 'guards' and 'carpenter', conventions or context were usually consulted to provide 'clues'. This has serious implications for neutral language – if readers are unable to imagine a neutral being, and further, predominantly associate male, is linguistic neutrality a viable option? As Jennie reflected in relation to *The Left Hand of Darkness*, 'they made a big deal of the first time they gendered somebody and then that was the point that anybody got an identity. So yeah, the name and the description of the person only followed after having been gendered.' Sex/gender was linked to identity, and readers made sense of characters through its classification. Pronouns played a considerable role in 'revealing' sex/gender; in the following section I evaluate how ambiguous anaphors complicate perception.

Considering the impact of pronouns: How they shape readers' perceptions

The use of 'I' in *The Left Hand of Darkness* and of 'na' in *The Cook and the Carpenter* had considerable impact on participants' readings. The lack of specificity connoted by these two pronouns led respondents to reflect on the potential sex/gender of a character and the meaning of their assumption. In the pilot focus group a central discussion emerged around the uncertainty of 'I'. While Janine was keen to know the sex/gender of the narrator, Martina argued that it was insignificant. Their conversation developed as follows: Janine commented first of all, 'so yeah the narrator usually uses "I" so you don't, he or she doesn't really, like, specify if we're talking about a male or a female.' This highlights an initial ambiguity around the sex/gender of the first person singular pronoun, which was, however, resolved by linking 'I' to the rest of the text. As quoted above, Janine 'came to the conclusion that with the rest of the text because it's only talking about men and kings and everything that we're talking only about men here.' Martina also reflected on the use of 'I' in *The Left Hand of Darkness*, but her position differed. She observed:

> Martina: yeah as you said it doesn't reveal the narrator's sex which, however, didn't make me feel the narrator could be male necessarily. For me it was more, like, [to Janine] not to say that
> Janine: yeah, no no no
> Martina: I mean you know it's just a perception that I had. It was more like it's not relevant
> Janine: Hmhm
> Martina: to the story and that's why I'm not seeing it

The theme of 'identifying sex/gender' versus 'sex/gender being irrelevant' continued beyond this initial exchange. After the third pilot focus group participant, Claudia, shared her perception of the text, Janine and Martina returned to their discussion:

> Janine: [to Claudia] yeah the thing you said … that you can't really know if it's a man or a woman, the narrator, until the end I was thinking, OK maybe at the end we're going to … have, like, kind of revealed that she is actually the only woman and that's why she is actually looking at the whole picture but because at the end we don't really

Martina: it doesn't matter
Janine: yeah
Martina: I think that's the, that's the
Janine: yeah
Martina: question, does it matter do we need to know whether this is a man or a woman?

Despite her initial declaration that the narrator was male, Janine was still undecided, which further highlights the ambiguity of 'I'. She also agreed with Martina on the surface that sex/gender might be irrelevant. This conflict over the narrator's sex/gender, however, was far from resolved. Janine still 'needed to know', as the following exchange illustrates:

Janine: in the book do you actually know who the narrator is?
Martina: it does matter now?
Janine: no, but just who the narrator is, like their story or
Researcher: yes
Janine: do you actually, do you actually get to know that?
Researcher: yes
Martina: you need to read the book, you need to read the book
Researcher: yeah
Janine: well that's good

It was a relief to Janine that the sex/gender of the narrator is revealed eventually. Additionally, the use of the phrase 'know *who* the narrator is' shows that sex/gender and identity were perceived as closely interlinked.

This becomes more poignant still in participants' reflections on their understanding of 'na' in *The Cook and the Carpenter*. Again, the pilot focus group data already brings key concerns surrounding the neutral pronoun to the fore. As Claudia commented, 'you read something and you need to picture what's going on in your head. What is that, like, an empty shell of a person?' This reminds of the limitations of any new language in a context that remains defined by the sex/gender binary. The image of 'an empty shell of a person' is a powerful cue of how central sex/gender is to readers' understanding of a character. She concluded, 'you can't portray a character without actually telling people who they are.' Without specificity, then, readers, according to the respondent, are unable to imagine 'who' a character is. Claudia related the impact of this ambiguity back to the use of 'I' in *The Left Hand of Darkness*, which resulted in the following discussion:

Claudia:	The same with the first one, the narrator, it's important in a sense that you need to know who's telling the story. Are they reliable? Are they making it all up? Am I going to believe it? Am I going to root for them? Am I going to like them or not? It's like
Martina:	yeah
Claudia:	if you don't tell me then what's the point in listening to your story?
Janine:	yeah
Martina:	I don't know, I found it different though, like in the first one it didn't really matter to me, … I don't find someone reliable because it's, they're a man or a woman

This exchange highlights how the identification of sex/gender potentially moves beyond ascertaining biology to being an indicator of reliability. While Martina openly disagreed with Claudia on this point, as she did with Janine over 'the need to know', she eventually conceded that, 'at the end of the day, to be fair that's how we see people.' She explained, 'when we see people, we want to identify because that helps us understand things kind of in [a] very stereotype way but still this is the way we make sense of reality, so I do understand what you mean.' Despite her reservations Martina admitted that the identification of sex/gender is key for many readers.

The theme of pronouns as a tool to help readers 'make sense of reality' emerged in all three focus group discussions. As Janine reflected on the use of 'na', 'the pronoun it feels weird … I think it's just because we're so used to hav[ing] "him" or "her".' This reliance on specific referents, which Wittgenstein terms 'menschliche Gepflogenheiten' [human customs], is explored also by participants from the postgraduate discussion and feminist writing group. Rich from the postgraduate group commented, for example, 'I found it quite difficult to place everything, as in I couldn't tell who was who, whether the "cook" was a man or the "carpenter" was a man or woman cause normally you'd rely so much on the pronouns to sort of build around.' Jessica from the feminist writers seconded this: 'I found it a little bit difficult to follow because we use "his", "her" so much as a shorthand for who the character is, to establish it.' Sarah from the postgraduate group explained this dependence: 'you have a set of assumptions that are just kind of, like, engrained and someone says "he" you see like a "man" and you kind of, you make certain assumptions, certain kind of associations with that.' She added, 'so when something like as basic as that, as a pronoun which you have to use or you use them all the time and [inaudible] you can't have sentences without them.' This feeling was shared by Rich from the same group: 'the main thing for me [is] just how unsettling it was to try and read it and how surprising that it's just such a small feature, that's so arbitrary and so easily replaceable.' He concluded, 'I couldn't get my head around it quite, I couldn't read it.' This illustrates Shaviro's argument in relation to Wittgenstein that language cannot be altered individually; any linguistic change needs to be agreed on by the speech community. And in the current context, a character might become unreadable if sex/gender is not 'revealed'.

Although the use of 'na' challenged respondents much more profoundly in their understanding than the use of nouns such as 'cook' and 'carpenter', for which convention or context could be consulted, most participants nevertheless found a tactic to reintroduce sex/gender to the neutral pronoun. Sarah from the postgraduate group reflected, 'I just had to replace it for "he", "she" or "they" with the "nan" because I was just kind of like, oh I need to just actually get to read, like, in my head.' To this Mandy from the feminist group added, 'I was sort of wondering what the effect of that was because all it did, it meant I went through and implanted my own "he", "his", "she", "hers".' She summarised, 'as much as they might want me to read it "na", my head was automatically planting in so it's, like, just how engrained that is I suppose.' However, this replacement is not necessarily permanent. As Alice commented, 'I think when you're first reading it, I'm replacing "nan" with "his", "her", "na" with "she", "he" and I'm doing that but I think as you read on you would get used to [it].' This was picked up also in the postgraduate discussion group where Rich stated, 'well I imagine if, once you read the whole book you probably get used to it.' Janine from the pilot focus group agreed: 'if we're going to use at some point in life a neutral pronoun, we're just going to get used to it like we got used to using "him" or "her".' As Davidson and Smith (1999) argue in extension of Wittgenstein's thought, language is not a fixed entity; it can and does evolve in accordance with new social practices. Martina, however, made an important point regarding the limitations of neutral language in the current sociocultural context:

> [T]he point for me is that I think there was an episode of, not violence, but something similar that was going to happen to the girl,

when the girl is named and I think this is important because you don't want to get this violence lost. Cause it was violence or threats or whatever from, done by specific people who were male on a specific person that … was female. And I think that if you kind of mix all the pronouns up and everything, this might get lost which is something important to bear in mind. And I'm very gender-conscious and I'd like to get rid of all the pronouns and everything but there are points in which you need to be strategic about the use of pronouns

While allowing readers to imagine either sex/gender, the very ambiguity of neutral pronouns could potentially do harm in certain instances. Neutralising the sex/gender of perpetrators in violent acts, especially those predominantly committed by men against women, obscures reality. And in doing so, neutral language could potentially weaken arguments for social change; for example, if a perpetrator is presented neutrally some might argue that both women and men are equally likely to commit violent acts against women. This could prevent the implementation of targeted initiatives to redress social norms and inequities. Martina's observation also moves us beyond considering the impact of pronouns and points toward the final two categories to be explored in this section: 'reflecting on effectiveness' and 'considering feasibility/reality'. She effectively asks whether neutral pronouns are a useful tool in all instances, which highlights a concern for the link between language and reality. I explore other responses relating to the 'effectiveness' and 'feasibility' of linguistic propositions in more detail next.

Reflecting on effectiveness: How literary texts thematise representation

When reflecting on the effectiveness of the literary excerpts, participants' readings fitted into two main strands. The first theme revolved around the intention of the texts and the second around their success in highlighting the issue of sex/gender and language. To begin with the first, comments on intent frequently surfaced during the focus group discussions. *The Left Hand of Darkness*, for example, puzzled many participants precisely because of its perceived lack of intentionality. As Martina reflected, 'I've got a preconception of *The Left Hand of Darkness* as being a kind of subversive text', but 'I was a bit surprised cause I didn't find much subversive stuff.' Rich from the postgraduate discussion group agreed with this interpretation: 'I didn't really quite know what to make of it', he said, 'cause I was sort of looking for a really blatant feminist point to come out of it, if you know what I mean, relating it to sort of, you know, real society let's say. And it did nothing.' This expectation of a 'feminist point' was influenced by the research context, as Rich explained at a later point: 'I found it difficult … to take any clear points out of it, of a let's say, regarding a feminist agenda specifically, which is what I was sort of on the lookout for given the topic of discussion.'

The perceived lack of making a 'clear point' was understood by other respondents as potentially useful in itself. As Jennie from the postgraduate group commented, 'even though the professions aren't gendered, they're like traditionally gendered professions so that's probably supposed to be leading so you think that like "masons" and "artisans" and stuff might be men.' While the language used in *The Left Hand of Darkness* might not provoke an instant reaction, the impact of 'traditionally gendered professions' on the imagination of readers did not go unnoticed. Further, when the excerpt did openly specify the sex/gender of a character, it had a powerful effect. As Sarah from the same group reflected on the sexing/gendering of Estraven, 'then the person [next] to her [the narrator] becomes a man and it's really, it's made really obvious, like, it's kind of trying to jolt you, like almost with force to make [inaudible] you to reflect on it.' This was seconded by Mandy from the feminist writing group:

> I quite liked the fact that it does that quite telling bit where it sort of says 'man I must say, having said he and his' that sort of points out to you what you've already made your mind up about and … how you've sort of already, and even though she [the narrator] said 'person on the left' very clearly, you've already made your mind up that it's a man

Jessica agreed: 'I feel like it's kind of intentionally drawing attention to itself.' The intention of the text was therefore perceived by some participants as knowingly understated. This approach, however, was considered problematic by Martina as the excerpt seemed to her 'a bit too subtle'. Sam from the postgraduate discussion group, on the other hand, saw power in this. She stated, 'I preferred the first one because it sort of just ambles along and then it hits you.' Overall, then, participants were undecided as to the text's effectiveness.

A different discussion emerged around *The Cook and the Carpenter*. The use of 'na' especially provoked debate on intent, with a key concern arising from the use of the neutral pronoun in conjunction with specific terms. Claudia from the pilot focus group argued, for example:

> [A]t some point I thought the text identified the 'na' or 'nan' person as a woman anyway cause they're like calling her a crazy woman and then they're calling her a girl so I don't understand, I didn't get the whole intention of well, if it's a woman why can't you say it's a woman, why can't you say it's 'her'

Other respondents agreed; as Sarah from the postgraduate discussion group reflected, 'when they talk about "woman" and "man" then you're almost surprised, you're like, oh we've just kind of avoided the whole issue of like who is a woman or a man so far.' This was supported by Jo from the feminist writing group: 'I was quite disappointed when I got to the use of "woman", I was like, ah it's not what I thought it's going to be … the use of the "woman" I did wonder then, oh what are they trying to achieve, what's trying to be achieved with the "na".' Participants were 'surprised' and 'disappointed' by this perceived inconsistency; however, that did not mean they considered the neutral pronoun ineffective. 'Na' was felt to cause a profound disruption to traditional pronoun usage. As Rich from the postgraduate group commented, 'I was finding it difficult to track who was saying what and who was, just obviously cause of not being used to the replacement of the pronouns.' He added, 'I think [this] is the whole point of it so as to make you rethink the arbitrariness of "his" and "her".' Martina, from the pilot focus group, agreed: 'I think for me on a deeper level, I think it's trying to show us what it says on the last page which is "it was the same thing either way". Maybe we shouldn't give too much importance to "he", "she", "her", "him".' In effect, the new language leads to reflections on the linguistic status quo and, in consequence, to the imagination of a new form of life – one that is not as centrally defined by the sex/gender binary.

In terms of overall effectiveness *The Cook and the Carpenter* was ranked highly by Martina. She explained, 'I think the most successful is the one we all got frustrated and confused about, cause that is actually pointing out that we do work by binaries, we do want to know whether it's a man or a woman cause otherwise we don't understand, we can't make sense of things.' However, Martina's description of the text as 'the one we all got frustrated and confused about' also highlights a central struggle participants experienced – one that was upheld across all focus group discussions. As linguistic changes were at odds with what Wittgenstein terms 'menschliche Gepflogenheiten' (Wittgenstein 1998, 108), they fundamentally challenged the participants' understanding. But respondents were unsure whether the experience of 'frustration/confusion' was due to the inability to identify the sex/gender of the referent or down to different reasons entirely. Either way, it had a profound impact on the perception of the text. Responses regarding the use of the neutral pronoun were strong, ranging from 'alienating' and 'disorientating' to 'clunky'. In consequence, 'it made it very difficult to read as well, like, I had to go back a thousand times and try and understand it … and then the next sentence you have to do the same, it just made it really slow, it kind of interrupted the flow', according to Martina. For many participants this 'slow' and 'interrupted' reading experience was linked to the writing style of the excerpt. For example, several postgraduate group respondents considered the text a 'language exercise' or 'linguistic exercise', while participants from the feminist writing group commented on 'the way that the story's told' from a stylistic perspective. A discussion between feminist writing group respondents illustrates this:

> Alice: just on this technique … I think some of the writing style isn't very clear and I think that's what makes this difficult is, I mean I kind of think 1973, I think if someone submitted this as a manuscript now I don't think it would get published based on this little intro about, you know, kind of talking about a warning but there's no idea what that is and a threat but there's no sense
> Jessica: it's a, it's a challenge
> Mandy: it is
> Jessica: to the reader I think, you know, it's a real laying down of the gauntlet because, you know, as first chapters go it's not the easiest or most you know
> Alice: and all they're doing is just hanging about like collecting some eggs and doing some
> Jessica: yeah
> Alice: woodwork
> Mandy: yeah it's confusing and who's speaking when … cause sometimes it's reported and then you know it's, like, what I don't understand how this happened

Alice concluded, 'I suppose what I'm saying is, I'm happy to read something with gender-neutral pronouns, I think it's good but it just, the writing there has to be, you know, compelling writing underneath it for me to read on.' Janine, from the pilot focus group, also pointed to the narrative style as the key obstacle to understanding:

> The story's really confusing I don't think it's because of the pronouns, it's just you don't know who's who so I spent my time going back and trying to actually figure out who's talking and who's doing what, so yeah the story is really frustrating because you can't actually understand it

In her subsequent conversation with Martina, however, the use of 'na' is explored as a key contributor rather than a mere addition to the confusion:

> Martina: the pronouns don't help though
> Janine: yeah that's true because actually, actually yeah if you know they are man or woman I can, they use 'her' or 'he', 'his' or so actually you can sort of place yourself in the story

In effect, Janine felt that specific pronouns are central to understanding and concluded that 'the second one with the gender-neutral pronoun, well it's a failure for me, I can't understand who's who so it's just I don't want to keep reading the story basically.' That is, the respondent is reluctant to engage with linguistic practices that are at odds with the status quo. And while Alice, from the feminist writing group, shared similar feelings about the limitations of the text, she concluded, on the other hand:

> I think the, you know, kind of in terms of language and gender, the male is the default and the female is the exception so when an author disrupts that and has these gender-neutral pronouns I think that's when like people get really annoyed by it as well cause they're like who but is it male or is it … I don't know are they female but I think that is the most kind of, you know, destabilising this kind of binary, you know, that you've got this kind of dominant and then this … other so I would say *The Cook and the Carpenter* is the most interesting kind of linguistically even though it's unfortunate the way that the story is told

So while the effectiveness of the text might be impaired by the style of the narrative for some respondents, the neutral pronoun was perceived as effective by Alice.

Participants were much less divided over the effectiveness of the excerpt from *The Daughters of Egalia*. While respondents did not necessarily reflect on the text as thoroughly in relation to the other categories, *The Daughters of Egalia* was frequently mentioned in relation to its perceived success. Martina, from the pilot group, for example, thought it was 'engaging' and 'funny', while Janine stated, 'it's so over-the-top it's, … it's kind of a parody, right? So it's, so I guess for me that just that might be the most useful.' This was supported by postgraduate discussion group participants, who described the excerpt as 'in-your-face' and 'striking', to which respondents from the feminist writing group added 'clear', 'vivid' and 'in the context of 1977 where, like, you'd be like this is revolutionary.' In effect, these reflections illustrate the potential of humour to liberate, as proposed by Freud's theory – the use of 'revolutionary' points to both 'Auflehnung' and 'Befreiung'. To explore these responses in more depth, Martina's comment is useful:

> It's a good way perhaps to make people realise how sexist society is and how, you know, sexist terms that apply to women, … everything that is usually said of women very stereotypically patronising, patriarchal, sexist and whatever you want is applied to men. … it's good to make people realise certain things, double standards

Jennie from the postgraduate discussion group supported this understanding: 'I thought it did a really good job of showing like how instrumental language is in kind of defining the normative and the aberrant so, like, the fact that it's "men" so that's the, like, the standard kind of position of personhood and then "women" is a sort of lesser secondary type of "man".' Jessica from the feminist writing group elaborated, 'I liked the inventiveness of the director's "housebound" and the "man-wom" and, you know, I thought they were interesting collisions of different, you know, ideas.' This reminds of Redfern's (1984) argument that wordplay helps to reveal double standards and thereby the role of language in upholding the status quo. As emerged from the data, participants felt the text was 'obvious' in its intentions and therefore generally effective.

The 'ease of reading' *The Daughters of Egalia* in comparison with *The Cook and the Carpenter* might have contributed to the above perceptions of textual effectiveness. And reflections on the feasibility of the proposed language change arguably also played into such perceptions. I explore comments on the category 'considering feasibility/reality' in the next section.

Considering feasibility/reality: How literary proposals could be transferred

This final category overlaps in many ways with the other core themes. However, as reflections on the feasibility/reality of language use distinctly emerged from the data, it is important to present them separately. Participants from the pilot focus group were the first to comment on the relationship between proposed linguistic changes and their place in the 'real' world. As Martina commented on *The Daughters of Egalia*, 'I don't think it's feasible in normal – it's good of a literary text, I find it really engaging and funny – I think it pushes the point a bit too far.' She clearly felt there is a difference between what is possible in a literary text and 'normality'; as she explained, 'I don't know how feasible it is in real, as in language use on a day-to-day basis.' Martina believes literary language is not necessarily transferable to 'language use on a day-to-day basis' – concerns that were shared by other respondents. As Claudia, this time in relation to *The Cook and the Carpenter*, stated, 'what's the point in trying to be neutral when you then, to illustrate a character, need to resort to the normal language anyway.' She elaborated, 'like normal as in a guy like this would use a language like this and that's why you need him in the story, that's why you have him use this language in the story because otherwise you couldn't tell the story.' Claudia was referring to the 'episode of violence', which Martina also took issue with. And like Martina, who felt the use of 'na' might potentially obscure the sex/gender of perpetrator and victim, Claudia pointed out the need for 'normal language' to 'tell the story'. To her, the narrative cannot be told if readers are unable to understand characters, and this understanding includes the identification of their sex/gender, which 'na' complicates.

In fact, reflections on the feasibility of the neutral pronoun emerged across all focus groups. Martina set the tone when commenting, 'as much as I want to believe in the fact that we can actually use a neutral pronoun to refer to people and etc. etc., I got so confused at some point that I stopped reading it.' She added, 'as much as I want to believe that it can actually work, sometimes it doesn't.' In short, the proposed changes seem still too profoundly at odds with 'menschliche Gepflogenheiten'. This perceived failure of 'na' was justified by participants in a variety of ways. Jennie from the postgraduate group felt, for example, that '"nan" would be too much of, like, a sort of glottal stop I suppose', and explained, 'I would have been interested to see what it would have been like if they'd just used "they" instead … cause it's having to get used to a whole new word.' An existing pronoun, such as 'they', seemed more viable because it is already in common usage. However, Martina questioned: 'are we ready to get rid of [sexed/gendered] pronouns completely?'. She reflected, 'I'm not sure in language use.' This was seconded by Jennie from the postgraduate discussion group, who queried the use of a neutral pronoun, which presumably includes 'they', in a narrative context defined by specificity. '[T]hey were linguistically just changing the pronouns but actually it did still seem like a sexist society so then it was, like, will that change anything? Will that matter? Will we still kind of see, like categorise things?', she asked. Such questions inspired the following discussion between two participants of the postgraduate group, who explored the issue further. In particular, their exploration reveals the popular premise that linguistic change is essentially ineffective.

> Rich: it sort of highlights that changing the language without changing the concepts or the sort of prejudices and the stigmas attached to it doesn't necessarily solve anything, if that makes sense, because you could call everyone 'na' and women could still be oppressed …
> Jennie: I think you're right
> Rich: What do you mean?
> Jennie: I think you're right, I agree that it's, yeah it could be a thing about, will just changing pronouns actually change anything cause obviously like in this text the concepts of 'man' and 'woman' and the associations of like negative and positive gender are still like really present

Martina agreed that changing pronouns might be problematic in an unequal social context. She stated, 'let's try and change the perspectives and the stereotypes rather than, when they're ready then we'll get rid of the pronouns.' To this Janine added, 'maybe we should try to educate people to actually understand that men and women, we're different but we're still equal … instead of trying to change everything.' A neutral pronoun was consequently considered ineffective if society remained defined by sex/gender.

However, reflections on the feasibility of 'na' were not restricted to concerns around how to best address inequality in an unequal social setting. Linguistic questions also played a central role. While some respondents felt they would 'get used to' the neutral pronoun, two respondents from the postgraduate group reflected on the stylistic hurdles to any wide-scale acceptance:

> Sarah: we're used to like adding new nouns to our vocabulary as well, technological concepts come out and you just, you add them, you get used to them …

Jennie: that's a good point about that we're really used to adding new nouns to our vocabulary so that doesn't pose too much of a problem, cause I thought one of the problems with the second [*The Cook and the Carpenter*] was that because pronouns are such common words

These comments emerged from a comparison of *The Cook and the Carpenter* and *The Daughters of Egalia* in terms of linguistic changes. While 'Egalia' remained 'readable' to most participants despite considerable modifications, Arnold's text caused a profound disruption to the reading experience. As Jo from the feminist writing group commented, 'even when I saw that the roles were reversed [in the English translation of Brantenberg's excerpt] I still had a woman and a man in my head whereas I didn't with this one … and that was simply "he" and "she", and "na" and "nan" that made that difference.'

Disrupting traditional pronoun usage therefore clearly challenged respondents' understanding, as pronouns support the specific interpretation of characters. As Janine stated, 'the pronoun ["na"], it feels weird not because, I think it's just because we're so used to hav[ing] "him" or "her".' This familiarity has a central impact, Janine explained: 'if, you know, they are man or woman I can, they use "her" or "he", "his" or so actually you can sort of place yourself in the story.' The reference to 'placing yourself in the story' highlights the importance of 'knowing' the sex/gender of referents. Readers occupy a specific 'place' in society, and so do characters in the fictional world. This is potentially why *The Left Hand of Darkness* and *The Daughters of Egalia* did not cause any great concern in terms of feasibility – except for the narrative voice in the first excerpt, sex/gender can be clearly identified. And if language use was ambiguous, such as in the use of 'I', participants found relevant clues to aid identification. The narrator of *The Left Hand of Darkness*, for example, was interpreted by respondents as 'female' or 'male' on the basis of the sex/gender of the author, the sex/gender of the reader and the sex/gender of a traditional central character. If such clues were missing, however, or were not accessible at first instance, feelings of frustration and confusion frequently emerged from the data relating to *The Cook and the Carpenter*. Repeated concerns around 'needing to know' consequently resulted in the formation of a new central category. The next section presents the results of theoretical sampling, which tests the boundaries of this new core. I employ the data emerging from the German focus groups to further explore the impact of the literary excerpts in relation to raising awareness of the issue of sex/gender and language.

Theoretical sampling – Native German responses

Identifying sex/gender is, according to Martina, 'the way people actually make sense of reality'. She explained that 'we do want to know whether it's a man or a woman cause otherwise we don't understand, we can't make sense of things.' Without linguistic clues as to whether a character was 'female' or 'male', Janine felt 'you don't really know who is who', and, as Claudia termed it, encounter only 'an empty shell of a person'. This core theme of 'needing to know' emerged across all focus groups and informed the subsequent analysis of the two native German transcripts. This specific focus further contributed to the formation of grounded theory from the data.

The research context for the native German discussions differed in several ways from that of the native English groups. First of all, I recruited participants via a general call for respondents within the university. Participants therefore did not have any previous familiarity with one another or with me. Secondly, I asked respondents to complete 'The Inventory of Attitudes Toward Sexist/Nonsexist Language – General (IASNL-G)' online. While the results of the questionnaire did not impact on the formation of the native English-speaking groups, this time they informed the selection and grouping of participants. Thirteen respondents completed the questionnaire and eight took part in two focus groups conducted in German. Of these, five, Matthias, Antje, Ines, Jochen and Katrin, had a supportive attitude toward non-sexist language, with an average score of 84. The remaining three respondents, Sebastian, Doreen and Berit, held neutral attitudes, with an average of 69 – 'total scores between 52.6 and 73.5 reflect a neutral attitude' (Parks and Roberton 2000, 434). The groups were led with a translated script as well as translated materials; both *The Left Hand of Darkness* and *The Daughters of Egalia* exist in German translation; I translated the excerpt from *The Cook and the Carpenter* for the purposes of this study. All other processes and procedures remained the same.

The participants identified as white and native German speakers. The group with supportive attitudes consisted of three female and two male participants, and respondents were on average 26 years old. Two female and one male participant took part in the focus group formed of those with a neutral attitude toward non-sexist language; respondents were slightly younger, with an average age of 21. As the focus groups did not originate from pre-existing connections, individual motivations played a more central role in the decision to participate. These ranged from a general curiosity about the study – as one respondent commented, 'eigentlich war's ganz spontan weil ich auch noch nie sowas gemacht habe und ich dachte ja das klingt nach einem interessanten Thema, daher wollt ich einfach mal schauen wie das überhaupt so abläuft' [it was quite spontaneous actually, as I have never done anything like this before and I thought it sounded like an interesting topic, so I wanted to have a look what it's like]– to a comparative interest in the issue of sex/gender and language: 'so eine Sprach- und Geschlechterstudie ist interessant besonders wenn man halt diesen Deutsch-Englischen Kontrast sieht' [such a language and sex/gender study is interesting, especially when one sees the contrast between German and English]. The appeal of speaking German was also mentioned by a third, 'ich mach hier mit, weil ich Deutschunterricht vermisse und weil ich schon richtig lange kein Deutsch mehr geredet hab' [I'm taking part because I miss German classes and because I haven't spoken German in a long time]. Owing to the lack of prior relationships between participants, the dynamics of both native German-speaking groups were consequently different. However, as I explore here, the concerns of respondents were similar to those who took part in previous meetings. As indicated above, particular attention is paid to reflections on the new core category 'needing to know'.

A first close reading of the transcript of the German group with supportive attitudes brought five initial codes to light. These were: 1. 'perceiving sex/gender clearly (due to language and/or context)', 2. 'perceiving a disruption to the assumed sex/gender', 3. 'potentially perceiving no sex/gender', 4. 'not knowing who is who' and 5. 'perceiving sex/gender as helpful to understanding'. An example helps to illustrate how one of these codes emerged. When asked to reflect on *The Cook and the Carpenter*, Matthias from the first group commented as follows: 'ich hab das dann als letztes tatsächlich durch … "er" [ersetzt] also eigentlich hab ich ihn dann als männlichen genommen, aber ich hätte es auch als weiblichen nehmen können, aber es macht dann den Text viel einfacher zu lesen' [I have eventually actually [replaced it] with … 'he', so actually I took it as male, but I could have also understood it as female, but it makes the text much easier to read]. That is, only by referring back to linguistic norms was the participant able to engage with the narrative. The respondent decided to replace 'na' with 'er' as the specific pronoun facilitated reading. He elaborated, 'also einfach nur weil man, glaub ich, dann mit dieser grammatischen Funktion einfach vertrauter ist, … dann dachte [ich], na ja wenn ich das ersetze … also dann wenn ich einfach nur irgendein Geschlecht einsetze, dann liest sich der Text viel einfacher' [simply because one, I think, is more familiar with this grammatical function, … I thought, if I replace it … so if I simply insert any sex/gender, then the text is much easier to read].

Matthias reflected that traditional pronouns were a familiar grammatical feature. And further, he felt that this familiar feature supported the reading of the text. Replacing a neutral pronoun with a specific one, according to the participant, therefore resulted in an 'einfacher' reading experience. Essentially, he was 'perceiving sex/gender as helpful to understanding', which along with similar comments made by other participants, led to the emergence of this particular code.

Evidence for all five codes above also surfaced from a close reading of the second German transcript. As in the evaluation of the pilot and English-speaking focus groups, diagrams enabled me to compare data within and across both transcripts as well as observe connections between codes. For example, I noticed a link between comments made on 'potentially perceiving no sex/gender' and 'not knowing who is who', which allowed me to test and develop each category. Through this comparative process, four final subcategories emerged: 1. 'perceiving sex/gender clearly', 2. 'perceiving sex/gender as helpful', 3. 'having doubts about sex/gender', which now included 'perceiving a disruption to the assumed sex/gender' and 'not knowing who is who', and 4. 'potentially perceiving no sex/gender'. In the following sections I test the boundaries of each and explore whether they hold up to scrutiny. This classification expands my previous investigation into the effectiveness of literary texts thematising sex/gender and language, and their impact on readers.

Perceiving sex/gender clearly: How language categorises human beings

Repeated identification of the sex/gender of characters by participants resulted in the creation of this category. As in the pilot and English-speaking focus groups, respondents perceived certain characters as specifically male or female. As Katrin from the first German group (supportive attitudes) commented in relation to *The Left Hand of Darkness*, this understanding was often shaped by the language used in the excerpt. '[A]lso was mir schon aufgefallen ist, also jetzt die "Herrschaften" wurden auch alle als "Herrschaften" benannt … also aus meiner Sicht wirkt das wie gezielt männlich bezeichnet' [[S]o what I noticed is, the lords [Herren = men] were all described as lords … so from my point of view it appears as if purposefully described as male], she stated. Berit from the second German group (neutral attitudes) agreed with this interpretation. When prompted to reflect on whom she imagined when reading the excerpt, she said, 'ich finde männlich … also es werden auch manchmal Männer explizit erwähnt und dass, dann denkt man sich, dass bestimmt auch ansonsten nur Männer da sind, zum Beispiel wird gesagt "dann kommen die Herren, Bürgermeister und Vertreter"' [I think male ... sometimes men are also explicitly referred to and that, one thinks that there must be only men otherwise as well, for example when it's said 'then come the lords/men, mayors and representatives']. This again illustrates the relevance of the hypothesis that language influences thought, and more specifically, perception. However, Sebastian from the same group doubted whether such nouns necessarily referred to men only. He argued that certain terms are 'theoretisch' open to interpretation. Nevertheless, he also admitted that in combination with specific nouns these quickly become restricted:

> [D]as stimmt, also im Bezug auf die eine Textstelle, wo nur 'Herren' kommt, da ist es sehr komisch, dass nur 'Herren' steht und nicht 'Frauen' ... manche Bezeichnungen sind ja an sich offen, zum Beispiel, also meiner Meinung nach 'Bürgermeister' und 'Vertreter', aber dadurch, dass eben ein Begriff 'Herren' sehr explizit ist, stimmt das, das wird abgeschwächt. Die Herren an sich also sind, das sind nur Männer und könnte man die Schlußfolgerung daraus ziehen, dass die anderen Teilnehmer auch nur männlich sind

> [[T]hat's true, in relation to the one passage where there are only lords men, that is very strange that it only says lords and not women ... some descriptions are open in themselves, for example, from my point of view 'mayors' and 'representatives', but because, as the term lords is very explicit, it's true, it is diminished. The lords in themselves are, they are only men and one could therefore come to the conclusion that the other participants are only male as well]

He agreed that the language used in the excerpt seemed to encourage the identification of one particular sex/gender, and further, one rather than the other.

Context and association were another aid in deciding whether characters were female or male. As Jochen from the first group commented in relation to *The Cook and the Carpenter*, 'beim Tischler war es irgendwie so, weil der auch irgendwie mit der Arbeit assoziiert wurde, dass um irgendwelche[s] Brettersägen oder so was ging, da hab ich mir den einfach als männlichen Tischler vorgestellt, so assoziiert' [for the carpenter it was somehow, because he was somehow associated with the work, that it was about sawing boards or something, I simply imagined him as a male carpenter, associated]. In addition, context encouraged specific interpretation, as Sebastian from the second group suggested: 'das gab es ja früher auch, dass eben manche Berufsbilder eben vor allem männlich geprägt sind und … dieses Berufsbild dann dort in dieser Prozession langmarschiert, dass es dann sozusagen indirekt auch nur Männer sind' [that existed in the past as well that some job profiles are predominantly linked to male and … this job profile marches in this procession, that it is, so to speak, indirectly only men as well]. This line of reasoning was similar to participants' reflections during the pilot and English-speaking focus groups; most participants found evidence for sex/gender either in convention or context. However, the German groups also drew on grammatical gender to identify whether a character was male or female. For example, in my translation of *The Cook and the Carpenter* I replaced the default article 'der' (masc.) with 'de' (neut.) – in line with the Low German article – to obscure the immediate connotations of the grammatical gender. Consequently, 'der Koch' was referred to as 'de Koch', and 'der Tischler' as 'de Tischler'. Nevertheless, the neutral article was unable to override the dominant associations for most respondents. Ines from the first group explained that 'war das "de" für mich einfach nur, da hat jemand das "r" vergessen und damit war das nach wie vor männlich und dann "de Koch" blieb einfach "Koch", "der Koch"' [the 'de' was for me simply, someone forgot the 'r' and therefore it was still male and 'de Koch' simply remained 'cook', 'the (masc.) cook']. Doreen from the second group agreed that the dominant connotation remained, 'da ja auch "Koch" und "Tischler" ja die männliche Variante der Berufsbezeichnungen sind, ansonsten wär es ja "de Köchin" und "de Tischlerin"' ['cook' and 'carpenter' are the male version of the job titles, otherwise it would be 'de Köchin' and 'de Tischlerin']. The familiar grammatical gender of terms therefore also played a key role in identification.

As clearly emerged from the data, language contributed to the perception of sex/gender. It generally seemed to guide readers to decide whether a character was one *or* the other. However, as Berit from the second group argued, this linguistic sexing/gendering goes further than nouns referring to characters directly, and also included actions and emotions. She reflected in relation to *The Daughters of Egalia*:

> [I]ch glaub es will halt auch darauf anspielen, dass Leute, dass viele Leute sagen zwar ja es macht doch gar nichts, dass halt die Sprache so männlich geprägt ist, zum Beispiel mit 'Beherrschung' also wenn ich sag, ich verlier die Beherrschung … also ich hab noch nie bei dem Wort 'Beherrschung' darüber nachgedacht, dass das irgendwie so männlich geprägt ist. Das ist einfach nur ein Wort und viele Leute sagen, ja ach lass doch die Sprache die Sprache sein, und das

find ich auch meistens, aber dieser Text zeigt halt wenn [man] das dann mal vertauscht und sagt 'Befrauschung' das klingt direkt total seltsam

[I think it wants to allude to the fact that many people say, it doesn't matter that language is androcentric. For example, 'composure', when I say I'm losing my composure ... when using the term composure [Be-herr-schung] I have never thought about it being androcentric. It's just a word and many people say, just let language be language and most of the time I agree, but this text shows that when you reverse it and say 'Befrauschung' then it sounds completely strange]

As 'Egalia' illustrated to the respondent, even terms that do not connote sex/gender directly are weighted. Antje from the first group agreed that the third excerpt made this particularly obvious. She stated, 'teilweise wurde einem dann so ein bisschen vor Augen geführt was man gar nicht merkt in der Alltagssprache, wie also, wo überall solche Geschlechtssachen auftauchen' [to some extent one was made aware a bit of what one doesn't notice in everyday language, where all these sex/gender things appear]. As Barr (1989) argues in relation to Brantenberg's text, the subversion of dominant norms renders it 'a social corrective – a weapon'. Through wordplay the novel effectively highlights the extent and impact of the status quo. Participants noticed how used they are to 'reading' sex/gender, and often, they felt led to interpret one sex/gender rather than the other; that is, in line with male-as-norm. As Sebastian from the second group responded in relation to *The Cook and the Carpenter*:

[A]lso was bei mir dazu geführt hat, dass ich als Männer wahrgenommen hab, ist vielleicht eher so die grundlegende Voreinstellung – ist vielleicht komisch, da müsste man auch länger drüber nachdenken, das ist nur das Erste was mir in den Sinn gekommen ist. Dass ... man solange dazu neigt von einem Mann auszugehen, bis im Text das Gegenteil kommt

[What made me perceive them as men is perhaps more of a default position – it's perhaps strange, one needs to think about this more deeply. But it's the first thing that came to my mind. That ... one tends to assume it's a man until the text says otherwise]

In support of the pilot and English focus group data, sex/gender was also perceived clearly by most German focus group members. Further, respondents reflected that 'knowing' the sex/gender of a referent was helpful when reading and understanding a text. I will now evaluate such comments in more detail.

Perceiving sex/gender as helpful: How linguistic norms rely on classification

Participants did not comment as frequently as in the English-speaking focus groups on the helpfulness of sex/gender; that is, that this marker enabled them to imagine a particular character. However, reflections were strong enough to merit the creation of this particular category. A good example is the following observation by Matthias from the first German-speaking focus group. As quoted earlier, he explained the replacement of 'na' with 'er' in *The Cook and the Carpenter* by stating, 'ich hab das dann als letztes tatsächlich durch ... "er" [ersetzt] also eigentlich hab ich ihn dann als männlichen genommen, aber ich hätte es auch als weiblichen nehmen können, aber es macht dann den Text viel einfacher zu lesen' [I have eventually actually [replaced it] with ... 'he', so actually I took it as male, but I could have also understood it as female, but it makes the text much easier to read]. This perception of an easier reading experience was seconded by Antje from the same group. She stated, 'irgendwann hat man es dann ersetzt, dann ging es eben wieder, weil irgendwie es war mühsam' [at some point one replaced it, then it was okay again, because somehow it was cumbersome]. When prompted to reflect on the choice of pronoun, she added, 'jeweils manchmal ausprobiert, bezieht es sich jetzt auf die Person ... und dann ja jetzt macht es Sinn OK' [experimented sometimes, does it refer to this person ... and yes, now it makes sense OK]. Antje considered the use of 'er' or 'sie' less 'mühsam' than the neutral pronoun: 'dann ging es eben wieder' and 'jetzt macht es Sinn', she confirmed. The data from the second group supported these findings. Berit, for example, mentioned that she also replaced 'na' when reading: 'ich hab das immer ersetzt durch das passende normale Pronomen' [I always replaced it with the appropriate normal pronoun]. The use of 'normal' is here revealing – having linguistic access to the referent's sex/gender is consequently judged routine, a familiar grammatical function.

In fact, as long as specification followed traditional conventions, it was not even perceived as a feature of language. Matthias from the first group stated in relation to *The Left Hand of Darkness*, 'also der erste Text war einfach ein Text, der sich mit de[r] Geschlechtersache vielleicht gar nicht so explizit beschäftigt' [so the first text was simply a text, which perhaps didn't engage with the sex/gender subject explicitly]. Linguistic specificity was not noticed precisely because it was considered ordinary. Antje agreed that 'beim ersten Text ja stimm ich dir auch zu … es wurde halt ein Bild gezeichnet und dadurch, dass das eh in so einer nicht-realen Welt war, hat man es halt einfach so akzeptiert wie es ist … halt viele Männer waren da und die sind diejenigen, die in den hohen Positionen sind' [with the first text I agree with you … a picture was created and as a result, that it was in an unreal world anyway, one simply accepted it as it was … that many men were there and they are the ones who have status]. The predominance of male terms and associations might have been frequently reflected on by focus group members as problematic; however, specification in itself was understood as commonplace. Katrin confirmed: 'weil es halt realistisch eben in der Zeit, aber eben auch in der Sprache auch so rüberkam, weil eben die meisten patriarchalischen Bezeichnungen eben männlich waren, weil dass eben alles Männer sind … also unter dem fand ich das gar nicht so unpassend' [because it was realistic of the time, but was also portrayed in the language, because most patriarchial terms were male, because they are all men … therefore I didn't find it necessarily inappropriate]. Further, as became obvious from the data leading to the emergence of the next subcategory, sex/gender was a central requirement to comprehend a text and its portrayed characters. In the following section I focus on participants' comments regarding 'having doubts about sex/gender' and the consequences of this uncertainty.

Having doubts about sex/gender: How neutral terms complicate classification

Similar to the responses by pilot and English-speaking focus group members, the German participants struggled when unable to identify sex/gender. Antje from the first group, for example, commented in relation to the use of 'na' in *The Cook and the Carpenter*: 'man weiß eigentlich nicht um wen es sich handelt … ja ob es nun ein Mann oder eine Frau ist oder ein Mädchen oder ein Junge, was aber sehr verwirrend ist, weil man selten weiß, auf wen sich das jetzt genau bezieht' [one doesn't know who is being referred to … if it is a man or a woman or a girl or a boy, which is very confusing, because one rarely knows who is definitely being referred to]. She added, 'dadurch dass immer nur "na" [verwendet wurde] war das sehr ungenau in meinem Kopf auf wen es sich jetzt bezieht' [because only 'na' was used at all times it was very unclear in my mind who is being referred to]. As the proposed changes are at odds with linguistic norms, readers were unable to 'make sense' of the narrative. 'Verwirrend' was also a key term employed by respondents from the second group. However, not only the neutral pronoun caused confusion, the use of 'de', rather than 'der', as default article was also perceived as problematic. Berit from the second group argued: 'ich fand das ganz verwirrend mit dem "de" das hat mich total gestört', and added, 'das hat mich mehr gestört als das "na" weil das "na" konnte ich ganz einfach ersetzen im Text' [I found it really confusing with the 'de', it really bothered me … it bothered me more than the 'na' because the 'na' I could easily replace in the text]. She explained, 'soll ich da jetzt sagen "de" oder "der" oder meint jetzt halt das einen komischen Eigennamen? Das hat mich total gestört' [should I now say 'de' or 'der' or does it mean a strange personal name? That really bothered me].

A name, however, is often associated with a particular sex/gender. As explored above, respondents interpreted terms referring to characters as either female or male. And 'de Koch' and 'de Tischler' were often classified according to their default grammatical gender and/or dominant associations, whether understood as names or job titles. For example, Doreen from the second group reflected, 'das "de" kann ja auch ein Adelstitel "von" sein, deswegen hab ich das dann nachher als Eigennamen gewertet, aber ich konnte es von diesen Berufsbezeichnungen … nicht lösen … also bei "de Tischler" hab ich die ganze Zeit an einen Tischler gedacht, das war so verbunden' [the 'de' could also be a title of nobility 'von', therefore I took it as a personal name in the end but I couldn't detach it from these job titles … so with 'de Tischler' I thought of a carpenter the whole time, that was linked]. I prompted both German-speaking groups to consider whether the use of the female/neutral suffix '-In', as in 'KöchIn' or 'TischlerIn' – with capital 'I' indicating inclusivity – would have had an impact on their perception. And while I evaluate specific responses in more depth in the final section, one comment was instructive in relation to this subcategory. As Doreen from the second group reflected on the potential use of the 'Binnen-I':

> [I]ch hätte mir auf jeden Fall darüber Gedanken gemacht ob es ein Mann oder eine Frau ist, weil so hab ich direkt vom ersten Satz an, war mir klar das sind beides Männer 'de Koch' und 'de Tischler'. Es wär aber auch an sich nicht nur wegen des Geschlechts merkwürdig gewesen, sondern einfach bei einer Einzelperson das einzufügen, weil das, müsste es eigentlich klar sein ob es männlich oder weiblich ist
>
> [I would have definitely thought about whether it is a man or a woman, because this way I have directly from the first sentence, it

was clear to me that they are both men 'de Koch' and 'de Tischler'. It would have been strange, however, not only because of the sex/gender, but because including it for a single person, because that should be actually clear whether it is male or female]

The expectation of the respondent was that the sex/gender of an individual referent would be known. Neutrality or 'doubts about sex/gender' would consequently be an oddity. So when sex/gender was obscured, such as by the use of 'na', it created difficulties for the reader. And these difficulties manifested themselves not only in the understanding of characters, but also in terms of engaging with the text in general.

As Ines from the first group stated, 'ich find das baut Distanz zum Text auf. Dadurch, dass man auf diese Art und Weise denken muss, ist es ein bisschen Analysearbeit und wenn das Prosa ist, die zur Unterhaltung dient, das würde ich nicht in meiner Freizeit lesen' [I think it creates a distance to the text. As one has to think in this particular way, it is a bit of analytic work and when it's prose that intends to entertain, I wouldn't read it in my free time]. She explained, 'das ist ein Gefühl wissenschaftlichen Arbeitens, wo ich gucken muss, OK was bezieht sich auf was, wer ist wer, was möchte gesagt werden … also ich würde nicht so in die Handlung reinfallen' [it's a feeling of scientific work, where I have to look, OK what refers to what, who is who, what does it intend to say … I wouldn't become immersed in the plot]. This reminded of Janine's comment during the pilot focus group: 'the second one with the gender-neutral pronoun well it's a failure for me, I can't understand who's who so … I don't want to keep reading the story basically.' That is, the perceived clash with 'menschliche Gepflogenheiten' leads participants to disengage, highlighting the limitations of a new language proposed in isolation. Not all respondents agreed with this position, however. Alice from the English feminist writing group felt that the use of the neutral pronoun helped to disrupt binaries and thereby made a valuable point regarding sex/gender and language. Matthias from the first German group agreed: 'der mittlere Text, der war viel sprachlicher für mich, weil der halt durch dieses "na", was ich halt nicht so wirklich verstanden habe am Anfang … und das hat halt diese Sprache viel mehr hervorgehoben und das damit zu experimentieren' [the middle text was more linguistic for me because of this 'na', which I didn't really understand in the beginning … and that has highlighted this language a lot more and to experiment with it]. 'Having doubts about sex/gender' can therefore be perceived as fruitful as well as 'verwirrend'. I evaluate responses to the final subcategory, 'potentially perceiving no sex/gender', in the next section.

Potentially perceiving no sex/gender: How classification can be obscured

The final subcategory of 'needing to know' emerged from participants' reflections on potentially neutral terms. While most nouns referring to characters were understood as sexed/gendered for linguistic and/or contextual reasons, some remained 'theoretisch' open to interpretation. For example, Matthias from the first German group commented on his understanding of 'Tischler': 'ich denke, das war eher so als Name hab ich das wahrgenommen als jetzt, also ich hab da kein Geschlecht [wahrgenommen] keine Ahnung' [I think I perceived it as more of a name, so I didn't perceive a sex/gender, no idea]. 'Koch' also remained potentially neutral, as Jochen from the same group reflected, 'während ich mir "de Koch" irgendwie gar nicht vorgestellt habe, war es beim "Tischler" irgendwie so, weil der auch irgendwie mit der Arbeit assoziiert wurde' [while I didn't really imagine 'de' Koch', for the carpenter it was somehow, because he was somehow associated with the work]. However, it was the prompt to consider the use of the '-In' suffix instead that resulted in most reflections on neutrality. Matthias from the first group suggested: 'so ein Binnen-I, dann würde das halt ganz explizit meinen Gedanken darauf gehören, dass es geschlechterneutral ist. Also ich … hätte mir dann kein Geschlecht vorgestellt, dann wäre ehrlich gesagt das egal quasi' [such a Binnen-I, then it would have explicitly made me think about that it is neutral. So I … wouldn't have imagined a sex/gender, then to tell the truth it wouldn't have mattered]. Sebastian from the second group agreed: 'das [Binnen-I] hätte einen Unterschied gemacht, weil dann konkret darauf hingewiesen wird, dass es geschlechtsneutral sein soll' [the Binnen-I would have made a difference, because then it would have been concretely shown that it's meant to be neutral]. He explained, 'für mich war das bis jetzt einfach nur ein Name, hinter dem sich eine verborgene Persönlichkeit eben verbirgt und wenn man "TischlerIn" oder "KöchIn" geschrieben hätte, dann hätte man explizit gemacht, dass es neutral ist' [for me it was until now just a name which refers to a hidden personality and if one had written 'TischlerIn' or 'KöchIn' then one would have made explicit that it's neutral]. This illustrates the potential of a new language to evoke a new form of life. The 'Binnen-I' is a relatively new addition to German and continues to be contested. Nevertheless, its increasing familiarity is, judging from the responses, beginning to result in acceptance as well as the conception of a neutral alternative to the status quo.

But while characters might have potentially been perceived as neutral owing to the '-In' suffix, participants' difficulty in understanding the neutral pronoun suggests the suffix might have created equal complications. As Jochen from the first group reflected on the use of 'na':

> [A]n manchen Punkten war es aber einfach auch zweideutig, dass man nicht ganz genau wusste, bezieht sichs jetzt auf eine männliche Person oder auf eine weibliche Person und da war es dann besonders schwierig. Aber ich denke aus dem Zusammenhang vielleicht hat es sich dann ergeben, ich glaube das war schwieriger zu lesen auf jeden Fall
>
> [I think in some instances it was ambiguous, that one didn't really know, does this refer to a male person or to a female person and then it was particularly difficult. But I think from the context it perhaps became clear. I thought it was more difficult to read definitely]

However, whether the use of the suffix would have the same impact remains to be tested. What did emerge from the existing data is that most respondents reacted strongly when unable to categorise a character as either male or female. This reaction generally manifested itself in feelings of frustration/confusion, as well as a reduced engagement with the text. Despite the very different environments and social hierarchies presented in *The Left Hand of Darkness* and *The Daughters of Egalia*, the excerpts remained 'readable' to participants, arguably because of the recognisable specification of referents. *The Cook and the Carpenter*, on the other hand, disrupted the usual associations. Consequently, focus group members often felt unable to tell 'who is who' and struggled to make sense of the excerpt altogether.

Having access to the sex/gender of characters was key to understanding a narrative, just as knowing the sex/gender of human beings is key to understanding reality. Being able to identify whether someone is 'female' *or* 'male' is central to human interaction in the readers' sociocultural context, and this centrality visibly emerged from the data. Participants' responses across all focus groups highlighted that they 'needed to know' and voiced frustration and confusion if clues were not given by terms and/or contexts. The data from this study supports the new core category 'needing to know' – *The Cook and the Carpenter*, in particular, prompted readers to reflect on this central requirement. In the following section I draw some first conclusions before I assess the findings of my study in relation to my overall proposal that literary texts can help to promote inclusive language use.

Conclusions

Previous research in the field of sex/gender and language has illustrated the link between language and imagination, as well as its impact on speakers. As Gastil's study (1990) showed, the English pronoun 'he' largely evokes 'man' in participants' minds. Equally, German male generics lead respondents to predominantly presume 'male', according to Stahlberg et al.'s research (2001). This cognitive bias has profound consequences. For example, if a job advertisement is worded in male terms, women feel less motivated to apply for the position, as Stout and Dasgupta's study (2011) highlighted. And even if women apply for a male-worded role, respondents in Horvath and Sczesny's study (2016) considered them less suitable. Building on these findings, researchers have explored potential solutions to the linguistic male-as-norm. 'Beidnennung' [pair forms], for example, results in a more egalitarian conception of the sexes/genders, according to Braun et al.'s study (1998). Moreover, the impact of inclusive language has been investigated by Vervecken et al. (2013). As their results showed, when children are presented with job titles in pair forms, they perceive women and men as similarly successful. Additionally, girls show more interest in pursuing traditionally male positions when pair forms are employed.

However, inclusive language remains far from the norm. Despite revisions of official language use, wider linguistic change continues to be slow and contested. A big hurdle seems the reluctance of general language users to employ inclusive terms, as Sczesny et al.'s (2015) study showed. Lack of familiarity and awareness, in particular, are key inhibitors. However, as Koeser et al. (2015) highlighted in their research, speakers adapt their language use when presented with inclusive terms. Furthermore, male participants increase their usage after encountering awareness-raising texts. This was the starting point for my study: I hypothesised that literary texts can help to sensitise readers to and, in extension, promote inclusive language use. As the focus group responses showed, literary texts encourage engagement with the issue of sex/gender and language. Moreover, as the data highlighted, literary texts prompt readers to reconsider biased language use. But not all literary approaches illustrate the issue equally. For example, the excerpt from *The Left Hand of Darkness* was felt to be too subtle by many focus group members. Because of its 'traditional' use of nouns and pronouns – those that favour a male interpretation – respondents frequently did not notice that it was making a point about sex/gender and language at all. *The Cook and the Carpenter*, on the other hand, provoked many participants to think about the function and usefulness of neutral pronouns. Being presented with 'na', instead of the familiar 'she' or 'he', focus group members responded with frustration and confusion, on the one hand. On the other, they also reflected on the binaries inherent in language. In contrast, *The Daughters of Egalia* stimulated discussion on sex/gender and language by reversing androcentric terms. This approach was most readily understood as effective by participants – perhaps because it remained 'readable' in terms of clearly identifying either sex/gender. The impact of *The Cook and the Carpenter* and *The Daughters of Egalia*, in particular, is summarised by Martina as follows:

> I think, you know, all our reactions ... kind of show that they [the literary excerpts], even though we haven't understood anything about the second one, even though the third one was confusing ... it's proof of the fact that it's doing something to us even if we don't understand what they're talking about, we're getting frustrated, we're getting angry, we're kind of engaging with the text. And I think that's the whole point about texts and that's how things can perhaps change when you come across something like this

Prompting in-depth responses and reflections suggests that literary texts are highly effective, and in this case, in illustrating the issue of sex/gender and language. Additionally, as the emergence of grounded theory from the data highlighted, responses to the literary texts reveal the importance of the linguistic category sex/gender to begin with. Participants 'need to know' a character's sex/gender in order to make sense of a narrative. As McConnell-Ginet (1979) argues, in the current sociocultural context human beings are identified as either 'female' or 'male'. Consequently, this information seems essential to facilitate communication and understanding. Arnold's text particularly illustrated the reliance on the sex/gender binary to respondents, and in turn prompted them to reflect on the linguistic status quo.

In the Conclusions I relate the findings of my focus group study to the literary and linguistic insights. I draw together my evidence that literary texts can be a valuable tool to raise awareness of the issue of linguistic representation. As a result, I propose how this tool can be most effectively applied and explore its value for future research.

Notes

1. As becomes visible throughout my analysis, integrating this level of reflexivity is challenging.
2. Owing to time constraints I focused on the first few pages of each text.
3. All names have been changed.

6
Conclusions

Despite decades of research and empirical support, inclusive language use is far from the norm in the English and German language. While some progress has been made – many official guidelines today recommend inclusive terminology – changes remain contested, and many English and German speakers continue to employ male generic terms. As studies by Kuhn and Gabriel (2014) and Sczesny et al. (2015) showed, only a minority of speakers use inclusive terms spontaneously. However, the authors also found that raising awareness of the importance of inclusive language can make a tangible difference. After encountering texts that aim to sensitise readers, usage generally improved. This was the starting point for my proposal: I suggested literary texts can sensitise readers to the impact of biased language and thereby promote inclusive language use. To explore the validity of my proposal I employed an interdisciplinary approach: in the first part of this book I evaluated the effectiveness of literary texts thematising sex/gender and language from a linguistic and philosophical perspective; in the second, I conducted a focus group study to gauge their ability to raise awareness of the importance of inclusive language.

My premise was based on the findings of narrative research. As Green and Brock (2000) found, through the process of transportation readers accept narrative characters and events as 'real'. Moreover, depending on the level of transportation, readers adjust their beliefs in line with the fictional perspective. As Hoeken and Fikkers's research (2014) showed, this adjustment takes place even when readers hold different views from the ones presented in the narrative. That is, transportation encourages readers to tap into feelings of identification and empathy, and restrain critical faculties. The desire of readers to engage with a narrative therefore allows literary texts to 'get under the radar', as Dal Cin et al. (2004) term it, of certain preconceptions. This ability, I hypothesised, makes literary texts a useful tool for sensitising readers.

My analysis was guided by three clusters of literary approaches I identified, namely 'Problematising the linguistic status quo', 'Proposing linguistic neutrality' and 'Reversing the linguistic status quo'. The central texts I evaluated in the first cluster were *The Left Hand of Darkness* and *Häutungen*. Both problematise the linguistic status quo – Le Guin's novel queries the generic use of 'he' and 'man', while Stefan's text questions the indefinite pronoun and the default grammatical gender. Each text highlights that male terms are unable to represent human beings equally. My application of Leibniz's *salva veritate* principle supports that 'man' cannot be equated with 'a human being of either sex'. Both fulfil a different function in language; one is specific and the other generic. In fact, as my etymological analysis illustrates, 'man' and 'human' used to be separate concepts; it was a shift in world view that made them interchangeable. Le Guin's and Stefan's literary problematisations highlight the issues with this equation.

The texts I assessed in the second cluster build on this premise and experiment with linguistic revision. *The Cook and the Carpenter* and *Woman on the Edge of Time* suggest new terms of reference to enable a more inclusive understanding. Both employ epicene nouns and pronouns – Piercy's novel uses 'person' to refer to the inhabitants of a future society, while Arnold's text employs 'na' in relation to the carpenter's community. Wittgenstein's notion 'eine Sprache vorstellen heißt, sich eine Lebensform vorstellen' proved valuable for framing Piercy's and Arnold's proposals of linguistic neutrality; a change in terminology opens up conceptual possibilities. However new linguistic practices need to become widely accepted before they can have an impact. This was confirmed by my evaluation of epicenes; many attempts to introduce an English neutral pronoun have failed. On the other hand, I also illustrated that the familiar pronoun 'they' has been, and continues to be, employed as a neutral alternative to 'she' and 'he'. Consequently, neutral language is possible if aligned with 'menschliche Gepflogenheiten' – and these can certainly change, as illustrated by Piercy and Arnold.

The key texts I analysed in the final cluster, the English and German translations of *Egalias døtre*, reverse the linguistic status quo to highlight the extent and impact of biased terms. If linguistic practices privilege one sex/gender only, the novel shows, the other is rendered conceptually insignificant. *Egalias døtre*, and its English and German translations, accentuate this via female generics such as 'Direktorinnen' and linguistic innovations such as 'wom' and 'manwom'. Brantenberg's, and her translators', use of wordplay is particularly effective, as illustrated by my discussion of Freud's work on 'Humor'. Freud proposes that humour enables speakers to ridicule figures of authority and thereby experience release. While the long-term consequences of this release remain contested, the novel helps to expose the artificiality of the linguistic hierarchy. My etymological study further confirmed that male-as-norm is a historical and cultural product – *Egalias døtre* effectively brings this to the fore.

To evaluate the ability of the three approaches to raise awareness in readers, I conducted a focus group study. I asked English and German speakers to read the introductory pages of *The Left Hand of Darkness*, *The Cook and the Carpenter* and *Egalias døtre* in their native language and focus on the employed nouns and pronouns. In particular, I prompted participants to reflect on who they imagined when reading, and discuss which text(s) they considered most effective in illustrating the issue of linguistic representation. Respondents remarked that they predominantly pictured male characters in the scene described in *The Left Hand of Darkness* – German speakers even more so owing to the male grammatical gender of the terms. In reference to *The Cook and the Carpenter*, participants reflected that they felt confused and frustrated by the neutral pronoun. In order to 'make sense' of the narrative, respondents stated that they replaced 'na' with 'she' or 'he' in line with sociocultural expectations – with German speakers additionally relying on grammar to make the distinction. When reading the English or German translation of *Egalias døtre* most participants commented that they were able to picture either sex/gender clearly. The reversal caused little concern as the created terms could be interpreted in line with the familiar pronouns 'she' and 'he'.

I subsequently asked respondents to select the excerpt they considered most effective in highlighting the issue of sex/gender and language. Responses were generally split. While some participants considered subtlety a useful tool, most respondents felt that *The Left Hand of Darkness* was too understated. Outside the focus group context, participants remarked, they would not have noticed the text's problematisation. *The Cook and the Carpenter* again provoked a mixed response; some respondents considered the linguistic and conceptual challenge presented by the excerpt a powerful means to highlight the issue. The majority, however, considered the text too confusing and frustrating to have any real impact on general readers. The translations of *Egalias døtre*, on the other hand, were deemed effective by most participants. Respondents commented that the text was both accessible and engaging. It allowed readers to reflect on the linguistic status quo through its humorous reversal and thereby effectively raised awareness of the impact of biased language. Brantenberg's novel was therefore considered most useful by readers.

Consequences and possibilities

As my research shows, literary texts highlight the issue of linguistic representation in three distinct ways. Furthermore, as the outcomes of my focus group study illustrate, the texts raise awareness of the issue of sex/gender and language. However, as the results also highlight, the depth of engagement is directly related to the literary approach. *The Left Hand of Darkness* and *The Cook and the Carpenter* were both found to be lacking – one was considered too subtle, the other confusing. The English and German translations of *Egalias døtre*, in contrast, were deemed accessible and effective. Judging from participants' responses, Brantenberg's novel could be employed to sensitise readers to the importance of inclusive language, whereas Le Guin's and Arnold's texts might additionally need a guided setting. Respondents' estimations provide a useful insight into the excerpts' effectiveness; however, they also give an indication of attitudes toward the issue of the linguistic representation of women and men. In effect, reader responses clearly indicate the boundaries of acceptable change. Despite the use of wordplay, the translations of *Egalias døtre* remained recognisable to readers as the reversal was linked to familiar nouns and pronouns. Consequently, Brantenberg's novel, while subverting the linguistic status quo, did not challenge readers' binary understanding. Similarly, *The Left Hand of Darkness* reproduced the familiar sex/gender constellation linguistically. And while the text's problematisation gave cause for concern in terms of wider effectiveness, it again did not compromise the binary conception of human beings – at least in the opening section that respondents encountered. Both excerpts reproduced the sex/gender hierarchy and therefore remained 'readable'.

The Cook and the Carpenter, on the other hand, profoundly disrupted the norms of the reader's sociocultural context. By referring to characters as 'na' and 'carpenter', Arnold's novel set out to render sex/gender linguistically irrelevant. Readers were consequently unable to instantly categorise according to the familiar 'she' or 'he'; that is, divide characters into 'male' or 'female'. While most participants tried to replace the epicene pronoun in order to 'make sense' of the narrative, the inability to distinguish sex/gender with certainty resulted in frustration and eventual disengagement. This response is of course problematic in terms of the text's ability to connect with general readers; however, it also exposes participants' dependence on linguistic sex/gender. Without the categories 'female' and 'male', respondents felt lost. In effect, participants felt they 'needed to know' a character's sex/gender in order to understand the excerpt. As this need was not met, they struggled to engage with the narrative. Arnold's novel thereby provides a telling commentary on the linguistic status quo – speakers seem unable to conceive human beings as simply people, that is, as unsexed/ungendered. Moreover, *The Cook and the Carpenter* revealed both the profound relevance of sex/gender and language's central role in conveying a binary conception of human beings. By highlighting the link between language and imagination, the excerpt proved a valuable resource for discussions: it directly illustrated opportunities for and boundaries of linguistic change.

Interestingly, as part of their response, participants reflected on existing neutral terminology in either language, such as the use of 'they' in English and, when prompted, 'Binnen-I' in German. Respondents commented that these forms would be less likely to cause frustration and confusion – first, because they are already familiar to speakers, and secondly, because they are understood neutrally. Whether the use of 'they' instead of 'na' would indeed override the 'need to know' needs to be assessed in future research. However, current studies certainly illustrate that attitudes toward neutral language are shaped by familiarity. That is, if a term is known to speakers they seem less likely to reject it. Oriane Sarrasin, Ute Gabriel and Pascal Gygax's 2012 research 'Sexism and Attitudes Toward Gender-Neutral Language: The Case of English, French, and German', for example, evaluates whether the official commitment to and promotion of neutral terms influenced speakers' attitudes. The authors asked participants to complete a series of questionnaires and hypothesised that English speakers who have been familiar with neutral terminology since the 1970s would be more supportive in their assessment. True enough, the data confirmed that 'attitudes toward gender-neutral language were more positive among British students … compared to Swiss students' (Sarrasin et al. 2012, 121). It is important to remember that neutral terminology was contested in the UK context when first introduced, and, in fact, continues to be to this day. Nevertheless, the responses of British students highlight that linguistic change is possible, leading Sarrasin et al. to conclude that 'if opposition to gender-neutral language exists, it is likely to decrease over time, as shown by the more positive attitudes held by the British students' (Sarrasin et al. 2012, 122). That is, if it becomes common practice, neutral language can eventually become a new norm.

Another example of the profound impact of familiarity on usage is the epicene Swedish pronoun 'hen'. Marie Gustafsson Sendén, Emma A. Bäck and Anna Lindqvist assessed the change in attitudes toward the neutral pronoun between 2012 and 2014 in their 2015 research 'Introducing a Gender-Neutral Pronoun in a Natural Gender Language: The Influence of Time on Attitudes and Behavior'. The authors found that 'the very negative attitudes … decreased over time' and 'the very positive attitudes increased' (Sendén et al. 2015, 6). Despite strong initial resistance to the neutral pronoun – heightened by factors such as political orientation and sex/gender – 'time was the most important predictor of the attitudes, even after controlling for various other factors' (Sendén et al. 2015, 8). Therefore, aversion to change, including to a novel epicene, can be overcome in a relatively short time period.

Still, 'hen' was first introduced in the 1960s and has been used more widely since 2010; in contrast, speakers are entirely unfamiliar with Arnold's pronoun. As such, the novel needs to be read in a guided environment in order to reach a deep level of engagement with its linguistic revision. Read on its own, as the focus group responses highlighted, it might be considered too disruptive to have a profound impact on speakers' attitudes. However, I would argue that this is essentially the case for all three literary texts – including the translations of *Egalias døtre*. The reasons might be different, but major hurdles also limit a wider impact of Brantenberg's novel. First, by belonging to the genre of '1970s feminist literature', general readers are unlikely to encounter the text. Moreover, *Egalias døtre* and its translations are neither widely available nor listed on contemporary bestseller lists. Additionally, readers who seek out the text are likely to already subscribe to Brantenberg's problematisation. As a result, it might only be able to 'preach to the converted'. Consequently, even if considered the most accessible and effective by focus group participants, the text is unlikely to be read widely enough to shape attitudes toward the linguistic representation of women and men. To reach general readers and encourage in-depth engagement, I believe, one of the most useful environments for the English and German translations of *Egalias døtre* is an educational setting. In fact, in this environment, all three texts are valuable tools to progress debates. My own experience of employing these excerpts in secondary education provides first evidence of their effectiveness. In 2015, I designed and taught a six-week course for Key Stage 5 students (ages 16–18) that aimed to give an introduction to the issue of sex/gender and language. The course combined different approaches, such as theoretical perspectives, empirical studies and examples of general language use, to set the linguistic frame. It then dedicated one session each to the discussion of the three literary excerpts – beginning with *The Left Hand of Darkness*, followed by *The Cook and the Carpenter* and concluding with the English translation of *Egalias døtre*. In the final two sessions, students developed their argument on how the excerpts relate to the theoretical positions. They also explored which of the texts they considered most effective in illustrating the issue of linguistic representation.

I taught this course at a UK state school and the literary excerpts, especially in comparison, encouraged plenty of debate. For example, some students initially felt that the use of inclusive language was no longer contested; however, when encountering *The Left Hand of Darkness* they recognised both the presented norms and their continued prevalence. Moreover, students' mixed responses to the neutral pronoun in *The Cook and the Carpenter* highlighted concerns around unsexed/ungendered terms of reference. At the same time, the novel allowed them to consider the possibilities, and limitations, of change. In addition, the translation of *Egalias døtre* illustrated the cultural and historical origins of linguistic bias. The outcomes of this teaching experience highlighted the value of literary texts for linguistics education, in particular. Rather than being confronted with rhetorical arguments and empirical findings in isolation, students were able to engage with language-in-use and, moreover, language as an experimental space. Through this engagement, students gained a deeper understanding of why linguistic representation matters and what is at stake: disparate linguistic representation leads to disparity in imagination.

This is a valuable experience for English and German speakers of any age – language is not the preserve of linguists or official bodies but a malleable tool to express human relations. In a guided group setting, readers are able to reflect on linguistic norms and the possibilities of change. However, this experience should not be restricted to education, and higher education, in particular. In fact, it needs to reach a much wider audience for profound changes to take place. As outlined above, the literary texts discussed throughout face substantial hurdles to connect with general readers; but this is not to say that these obstacles are insurmountable. There are multiple ways in which language users can be engaged beyond formal education. First of all, debates on sex/gender and language are already part of the public realm. As an exchange over the use of 'Studenten' and 'Studierende' in a *ZEIT Campus* piece indicates (Scholz and Kerstan 2016), both opponents to and proponents of inclusive language are given public platforms. However, as media coverage also highlights, the anti-change position remains audible, to say the least – see, for example, *the Daily Express* headline 'EU to kill off MEN: Brussels demands end to words like "mankind" and "manpower"' (Nellist 2018). To counteract adverse viewpoints and to provide an alternative perspective, feminist linguists and activists employ a variety of formats.

Luise F. Pusch, for example, has been publishing accessible essays and 'Glossen' since 1984 to reach general language users; since 1998, she has also published online. Equally, English- and German-language activists create zines, write blogs and contribute to online forums to present their pro-change arguments.

I believe these existing channels could help to bring literary texts to a wider audience. For example, blogs could publish excerpts from *The Left Hand of Darkness*, *The Cook and the Carpenter* and the translations of *Egalias døtre*, and also more recent texts such as Ann Leckie's 2013 award-winning novel *Ancillary Justice*. The excerpts could be framed with questions, such as 'Who did you imagine when reading the text?' and 'Why did you imagine a particular person?', to encourage readers to engage more deeply. Publications could additionally be linked to an online forum to allow readers to exchange ideas, or they could advertise reading groups to bring language users together to explore the excerpts' impact and implications. This could help to reproduce the guided reading environment of my focus group study and raise awareness more widely. I am encouraging readers to discuss the above texts via my research blog 'A Little Feminist Blog on Language' (Luck 2018). The aim of the blog is to publicise literary texts thematising sex/gender and language more widely and to get further feedback on whether and how they are useful tools to sensitise readers. Another option could be an official drive to encourage language users to engage with texts such as *The Left Hand of Darkness*, *The Cook and the Carpenter* and *Egalias døtre*, and its translations. A 2015 Swedish campaign, led by the Swedish Women's Lobby and publisher Albert Bonniers, distributed a copy of Chimamanda Ngozi Adichie's essay *We Should All Be Feminists* to every high-school student. The aim was for Adichie's text to 'work as a stepping stone for a discussion about gender equality and feminism' (Flood 2015, n. pag.). Similarly, via a public programme, Le Guin's, Arnold's and Brantenberg's texts could be made available to English- and German-speaking students to stimulate discussions. Associated reading groups could encourage in-depth reflection.

However, such initiatives still potentially exclude a wider audience. For example, feminist blogs are usually sought out by readers who already prescribe to the presented viewpoints. Equally, official campaigns, such as the one conducted in Sweden, are likely to predominantly reach speakers of a certain background and education – if they are restricted to high-school students. Consequently, the texts would be unable to fundamentally sensitise all readers and thereby effectively promote inclusive language use. The literary problematisation of sex/gender and language might therefore have to be presented more accessibly to begin with. To address this hurdle two avenues seem particularly fruitful: first, the English and German translation of *Egalias døtre*, in particular, could be adapted for film or TV in order to connect with adult speakers, and secondly, children's and young adult fiction could be employed to raise awareness from a young age. The satiric tone of Brantenberg's novel renders it a valuable resource for visual adaptation. As film and TV typically reach a much larger demographic than literary texts, it could play a profound role in sensitising speakers. A potential downside is of course the high cost associated with film production; however, an online series could circumvent this issue. Furthermore, when effective, online resources are widely shared – the short film *Majorité Opprimée* by Eléonore Pourriat is a good case in point. Like *Egalias døtre*, the film illustrates a reversal of the linguistic (and social) status quo. Moreover, the English version, *Oppressed Majority* (2014), attracted 12.5 million viewers in the first two years of its release. A short adaptation of *Egalias døtre* could potentially reach a similar number of viewers. The novel could be advertised alongside to encourage deeper engagement; in effect, the film could function as an introduction to the novel, which would be likely to be read by a much wider audience as a consequence. Again, associated forums and reading groups would allow speakers to engage more deeply with the issue of linguistic representation.

Children's and young adult fiction have even more potential for sensitising readers to the importance of inclusive language. By shaping understanding from an early age, this literature could provide the basis for broad linguistic change. Just as children are trained to learn the dominant norms – Wittgenstein terms it 'Abrichten' (Wittgenstein 1998, 4) – they can equally acquire a different point of view. On the one hand, a simplified version of *Egalias døtre* could familiarise children with the notion that both language and sex/gender roles are cultural constructs. On the other, existing storybooks such as Andrea Beaty's *Rosie Revere, Engineer* (2013), enable children to imagine a girl in a historically 'male' career, while Tanja Abou's *Raumschiff Cosinus: Der Bordcomputer hat die Schnauze voll* (2011) avoids sex/gender-specific nouns and pronouns to allow for a neutral conception of characters. Exploring and discussing these books with parents and in classrooms would allow children to develop a more inclusive understanding. As a result, children would grow up to become more flexible and tolerant thinkers, and therefore more receptive to inclusive language. But it is not only early exposure that can have a profound effect; young adults are also open to new understandings. Suzanne Collins's *The Hunger Games* trilogy (2008, 2009, 2010), for example, has captured the imagination of teenagers. By challenging what girls can and cannot do, *The Hunger Games* is presenting an effective counterpoint to the status quo. The trilogy also addresses the implicit norms of language; that is, the assumption that concepts such as 'leader' are linked to 'he' not 'she'. The mass appeal of texts such as Collins' novels holds a powerful potential for promoting inclusive language use.

A shift in usage and attitudes is crucial to move forward. Norms have changed throughout history, and while male-as-norm remains a remnant of a former understanding, society is progressing toward a more inclusive picture of humanity. Language can, and must, express this shift to reflect and reinforce this new conception. As empirical research shows, changing the linguistic status quo is paramount, as language and imagination are closely interlinked. That is, if only 'men' are mentioned, speakers imagine predominantly 'male'. Literary texts effectively illustrate this bias but also provide suggestions for alternatives. Making them more widely accessible, particularly in guided educational or reading group settings, can contribute to sensitising readers and thereby further promote inclusive language use. However, that is not to say that all kinds of revision are helpful at this stage. For example, I believe that as long as the premise male-as-norm remains prominent, neutral terminology will be interpreted accordingly. As my focus group study illustrates, neutral nouns and pronouns continue to be categorised according to sex/gender, and moreover in line with social and grammatical expectations. In the current sociocultural context, female visibility is therefore key to undermining androcentric interpretation. My understanding of inclusive language therefore means addressing both sexes/genders specifically. Linguistic strategies, such as mentioning 'she' and 'he' in conjunction with personal nouns and extending German terms with the suffix '-in', are consequently crucial to ensuring women's conceptual availability.

However, inclusive language presents challenges as well as opportunities. While split forms, such as 'Direktor/Direktorin' or 'carpenter, she or he', or female generics, such as 'Direktorin' or 'woman', can be argued to address both sexes/genders, they also raise concerns. First of all, split forms ensure that each sex/gender is specifically mentioned, while the generic use of female nouns and pronouns is shorter and therefore more economical. But at the same time, these very advantages present issues: split forms are lengthier, while female generics predominantly evoke one sex/gender. In writing, the length of terms might be negotiable; however, in speech, shorter terminology is often preferred. And while this might speak for female generics, the issue of bias remains – 'Direktorin' might be linguistically inclusive of 'Direktor';

however, it undeniably evokes 'woman' more than 'man'. Nevertheless, the use of female generic terms has a valuable shock factor; as the English and German translations of *Egalias døtre* effectively illustrate, reversing male-as-norm has a powerful impact. When confronted with gynocentric language, speakers are prompted to realise both the extent and implications of linguistic norms – female generics can therefore be a useful strategy to raise awareness. On the other hand, using split forms is most egalitarian; both sexes/genders are named and therefore visible. However, not only naming is paramount; the positioning of each sex/gender is equally important. That is, alternating between 'Direktorin/Direktor' and 'Direktor/Direktorin' or 'carpenter, she or he' and 'carpenter, he or she', is equally crucial to undermining the notion of 'default male'.

While alternating split/pair forms is my preferred choice, two key concerns remain for the German language. In particular: the implications of the suffix '-in' and potential slippage into male generics. First of all, the suffix signifies female deviation – as terms are created by extending male nouns with '-in', it enshrines male-as-norm. This problematises the use of existing female terms altogether. On the other hand, however, speakers are familiar with suffix-creations, and as studies show, familiarity is the first step toward linguistic change. In a sociocultural context where wider change is slow at best, a compromise might be needed to move forward. As female nouns and pronouns are becoming more commonly placed next to male terms, a more thorough revision might eventually take place. However, split forms are still far from common practice and speech economy remains a key hurdle to change. I myself am much more successful at writing than at speaking inclusively in German – I frequently slip back into male generic terms in speech both out of training and convenience. I am aware of the impact and attempt to correct slippages whenever possible; however, I lack consistency. Nevertheless, I believe it is this awareness, in addition to familiarity, that is paramount for any fundamental revision to take place. Employing alternated split forms, even if not consistently, is the first step to wider change. Once speakers, myself included, get into the habit of employing inclusive terms, they are more likely to persevere.

This is not to say, however, that my ambitions for linguistic change are guided only by pragmatic considerations. In fact, my ambition for the long term is a truly inclusive language – one that no longer categorises between 'women' and 'men'. Terms would be economical and representative at the same time because sex/gender would no longer be relevant to understanding. In this future language, human beings would simply be referred to as people; that is, neutrally. Both *The Cook and the Carpenter* and *Woman on the Edge of Time* provide useful illustrations of this potential. However, this new conception of humanity need not be a preserve of a future world only – as Wittgenstein proposes, imagining new linguistic practices enables imagining a new way of life. However, these new practices need to become commonly accepted to result in any profound revision. Current sociocultural norms remain informed by the sex/gender binary, and therefore any different conception of human beings inevitably remains contested. This is illustrated in Piercy's and Arnold's narratives, highlighted by the general rejection of neutral terms by focus group participants, and confirmed by persisting verbal and physical attacks on people who do not conform to the sex/gender binary. Nevertheless, it is the suggestion of a new language that allows for the very imagination of a new form of life to begin with. Consequently neutral, or non-binary, terms are crucial for pushing the boundaries of what can be said and what can be imagined. I believe inclusive and neutral language should therefore function in tandem – women need to be named to be linguistically and conceptually visible, but at the same time, neutral terminology will allow speakers to eventually move away from the restrictions of binaries. Alternating between 'carpenter, she or he' and 'carpenter, they',[1] I believe, will help to open speakers' minds to both inclusive linguistic representation and linguistic neutrality. The same applies for the German language – employing forms, such as 'Tischlerin und Tischler', as well as the 'Genderstern' [gender star], as in 'Tischler*in', can help to open up our conception of the sexes/genders and challenge a binary understanding.

Literary texts can contribute to sensitising readers in a profound way. As I have shown throughout this book, the texts provide a fruitful experimental space in which to explore the issue of linguistic representation. *The Left Hand of Darkness* and *Häutungen* illustrate the extent and impact of male generic terms; *The Cook and the Carpenter* and *Woman on the Edge of Time* frame discussions around language's role in creating and reinforcing binaries; and *Egalias døtre*, and its translations, highlight the link between linguistic practices and world view. In combination, the three approaches make the case for why inclusive language matters and thereby effectively promote change. This is particularly valuable in the context of education – literary texts help to bring theoretical arguments and empirical evidence to life. Moreover, fiction provides an immersive counterpoint to the position that grammar and sex are separate entities and that the issue of sex/gender and language is irrelevant. By engaging readers, literary texts can sensitise them to why linguistic change is necessary. Additionally, readers' desire to immerse themselves encourages them to reflect on perspectives they might otherwise reject – literary texts therefore enable a more open discussion of the linguistic representation of women and men. Furthermore, through the experiments presented by authors, readers are prompted to consider the possibilities and limitations of linguistic change. As the authors discussed in this book highlight, language is neither a fixed nor abstract entity. '[E]ine Sprache vorstellen heißt, sich eine Lebensform vorstellen' (Wittgenstein 1998, 8), that is, a change in language allows speakers to arrive at a different understanding of reality. Literary texts enable readers to see linguistic norms in a new light and imagine alternatives. However, to be effective literary texts need to reach a larger audience. To do so, guided reading in both educational and activist settings is most fruitful. In these contexts, especially if widely implemented, literary texts can engage readers with the issue of sex/gender and language, and sensitise them to why linguistic change matters.

Future research

The research presented in this book could be built upon in four ways. First, researchers could test whether the three clusters of literary approaches I identified are able to encompass more recent writing or need to be extended. Secondly, they could investigate the ability of other forms of writing to sensitise readers to the importance of inclusive language use. Thirdly, they could expand my focus group study to test the emerging core category, 'needing to know' sex/gender, as well as measure the short- and long-term impact of the texts. And fourthly, researchers could assess the impact of reading and discussing the whole texts in a reading group setting.

Literary approaches to the linguistic representation of women and men are not confined to the 1960s and 1970s. In fact, writers continue to engage with the issue of sex/gender and language to this day. One focus guiding future research, for example, could be how more recent texts confirm and expand the clusters I identified throughout this book. Three useful literary texts are Barbara Köhler's 1999 *Wittgensteins Nichte*, Leslie Feinberg's 1993 *Stone Butch Blues* and Ann Leckie's 2013 *Ancillary Justice*. Köhler's texts problematise the German linguistic status quo akin to *Häutungen*, Feinberg's novel challenges linguistic binaries in a similar vein to Arnold's, and Leckie's text employs female generics comparable to those in *Egalias døtre* – at first instance these texts could therefore be argued to fit into the clusters I identified. However, two issues emerge from the outset. First, the above differ profoundly from the ones evaluated in this book. Köhler's work consists of essays, rather than perspectival narrations. *Stone Butch Blues* and *Ancillary Justice* do not engage as thoroughly with disparate linguistic representation as Arnold's and Brantenberg's texts. Additionally, of the three, only *Wittgensteins Nichte* broadly corresponds with the approaches employed in the cluster 'problematising the linguistic status quo'. *Stone Butch Blues* is concerned with exploring linguistic liminality rather than neutrality. Jess Goldberg, the novel's protagonist, employs the noun 'he-she' (Feinberg 1993, 7) and explains, 'I didn't feel like a woman or a man' (Feinberg 1993, 143). Consequently, the text pushes the boundaries of 'proposing linguistic neutrality', potentially leading to the creation of a new category altogether. Equally, *Ancillary Justice* is not an outright reversal like Brantenberg's; Leckie's novel additionally problematises the sex/gender binary. 'She was probably male' (Leckie 2013, 3), the protagonist Breq remarks in reference to another character. Again, this extends, if not surpasses the cluster 'reversing the linguistic status quo'. New clusters emerging from such a study could consequently be employed to revise or extend my framework for categorising literary texts thematising the issue of sex/gender and language.

The second focus for future research could be to investigate the ability of other types of writing – online pieces in particular – to sensitise readers. Today, many speakers engage with social media to inform themselves about issues and gain new perspectives. Equally, activists and linguists participate in discussions to share their views and shape debates. For example, Luise F. Pusch and Deborah Cameron write blogs to connect with language users. Blog posts are both accessible and often widely read; Cameron's blog, 'language: a feminist guide', has over 7,000 followers to date. And while statistics are not as readily available for Pusch's blog, 'Laut & Luise', she has been blogging since 1998 and is well known because of her public stature. Activists also use social media to communicate their views and ideas. They publish via blogs, such as 'Gender Neutral Pronoun Blog' and 'Frauensprache', and Twitter accounts. Potential resources are therefore plentiful and diverse, and researchers could investigate whether online pieces are as, or even more, effective than literary texts in illustrating the issue of linguistic representation. From my own experience of writing a blog, online outlets, whether fictional or non-fictional, allow a more explorative space than other publications. First, authors are able to self-publish and therefore circumvent gatekeepers; allowing writers to present works-in-progress. Secondly, blog posts can be any length; authors are able to publish short experiments as well as longer pieces. And thirdly, blogs are interactive; therefore enabling readers to directly comment on their understanding of a text. Studies could investigate whether or not the above contentions are borne out by evidence.

A third potential focus could be to test the emerging core category of my focus group study, 'needing to know' sex/gender. Researchers could reproduce or adjust my materials and procedures to undertake further theoretical sampling. Taking my four subcategories as the frame, 1. 'perceiving sex/gender clearly', 2. 'perceiving sex/gender as helpful', 3. 'having doubts about sex/gender' and 4. 'potentially perceiving no sex/gender', it would be fruitful to evaluate whether these hold up to scrutiny or need revision. Future studies could explore, in particular, why readers experience the 'need to know' and what the consequences are of not knowing. Additionally, researchers could assess the different strategies readers employ to satisfy the 'need to know' and whether or not, and why, readers are willing to accept inclusive/neutral alternatives. Another useful empirical avenue could be to assess the short- and long-term impact of the literary texts on readers' attitudes and usage. Questions guiding such research could be, 'Are speakers more likely to use inclusive language after encountering a literary text?'; 'Do literary texts continue to shape speakers' attitudes two weeks later?'; 'If so, why?'; 'If not, why not?'. 'The Inventory of Attitudes Toward Sexist/Nonsexist Language – General (IASNL-G)' could be employed to collect responses before and after the study, and evaluate any shift. This could provide a valuable quantitative extension to my research and illustrate the value of literary texts statistically.

Finally, it would be valuable to assess the impact of reading one, or several, of the texts in a reading group setting. This would provide the opportunity to engage further with each literary approach and reflect on its implications. Questions might be 'How do reader responses compare to the above focus group setting?' and 'Do readers respond differently to *The Cook and the Carpenter* when they encounter the novel as a whole?'. Expanding on the educational potential of literary texts proposed in this book, scholars could also assess whether and how the novels can help to support pedagogic aims. It would be particularly interesting to conduct research with diverse groups of readers as well as with speakers who hold supportive, neutral and negative attitudes towards inclusive language. As suggested, a guided context will be required to make discussions most fruitful, especially as certain readers might be disinclined to engage with the texts from the outset. Careful framing of the study will therefore be necessary. However, the results could provide valuable further evidence for whether and how literary texts can sensitise readers and promote inclusive language use.

This book presents solid foundations for future interdisciplinary research. I have illustrated the merits of fiction for linguistics education and the usefulness of social research methods in literary research. I have shown from a linguistic and philosophical perspective that literary texts effectively engage with the linguistic representation of women and men. My focus group study provides clear empirical evidence; reader responses illustrated that fiction encourages speakers to reflect on dominant linguistic practices and, moreover, to consider alternatives. However, responses also highlighted that any reflection is directly linked to the linguistic status quo. Neutral terms of reference were deemed unimaginable because linguistic and conceptual norms depend on the binary female/male. Additionally, the presented terms were unfamiliar to readers. Linguistic change is therefore bound by what speakers consider 'possible' and what has been considered 'possible' so far. However, as I have also shown, what is possible is always subject to change. By problematising and pushing the boundaries of linguistic representation, literary texts bring this to the fore and highlight that language is flexible and malleable. Furthermore, by engaging readers, perspectival literary texts prompt speakers to reflect on the possibilities, and limitations, of linguistic change. Literary texts are a powerful tool to stimulate reflection on dominant linguistic practices, and do so particularly effectively in educational settings. In guided discussions, as the results of my focus group study illustrate, they help to raise awareness of linguistic norms and prompt exploration of alternatives.

Via an interdisciplinary approach, encompassing literary, linguistic and social research methods, I have shown the sensitising potential of literary texts. In educational and activist settings, I believe literary texts can have a profound impact on shaping attitudes and usage, precisely because they 'enable us to see that familiar reality with new eyes' (Iser 1978, 181). On the basis of my findings, I recommend the integration of literary texts into linguistics education and activism – in particular in guided reading and discussion group environments. In educational settings readers are able to engage in depth with the issue of sex/gender and language. This engagement can help to sensitise readers and thereby prompt a wider revision of biased linguistic practices. In effect, as I show throughout this book, literary texts can promote inclusive language use.

Note

1. As discussed earlier, devising a neutral alternative for the German language is decidedly more challenging. The SYLVAIN-Konventionen point to a potential solution, albeit a more comprehensive one owing to the grammatical structure of German.

Works cited

Abou, Tanja. 2011. *Raumschiff Cosinus: Der Bordcomputer hat die Schnauze voll*. Berlin: NoNo Verlag.
Albrecht, Terrance L., Gerianne M. Johnson and Joseph B. Walther. 1993. 'Understanding Communication Processes in Focus Groups'. In *Successful Focus Groups: Advancing the State of the Art*, edited by David L. Morgan, 51–64. Newbury Park, CA: SAGE Publications.
Allen, Julia M. and Lester Faigley. 1995. 'Discursive Strategies for Social Change: An Alternative Rhetoric of Argument', *Rhetoric Review* 14 (1): 142–72.
Annas, Pamela J. 1978. 'New Worlds, New Words: Androgyny in Feminist Science Fiction', *Science Fiction Studies* 5 (2): 143–56.
Appel, Markus and Tobias Richter. 2007. 'Persuasive Effects of Fictional Narratives Increase Over Time', *Media Psychology* 10 (1): 113–34.
Armstrong, Paul B. 2013. *How Literature Plays with the Brain: The Neuroscience of Reading and Art*. Baltimore, MD: Johns Hopkins University Press.
Arnold, June. 1973. *The Cook and the Carpenter: A Novel by the Carpenter*. Plainfield, VT: Daughters.
Bailey, Nathan. [1721] 1776. *An Universal Etymological English Dictionary*. London: R. Ware et al.
Baker, Lynne Rudder. 1984. 'III. On the Very Idea of a Form of Life', *Inquiry: An Interdisciplinary Journal of Philosophy* 27 (1–4): 277–89.
Baron, Dennis. n.d. 'The Epicene Pronouns: A Chronology of the Word that Failed'. Accessed June 2014. https://web.archive.org/web/20140509212627/http://www.english.illinois.edu/-people-/faculty/debaron/essays/epicene.htm.
Baron, Dennis E. 1981. 'The Epicene Pronoun: The Word That Failed', *American Speech* 56 (2): 83–97.
Baron, Dennis. 1986. *Grammar and Gender*. New Haven, CT: Yale University Press.
Barr, Marleen S. 1989. '"Laughing in a Liberating Defiance": *Egalia's Daughters* and Feminist Tendentious Humor'. In *Discontented Discourses: Feminism/Textual Intervention/Psychoanalysis*, edited by Marleen S. Barr and Richard Feldstein, 87–99. Urbana, IL: University of Illinois Press.
Beaty, Andrea. 2013. *Rosie Revere, Engineer*, illustrated by David Roberts. New York: Abrams Books for Young Readers.
Bem, Sandra L. and Daryl J. Bem. 1973. 'Does Sex-Biased Job Advertising "Aid and Abet" Sex Discrimination?', *Journal of Applied Social Psychology* 3 (1): 6–18.
Bernardo, Susan M. and Graham J. Murphy. 2006. *Ursula K. Le Guin: A Critical Companion*. Westport, CT: Greenwood Press.
Billig, Michael. 2005. *Laughter and Ridicule: Towards a Social Critique of Humour*. London: SAGE Publications.
Black, Maria and Rosalind Coward. 1999. 'Linguistic, Social and Sexual Relations: A Review of Dale Spender's *Man Made Language*'. In *The Feminist Critique of Language: A Reader*, edited by Deborah Cameron, 100–18. 2nd ed. London: Routledge.
Blake, Christopher and Christoph Klimmt. 2010. 'Geschlechtergerechte Formulierungen in Nachrichtentexten', *Publizistik* 55 (3): 289–304.
Bloor, Michael, Jane Frankland, Michelle Thomas and Kate Robson. 2001. *Focus Groups in Social Research*. London: SAGE Publications.
Bodine, Ann. 1975. 'Androcentrism in Prescriptive Grammar: Singular "They", Sex-Indefinite "He", and "He or She"', *Language in Society* 4 (2): 129–46.
Born, Marise P. and Toon W. Taris. 2010. 'The Impact of the Wording of Employment Advertisements on Students' Inclination to Apply for a Job', *Journal of Social Psychology* 150 (5): 485–502.

Brantenberg, Gerd. 1977. *Egalias døtre: En roman*. Oslo: Pax Forlag.
Brantenberg, Gerd. 1985. *The Daughters of Egalia*, translated by Louis Mackay. London: Journeyman Press.
Brantenberg, Gerd. 1987. *Die Töchter Egalias: Ein Roman über den Kampf der Geschlechter*, translated by Elke Radicke and Wilfried Sczepan. Munich: Verlag Frauenoffensive.
Braun, Friederike, Anja Gottburgsen, Sabine Sczesny and Dagmar Stahlberg. 1998. 'Können Geophysiker Frauen sein? Generische Personenbezeichnungen im Deutschen', *Zeitschrift für germanistische Linguistik* 26 (3): 265–83.
Braun, Peter. 1997. *Personenbezeichnungen: Der Mensch in der deutschen Sprache*. Tübingen: Max Niemeyer Verlag.
Brose, Karl. 1985. *Sprachspiel und Kindersprache: Studien zu Wittgensteins "Philosophischen Untersuchungen"*. Frankfurt am Main: Campus Verlag.
Bundeskanzleramt Österreich. 2012. 'Bundeshymne'. Accessed 30 August 2019. https://www.bundeskanzleramt.at/bundeshymne.
Butler, Judith. [1990] 2007. *Gender Trouble: Feminism and the Subversion of Identity*. New York: Routledge.
Cameron, Deborah. n.d. 'language: a feminist guide'. Accessed 30 August 2019. https://debuk.wordpress.com.
Carey, Martha Ann. 1994. 'The Group Effect in Focus Groups: Planning, Implementing, and Interpreting Focus Group Research'. In *Critical Issues in Qualitative Research Methods*, edited by Janice M. Morse, 225–41. Thousand Oaks, CA: SAGE Publications.
Carroll, John B., ed. 1956. *Language, Thought, and Reality: Selected Writings of Benjamin Lee Whorf*. Cambridge, MA: MIT Press.
Casper, Monica J. 2014. 'Marge Piercy: On Feminism, Politics, and Writing', TRIVIA: *Voices of Feminism* 16 (Spring). Accessed 30 August 2019. http://www.triviavoices.com/marge-piercy-on-feminism-politics-and-writing.html.
Charmaz, Kathy. 1990. '"Discovering" Chronic Illness: Using Grounded Theory', *Social Science and Medicine* 30 (11): 1161–72.
Charmaz, Kathy. 2014. *Constructing Grounded Theory*. 2nd ed. London: SAGE Publications.
Cieszkowski (Bydgoszcz), Marek. 2015. 'Zum geschlechtergerechten Sprachgebrauch am Beispiel deutscher und polnischer Stellenausschreibungen', *Linguistik Online* 70 (1): 23–42.
Classen, Brigitte and Gabriele Goettle. 1976. '"Häutungen" – eine Verwechslung von Anemone und Amazone', *Courage* 1: 45–6.
Clausen, Jeanette. 1982. 'Our Language, Our Selves: Verena Stefan's Critique of Patriarchal Language'. In *Beyond the Eternal Feminine: Critical Essays on Women and German Literature*, edited by Susan L. Cocalis and Kay Goodman, 381–400. Stuttgart: Akademischer Verlag Hans-Dieter Heinz.
Collins, Suzanne. 2008. *The Hunger Games*. New York: Scholastic.
Collins, Suzanne. 2009. *Catching Fire*. New York: Scholastic.
Collins, Suzanne. 2010. *Mockingjay*. New York: Scholastic.
Cummins, Elizabeth. 1990. *Understanding Ursula K. Le Guin*. Columbia, SC: University of South Carolina Press.
Cutcliffe, John R. 2005. 'Adapt or Adopt: Developing and Transgressing the Methodological Boundaries of Grounded Theory', *Journal of Advanced Nursing* 51 (4): 421–28.
Dal Cin, Sonya, Mark P. Zanna and Geoffrey T. Fong. 2004. 'Narrative Persuasion and Overcoming Resistance'. In *Resistance and Persuasion*, edited by Eric S. Knowles and Jay A. Linn, 175–91. Mahwah, NJ: Lawrence Erlbaum Associates.
Davidson, Joyce and Mick Smith. 1999. 'Wittgenstein and Irigaray: Gender and Philosophy in a Language (Game) of Difference', *Hypatia* 14 (2): 72–96.
De Sylvain, Cabala and Carsten Balzer. 2008. 'Die SYLVAIN-Konventionen: Versuch einer "geschlechtergerechten" Grammatik-Transformation der deutschen Sprache', *Liminalis* 2: 40–53.
Duden. 2016. Accessed 2016. http://www.duden.de.
Durkin, Philip. 2012. 'Old English – an Overview'. Oxford English Dictionary Blog, 16 August. Accessed 30 August 2019. http://public.oed.com/aspects-of-english/english-in-time/old-english-an-overview.
Eckert, Penelope and Sally McConnell-Ginet. 2003. *Language and Gender*. Cambridge: Cambridge University Press.

Evans, Vyvyan. 2010. *How Words Mean: Lexical Concepts, Cognitive Models, and Meaning Construction*. Oxford: Oxford University Press.

Everett, Caleb. 2011. 'Gender, Pronouns and Thought: The Ligature between Epicene Pronouns and a More Neutral Gender Perception', *Gender and Language* 5 (1): 133–52.

Fayad, Mona. 1997. 'Aliens, Androgynes, and Anthropology: Le Guin's Critique of Representation in *The Left Hand of Darkness*', *Mosaic* 30 (3): 59–73.

Feinberg, Leslie. 1993. *Stone Butch Blues: A Novel*. Ithaca, NY: Firebrand Books.

Flood, Alison. 2015. 'Every 16-Year-Old in Sweden to Receive Copy of We Should All Be Feminists', *The Guardian*, 4 December. Accessed 20 July 2016. https://www.theguardian.com/books/2015/dec/04/every-16-year-old-in-sweden-to-receive-copy-of-we-should-all-be-feminists.

Frank-Cyrus, Karin M. and Margot Dietrich. 1997. 'Sprachliche Gleichbehandlung von Frauen und Männern in Gesetzestexten: Eine Meinungsumfrage der Gesellschaft für deutsche Sprache', *Der Sprachdienst* 41 (2): 55–68.

Frauensprache. 2011. Accessed 26 September 2019. http://frauensprache.com.

Freedman, Carl, ed. 2008. *Conversations with Ursula K. Le Guin*. Jackson, MS: University Press of Mississippi.

Freud, Sigmund. [1960] 1975. *Jokes and Their Relation to the Unconscious*. In *The Standard Edition of the Complete Psychological Works of Sigmund Freud, Volume 8*, translated by James Strachey, Anna Freud, Alix Strachey and Alan Tyson. London: Hogarth Press.

Freud, Sigmund. [1905] 1948. *Der Witz und seine Beziehung zum Unbewussten*. In *Gesammelte Werke: Chronologisch geordnet. Sechster Band*. London: Imago Publishing Co.

Gabriel, Ute and Franziska Mellenberger. 2004. 'Exchanging the Generic Masculine for Gender-Balanced Forms: The Impact of Context Valence', *Swiss Journal of Psychology* 63 (4): 273–78.

Gagnier, Regenia. 1988. 'Between Women: A Cross-Class Analysis of Status and Anarchic Humor', *Women's Studies: An Inter-Disciplinary Journal* 15 (1–3): 135–48.

Galinsky, Adam D. and Gordon B. Moskowitz. 2000. 'Perspective-Taking: Decreasing Stereotype Expression, Stereotype Accessibility, and In-Group Favoritism', *Journal of Personality and Social Psychology* 78 (4): 708–24.

Garnham, Alan, Ute Gabriel, Oriane Sarrasin, Pascal Gygax and Jane Oakhill. 2012. 'Gender Representation in Different Languages and Grammatical Marking on Pronouns: When Beauticians, Musicians, and Mechanics Remain Men', *Discourse Processes* 49 (6): 481–500.

Gastil, John. 1990. 'Generic Pronouns and Sexist Language: The Oxymoronic Character of Masculine Generics', *Sex Roles* 23 (11/12): 629–43.

Gender Neutral Pronoun Blog. 2010. Accessed 30 August 2019. https://genderneutralpronoun.wordpress.com.

Gerrig, Richard J. 1993. *Experiencing Narrative Worlds: On the Psychological Activities of Reading*. New Haven, CT: Yale University Press.

GfdS (Gesellschaft für deutsche Sprache). 2019. 'Die GfdS zum Thema … geschlechtergerechte Sprache'. Accessed 31 August 2019. https://gfds.de/standpunkt-der-gesellschaft-fuer-deutsche-sprache-gfds-zu-einer-geschlechtergerechten-sprache/.

Glaser, Barney G. and Anselm L. Strauss. [1967] 1968. *The Discovery of Grounded Theory: Strategies for Qualitative Research*. London: Weidenfeld and Nicolson.

Goss, Jon D. and Thomas R. Leinbach. 1996. 'Focus Groups as Alternative Research Practice: Experience with Transmigrants in Indonesia', *Area* 28 (2): 115–23.

Green, Melanie C. 2004. 'Transportation into Narrative Worlds: The Role of Prior Knowledge and Perceived Realism', *Discourse Processes* 38 (2): 247–66.

Green, Melanie C. and Timothy C. Brock. 2000. 'The Role of Transportation in the Persuasiveness of Public Narratives', *Journal of Personality and Social Psychology* 79 (5): 701–21.

Grimm, Jacob and Wilhelm Grimm. 1878. *Deutsches Wörterbuch*. Leipzig: Hirzel.

Guentherodt, Ingrid, Marlis Hellinger, Luise F. Pusch and Senta Trömel-Plötz. 1980. 'Richtlinien zur Vermeidung sexistischen Sprachgebrauchs', *Linguistische Berichte* 69: 15–21.

Haig, David. 2004. 'The Inexorable Rise of Gender and the Decline of Sex: Social Change in Academic Titles, 1945–2001', *Archives of Sexual Behavior* 33 (2): 87–96.

Hamilton, Mykol C. 1988. 'Using Masculine Generics: Does Generic He Increase Male Bias in the User's Imagery?', *Sex Roles* 19 (11/12): 785–99.

Hoad, T.F., ed. 1986. *The Concise Oxford Dictionary of English Etymology*. Oxford: Oxford University Press.

Hoeken, Hans and Karin M. Fikkers. 2014. 'Issue-Relevant Thinking and Identification as Mechanisms of Narrative Persuasion', *Poetics* 44: 84–99.
Hoffmann, Wilhelm, ed. 1871. *Vollständiges Wörterbuch der deutschen Sprache*. Leipzig: Louis Zander.
Hokenson, Jan. 1988. 'The Pronouns of Gomorrha: A Lesbian Prose Tradition', *Frontiers: A Journal of Women Studies* 10 (1): 62–69.
Holder, R.W. 2008. *A Dictionary of Euphemisms*. 4th ed. Oxford: Oxford University Press.
Hord, Levi C.R. 2016. 'Bucking the Linguistic Binary: Gender Neutral Language in English, Swedish, French, and German', *Western Papers in Linguistics* 3 (1), Article 4: 1–29. Accessed 31 August 2019. https://ojs.lib.uwo.ca/index.php/wpl_clw/article/view/966/456.
Horvath, Lisa Kristina and Sabine Sczesny. 2016. 'Reducing Women's Lack of Fit with Leadership Positions? Effects of the Wording of Job Advertisements', *European Journal of Work and Organizational Psychology*, 25 (2): 316–28.
House of Lords Hansard. 2013. 'Legislation: Gender-Neutral Language'. Accessed 2 September 2019. https://hansard.parliament.uk/Lords/2013-12-12/debates/13121276000394/LegislationGender-NeutralLanguage.
Hunt, Earl and Franca Agnoli. 1991. 'The Whorfian Hypothesis: A Cognitive Psychology Perspective', *Psychological Review* 98 (3): 377–89.
Hyde, Janet Shibley. 1984. 'Children's Understanding of Sexist Language', *Developmental Psychology* 20 (4): 697–706.
Irmen, Lisa and Astrid Köhncke. 1996. 'Zur Psychologie des "generischen" Maskulinums', *Sprache und Kognition* 15 (3): 152–66.
Irmen, Lisa and Nadja Roßberg. 2004. 'Gender Markedness of Language: The Impact of Grammatical and Nonlinguistic Information on the Mental Representation of Person Information', *Journal of Language and Social Psychology* 23 (3): 272–307.
Iser, Wolfgang. 1978. *The Act of Reading: A Theory of Aesthetic Response*. London: Routledge and Kegan Paul.
Ishiguro, Hidé. 1990. *Leibniz's Philosophy of Logic and Language*. 2nd ed. Cambridge: Cambridge University Press.
Johnson, Samuel. [1755] 1983. *A Dictionary of the English Language*. London: Times Books.
Kalverkämper, Hartwig. 1979. 'Die Frauen und die Sprache', *Linguistische Berichte* 62: 55–71.
Khosroshahi, Fatemeh. 1989. 'Penguins Don't Care, but Women Do: A Social Identity Analysis of a Whorfian Problem', *Language in Society* 18 (4): 505–25.
Kienzler, Wolfgang. 2007. *Ludwig Wittgensteins "Philosophische Untersuchungen"*. Darmstadt: Wissenschaftliche Buchgesellschaft.
Kitzinger, Jenny and Rosaline S. Barbour. 1999. 'Introduction: The Challenge and Promise of Focus Groups'. In *Developing Focus Group Research: Politics, Theory and Practice*, edited by Rosaline S. Barbour and Jenny Kitzinger, 1–20. London: SAGE Publications.
Klein, Josef. 1988. 'Benachteiligung der Frau im generischen Maskulinum – eine feministische Schimäre oder psycholinguistische Realität?'. In *Das Selbstverständnis der Germanistik: Aktuelle Diskussionen*, edited by Norbert Oellers, 310–19. Tübingen: Max Niemeyer Verlag.
Kluge, Friedrich. [1883] 1989. *Etymologisches Wörterbuch der deutschen Sprache*. 22nd ed. Berlin: Walter de Gruyter.
Koeser, Sara, Elisabeth A. Kuhn and Sabine Sczesny. 2015. 'Just Reading? How Gender-Fair Language Triggers Readers' Use of Gender-Fair Forms', *Journal of Language and Social Psychology* 34 (3): 343–57.
Köhler, Barbara. 1999. *Wittgensteins Nichte: Vermischte Schriften: Mixed Media*. Frankfurt am Main: Suhrkamp.
Kohlheim, Rosa and Volker Kohlheim. 2013. *Duden – Lexikon der Vornamen*. 6th ed. Mannheim: Dudenverlag.
Kotthoff, Helga. 2006. 'Gender and Humor: The State of the Art', *Journal of Pragmatics* 38 (1): 4–25.
Krueger, Richard A. 1994. *Focus Groups: A Practical Guide for Applied Research*. 2nd ed. Thousand Oaks, CA: SAGE Publications.
Kuhn, Elisabeth A. and Ute Gabriel. 2014. 'Actual and Potential Gender-Fair Language Use: The Role of Language Competence and the Motivation to Use Accurate Language', *Journal of Language and Social Psychology* 33 (2): 214–25.
Kulp, Denise. 1986. 'Book Review – Egalia's Daughters, by Gerd Brantenberg', *Off Our Backs* 16 (4): 19.

Lakoff, Robin. 1973. 'Language and Woman's Place', *Language in Society* 2 (1): 45–79.
Landeshauptstadt Hannover. 2019. *Empfehlungen für eine geschlechtergerechte Verwaltungssprache*. Hannover: Referat für Frauen und Gleichstellung. Accessed 31 August 2019. https://www.hannover.de/content/download/756032/18968385/file/Flyer_Geschlechtergerechte_Sprache.pdf.
Leckie, Ann. [2013] 2014. *Ancillary Justice*. London: Orbit.
Lefanu, Sarah. 1988. *In the Chinks of the World Machine: Feminism and Science Fiction*. London: Women's Press.
Le Guin, Ursula K. 1976. 'Introduction'. In *The Left Hand of Darkness*. New York: Ace Books.
Le Guin, Ursula K. [1974] 1981. *Winterplanet*, translated by Gisela Stege. Munich: Heyne.
Le Guin, Ursula K. [1969] 1991. *The Left Hand of Darkness*. London: Futura.
Leibniz, Gottfried Wilhelm. [1686] 1982. *Generales inquisitiones de analysi notionum et veritatum = Allgemeine Untersuchungen über die Analyse der Begriffe und Wahrheiten*, edited and translated by Franz Schupp. Hamburg: Felix Meiner Verlag.
Litosseliti, Lia. 2007. *Using Focus Groups in Research*. London: Continuum.
Livia, Anna. 2001. *Pronoun Envy: Literary Uses of Linguistic Gender*. Oxford: Oxford University Press.
Lothane, Zvi. 2008. 'The Uses of Humor in Life, Neurosis and in Psychotherapy: Part 2', *International Forum of Psychoanalysis* 17 (4): 232–39.
Luck, Christiane. 2018. 'A Little Feminist Blog on Language. Accessed 30 August 2019. http://alittlefeministblogonlanguage.blogspot.com/2018/08/read-all-about-it.html.
Madriz, Esther. 192000. 'Focus Groups in Feminist Research'. In *Handbook of Qualitative Research*, edited by Norman K. Denzin and Yvonna S. Lincoln, 835–50. 2nd ed. Thousand Oaks, CA: SAGE Publications.
Malotki, Ekkehart. 1983. *Hopi Time: A Linguistic Analysis of the Temporal Concepts in the Hopi Language*. Berlin: Mouton.
Mandelbaum, David G., ed. 1949. *Selected Writings of Edward Sapir in Language, Culture and Personality*. Berkeley: University of California Press.
Mar, Raymond A. and Keith Oatley. 2008. 'The Function of Fiction is the Abstraction and Simulation of Social Experience', *Perspectives on Psychological Science* 3 (3): 173–92.
Maron, Monika, Wolf Schneider, Walter Krämer and Josef Kraus. 2019. 'Schluss mit Gender-Unfug!'. Accessed 30 August 2019. https://vds-ev.de/gegenwartsdeutsch/gendersprache/gendersprache-unterschriften/schluss-mit-dem-gender-unfug.
Martyna, Wendy. 1980. 'The Psychology of the Generic Masculine'. In *Women and Language in Literature and Society*, edited by Sally McConnell-Ginet, Ruth Borker and Nelly Furman, 69–78. New York: Praeger.
Mates, Benson. 1986. *The Philosophy of Leibniz: Metaphysics and Language*. New York: Oxford University Press.
McConnell, Allen R. and Russell H. Fazio. 1996. 'Women as Men and People: Effects of Gender-Marked Language', *Personality and Social Psychology Bulletin* 22 (10): 1004–13.
McConnell-Ginet, Sally. 1979. 'Prototypes, Pronouns and Persons'. In *Ethnolinguistics: Boas, Sapir and Whorf Revisited*, edited by Madeleine Mathiot, 63–83. The Hague: Mouton.
McGinn, Marie. 2013. *The Routledge Guidebook to Wittgenstein's Philosophical Investigations*. London: Routledge.
Merrill, Lisa. 1988. 'Feminist Humor: Rebellious and Self-affirming', *Women's Studies: An Inter-Disciplinary Journal* 15 (1–3): 271–80.
Mies, Maria. 1983. 'Towards a Methodology for Feminist Research'. In *Theories of Women's Studies*, edited by Gloria Bowles and Renate Duelli Klein, 117–39. London: Routledge and Kegan Paul.
Moberg, Verne. 1985. 'A Norwegian Women's Fantasy: Gerd Brantenberg's *Egalias Døtre* as *Kvinneskelig* Utopia', *Scandinavian Studies* 57 (3): 325–32.
Moser, Franziska and Bettina Hannover. 2014. 'How Gender Fair are German Schoolbooks in the Twenty-First Century? An Analysis of Language and Illustrations in Schoolbooks for Mathematics and German', *European Journal of Psychology of Education* 29 (3): 387–407.
Moulton, Janice, George M. Robinson and Cherin Elias. 1978. 'Sex Bias in Language Use: 'Neutral' Pronouns That Aren't', *American Psychologist* 33 (11): 1032–36.
Nellist, Tom. 2018. 'EU to kill off MEN: Brussels demands end to words like "mankind" and "manpower"'. *Daily Express* (28 December 2018). Accessed 27 September 2019. https://www.express.co.uk/news/politics/1064252/political-correctness-european-union-european-parliament-gender-neutral-words.
Ng, Sik Hung. 1990. 'Androcentric Coding of *Man* and *His* in Memory by Language Users', *Journal of Experimental Social Psychology* 26 (5): 455–64.

O'Briant, Walter H. 1968. *Gottfried Wilhelm Leibniz's General Investigations concerning the Analysis of Concepts and Truths: A Translation and an Evaluation*. Athens, GA: University of Georgia Press.
Olesen, Virginia L. 2010. 'Feminist Qualitative Research and Grounded Theory: Complexities, Criticisms, and Opportunities'. In *The SAGE Handbook of Grounded Theory*, edited by Antony Bryant and Kathy Charmaz, 417–35. Los Angeles: SAGE Publications.
Oltermann, Philip. 2014. 'Germans Try to Get Their Tongues around Gender-Neutral Language', *The Guardian*, 24 March. Accessed 30 August 2019. https://www.theguardian.com/world/2014/mar/24/germans-get-tongues-around-gender-neutral-language.
Oxford Dictionaries. 2016. Accessed 2016. https://www.oxforddictionaries.com.
Parks, Janet B. and Mary Ann Roberton. 2000. 'Development and Validation of an Instrument to Measure Attitudes toward Sexist/Nonsexist Language', *Sex Roles* 42 (5/6): 415–38.
Parks, Janet B. and Mary Ann Roberton. 2001. 'Erratum: Inventory of Attitudes toward Sexist/Nonsexist Language – General (IASNL-G): A Correction in Scoring Procedures', *Sex Roles* 44 (3/4): 253.
Partington, Alan. 2006. *The Linguistics of Laughter: A Corpus-Assisted Study of Laughter-Talk*. London: Routledge.
Penelope (Stanley), Julia and Cynthia McGowan. 1979. 'Woman and Wife: Social and Semantic Shifts in English', *Papers in Linguistics* 12 (3/4): 491–502.
Penn, Julia M. 1972. *Linguistic Relativity versus Innate Ideas: The Origins of the Sapir-Whorf Hypothesis in German Thought*. The Hague: Mouton.
Pennington, John. 2000. 'Exorcising Gender: Resisting Readers in Ursula K. Le Guin's *Left Hand of Darkness*', *Extrapolation* 41 (4): 351–58.
Piercy, Marge. [1976] 1989. *Woman on the Edge of Time*. London: Women's Press.
Piercy, Marge. [1996] 2000. *Frau am Abgrund der Zeit*, translated by Karsta Frank. Hamburg: Argument-Verlag.
Plowman, Andrew. 1998. *The Radical Subject: Social Change and the Self in Recent German Autobiography*. Bern: Peter Lang.
Polichak, James W. and Richard J. Gerrig. [2002] 2013. '"Get Up and Win!": Participatory Responses to Narrative'. In *Narrative Impact: Social and Cognitive Foundations*, edited by Melanie C. Green, Jeffrey J. Strange and Timothy C. Brock, 71–95. New York: Psychology Press.
Pourriat, Eléonore. 2014. 'Oppressed Majority (Majorité Opprimée English)'. Video. Accessed 2 September 2019. https://www.youtube.com/watch?time_continue=3&v=V4UWxlVvT1A.
Pugh, Meryl. 1999. '"You Canna Change the Laws of Fiction, Jim!": A Personal Account of Reading Science Fiction', *Changing English: Studies in Culture and Education* 6 (1): 19–30.
Pusch, Luise F. 1979. 'Der Mensch ist ein Gewohnheitstier, doch weiter kommt man ohne ihr: Eine Antwort auf Kalverkämpers Kritik an Trömel-Plötz' Artikel über "Linguistik und Frauensprache"', *Linguistische Berichte* 63: 84–102.
Pusch, Luise F. 1980. 'Das Deutsche als Männersprache – Diagnose und Therapievorschläge', *Linguistische Berichte* 69: 59–74.
Pusch, Luise F. 1984. *Das Deutsche als Männersprache: Aufsätze und Glossen zur feministischen Linguistik*. Frankfurt am Main: Suhrkamp.
Pusch, Luise F. 2017. 'Laut & Luise'. Accessed 30 August 2019. http://www.fembio.org/biographie.php/frau/blog.
Ragland, Mary Eloise. 1976. 'The Language of Laughter', *SubStance* 5 (13): 91–106.
Reali, Chiara, Yulia Esaulova, Anton Öttl and Lisa von Stockhausen. 2015. 'Role Descriptions Induce Gender Mismatch Effects in Eye Movements during Reading', *Frontiers in Psychology* 6, Article 1607: 1–13. Accessed 30 August 2019. https://doi.org/10.3389/fpsyg.2015.01607.
Redfern, Walter. 1984. *Puns*. Oxford: Blackwell.
Relf, Jan. 1991. 'Women in Retreat: The Politics of Separatism in Women's Literary Utopias', *Utopian Studies* 2 (1/2): 131–46.
Rhodes, Jewell Parker. 1983. 'Ursula Le Guin's *The Left Hand of Darkness*: Androgyny and the Feminist Utopia'. In *Women and Utopia: Critical Interpretations*, edited by Marleen Barr and Nicholas D. Smith, 108–20. Lanham, MD: University Press of America.
Richter-Schröder, Karin. 1986. *Frauenliteratur und weibliche Identität: Theoretische Ansätze zu einer weiblichen Ästhetik und zur Entwicklung der neuen deutschen Frauenliteratur*. Frankfurt am Main: Anton Hain.
Riessman, Catherine Kohler. 1987. 'When Gender is Not Enough: Women Interviewing Women', *Gender and Society* 1 (2): 172–207.

Riester, Susanne. 2006. '"Der Witz und seine Beziehung zum Unbewussten" von Sigmund Freud', *Dynamische Psychiatrie* 39 (1): 89–108.
Rothermund, Klaus. 1998. 'Automatische geschlechtsspezifische Assoziationen beim Lesen von Texten mit geschlechtseindeutigen und generisch maskulinen Text-Subjekten', *Sprache und Kognition* 17 (4): 183–98.
Rugenstein, Kai. 2014. *Humor: Die Verflüssigung des Subjekts bei Hippokrates, Jean Paul, Kierkegaard und Freud*. Paderborn: Wilhelm Fink.
Sarrasin, Oriane, Ute Gabriel and Pascal Gygax. 2012. 'Sexism and Attitudes toward Gender-Neutral Language: The Case of English, French, and German', *Swiss Journal of Psychology* 71 (3): 113–24.
Sato, Sayaka, Pascal M. Gygax and Ute Gabriel. 2013. 'Gender Inferences: Grammatical Features and their Impact on the Representation of Gender in Bilinguals', *Bilingualism: Language and Cognition* 16 (4): 792–807.
Schmidt, Ricarda. 1982. 'Körperbewusstsein und Sprachbewusstsein: Verena Stefans "Häutungen"'. In *Westdeutsche Frauenliteratur in den 70er Jahren*, by Ricarda Schmidt, 52–136. Frankfurt am Main: Rita G. Fischer Verlag.
Schneider, Joseph W. and Sally L. Hacker. 1973. 'Sex Role Imagery and Use of the Generic "Man" in Introductory Texts: A Case in the Sociology of Sociology', *American Sociologist* 8 (1): 12–18.
Scholz, Anna-Lena and Thomas Kerstan. 2016. 'Es heißt Stu- denten! dierende!', *ZEIT Campus*, 2 June. Accessed 30 August 2019. http://www.zeit.de/2016/24/sprache-gender-studenten-streit-studierende.
Schupp, Franz. 1982. 'Einleitung'. In *Generales inquisitiones de analysi notionum et veritatum = Allgemeine Untersuchungen über die Analyse der Begriffe und Wahrheiten*, by Gottfried Wilhelm Leibniz, vii–xxxv. Hamburg: Felix Meiner Verlag.
Sczesny, Sabine, Franziska Moser and Wendy Wood. 2015. 'Beyond Sexist Beliefs: How Do People Decide to Use Gender-Inclusive Language?', *Personality and Social Psychology Bulletin* 41 (7): 943–54.
Sendén, Marie Gustafsson, Emma A. Bäck and Anna Lindqvist. 2015. 'Introducing a Gender-Neutral Pronoun in a Natural Gender Language: The Influence of Time on Attitudes and Behavior', *Frontiers in Psychology* 6, Article 893: 1–12. Accessed 30 August 2019. https://doi.org/10.3389/fpsyg.2015.00893.
Serke, Jürgen. 1982. *Frauen schreiben: Ein neues Kapitel deutschsprachiger Literatur*. Frankfurt am Main: Fischer Taschenbuch Verlag.
Shane, Neala. 2015. *Inspired Baby Names from Around the World*. Novato, CA: New World Library.
Shaviro, Steven. 1986. 'From Language to "Forms of Life": Theory and Practice in Wittgenstein', *Social Text* 13/14: 216–36.
Short, Kayann. 1996. 'Do-It-Yourself Feminism', *Women's Review of Books* 13 (4): 20–21.
Skeat, Walter W. [1882] 1984. *A Concise Etymological Dictionary of the English Language*. Oxford: Oxford University Press.
Spender, Dale. 1980. *Man Made Language*. London: Routledge and Kegan Paul.
Stahlberg, Dagmar, Sabine Sczesny and Friederike Braun. 2001. 'Name Your Favorite Musician: Effects of Masculine Generics and of Their Alternatives in German', *Journal of Language and Social Psychology* 20 (4): 464–69.
Stanley, Julia P. and Susan W. Robbins. 1978. 'Going through the Changes: The Pronoun *She* in Middle English', *Paper in Linguistics* 11 (1/2): 71–88.
Stefan, Verena. [1978] 1979. *Shedding*, translated by Johanna Moore and Beth Weckmüller. London: Women's Press.
Stefan, Verena. [1975] 1994a. *Häutungen*. Frankfurt am Main: Fischer Taschenbuch Verlag.
Stefan, Verena. 1994b. 'Kakophonie: Vorwort zur Neuausgabe von 1994'. In *Häutungen*, by Verena Stefan. Frankfurt am Main: Fischer Taschenbuch Verlag, 7–29.
Steiger, Vera and Lisa Irmen. 2011. 'Recht verständlich und "gender-fair": Wie sollen Personen in amtlichen Texten bezeichnet werden? Ein Vergleich verschiedener Rezipientengruppen zur Akzeptanz geschlechtergerechter Rechtssprache', *Linguistische Berichte* 227: 297–322.
Stockwell, Sam, S. S., Carol Anne Douglas and Margie Crow. 1974. 'Four by Daughters, Inc.', *Off Our Backs* 4 (3): 14.
Stout, Jane G. and Nilanjana Dasgupta. 2011. 'When *He* Doesn't Mean *You*: Gender-Exclusive Language as Ostracism', *Personality and Social Psychology Bulletin* 37 (6): 757–69.

Sylvain, Cabala de, and Carsten Balzer. 2008. 'Die SYLVAIN-Konventionen – Versuch einer "geschlechtergerechten" Grammatik-Transformation der deutschen Sprache', *Liminalis* 2:40–53. http://www.liminalis.de.

Tanner, Laura E. 1987. 'Self-Conscious Representation in the Slave Narrative', *Black American Literature Forum* 21 (4): 415–24.

Taylor, Karen. 1996. 'Keeping Mum: The Paradoxes of Gendered Power Relations in Interviewing'. In *Challenging Women: Psychology's Exclusions, Feminist Possibilities*, by Erica Burman, Pam Alldred, Catherine Bewley, Brenda Goldberg, Colleen Heenan, Deborah Marks, Jane Marshall, Karen Taylor, Robina Ullah and Sam Warner, 106–22. Buckingham: Open University Press.

Tillman, Lynne. 2004. 'Telling Tales'. In *Biting the Error: Writers Explore Narrative*, edited by Mary Burger, Robert Glück, Camille Roy and Gail Scott, 139–47. Toronto: Coach House Books.

Timm, Lenora A. 1976. 'Book Review – Language and Woman's Place, by Robin Lakoff (1975)', *Lingua* 39 (3): 244–52.

Tohidian, Iman. 2009. 'Examining Linguistic Relativity Hypothesis as One of the Main Views on the Relationship between Language and Thought', *Journal of Psycholinguist Research* 38 (1): 65–74.

Trömel-Plötz, Senta. 1978. 'Linguistik und Frauensprache', *Linguistische Berichte* 57: 49–68.

Unger, Rhoda Kesler. 1979. 'Toward a Redefinition of Sex and Gender', *American Psychologist* 34 (11): 1085–94.

Varnhorn, Beate, ed. 2008. *Bertelsmann – Das grosse Lexikon der Vornamen*. Gütersloh: Wissen Media Verlag.

Vervecken, Dries, Bettina Hannover and Ilka Wolter. 2013. 'Changing (S)expectations: How Gender Fair Job Descriptions Impact Children's Perceptions and Interest Regarding Traditionally Male Occupations', *Journal of Vocational Behavior* 82 (3): 208–20.

Von Behr, Sophie. 1975. 'Etwas an seiner Seite', *Der Spiegel*, 8 December. Accessed 29 August 2019. http://www.spiegel.de/spiegel/print/d-41389603.html.

Von Humboldt, Wilhelm. [1810/11] 1973. *Schriften zur Sprache*, edited by Michael Böhler. Stuttgart: Philipp Reclam.

Weber, Christina D. 2010. 'Literary Fiction as a Tool for Teaching Social Theory and Critical Consciousness', *Teaching Sociology* 38 (4): 350–61.

Wilkinson, Sue. 1998. 'Focus Groups in Feminist Research: Power, Interaction, and the Co-Construction of Meaning', *Women's Studies International Forum* 21 (1): 111–25.

Wilkinson, Sue. 1999a. 'Focus Groups: A Feminist Method', *Psychology of Women Quarterly* 23 (2): 221–44.

Wilkinson, Sue. 1999b. 'How Useful are Focus Groups in Feminist Research?'. In *Developing Focus Group Research: Politics, Theory and Practice*, edited by Rosaline S. Barbour and Jenny Kitzinger, 64–78. London: SAGE Publications.

Williams, Christopher. 2008. 'The End of the "Masculine Rule"? Gender-Neutral Legislative Drafting in the United Kingdom and Ireland', *Statute Law Review* 29 (3): 139–53.

Wittgenstein, Ludwig. [1953] 1998. *Philosophische Untersuchungen = Philosophical investigations*, translated by G.E.M. Anscombe. 3rd ed. Oxford: Blackwell.

Zwaan, Rolf A. 1994. 'Effect of Genre Expectations on Text Comprehension', *Journal of Experimental Psychology: Learning, Memory, and Cognition* 20 (4): 920–33.

Index

address forms *see also* titles 111
activism 1–3, 51–5, 173–4, 179–82
ambiguity 40, 45, 93, 99
   of characters 64–5, 137–43, 151, 163
androcentric
   context 56, 65–7, 82, 88, 101, 105
   language, history 16–17, 116
   language, understanding 25–6, 60–4, 74, 176
   language use 59, 93, 103, 113, 119, 157, 165
androgyny 55, 58–66, 80
Annas, Pamela J. 59, 80–1
Arnold, June see also *The Cook and the Carpenter* 3–4, 81, 96
author
   sex/gender assumptions 151
   intentions 143–5

Baron, Dennis 69, 90–1, 115
Barr, Marleen S. 117–19, 157
belief system *see* world view
binaries, sex/gender
   understanding 88, 103–5, 138–40, 145, 170–1, 178–80
   language 43, 96, 147, 161, 165, 178–82
biology 5–8, 141
Black, Maria 16–17
bodies 80, 92
   female 57, 63–6, 83
Bodine, Ann 71, 91
boundaries
   linguistic 18, 75, 170–1, 178, 182
   sociocultural 76, 117
Brantenberg, Gerd see also *Egalias døtre* 3–4, 105–6, 120
Brose, Karl 77, 95
Butler, Judith 7–8

categorisation
   in literary texts 55, 61, 79, 83–4, 88
   of human beings 5, 17–18, 22, 150, 163, 170
Charmaz, Kathy *see* Grounded Theory
context *see also* social context
   historical 8, 77, 136–8, 148,
   linguistic 4, 10, 14, 27, 30–5, 39, 63, 92, 109, 130
   narrative 56–61, 79–90, 100–2, 107, 111–12
   reader responses 135–8, 150, 153–6, 162–3

research 1, 5, 10, 121, 144, 152, 169, 182
convention 31, 45, 59, 94, 99, 105, 118
   reader responses 130, 136–8, 142, 156–8
Cook and the Carpenter, The 11–12, 74–90, 93–7, 127, 168–174, 178, 180
   reader responses 130, 132, 137–59, 163–5, 169–73
Coward, Rosalind 16–17
Cummins, Elizabeth 58–9

Dal Cin, Sonya 46–7, 50–1, 167
data collection 12, 121, 124–8
Davidson, Joyce 95, 142
derogation, semantic *see* semantic derogation
derogatory terms 14–15, 18, 112, 115
dictionaries
   English 5–9, 56, 65, 68–71, 85–7, 91–2, 102, 108–14
   German 69–70, 86, 92, 108–11, 115–16

Egalias døtre 12, 46, 97–114, 117–21, 127, 172–5, 180
   reader responses 131, 148–51, 156–7, 165, 169–70, 173
Eckert, Penelope 6–7
educational settings
   literary texts in 13, 172–3, 176–82
   sex/gender in 40
empirical studies
   English 23–7, 39, 43
   German 31–7, 40–3
epicenes *see* neutral terms
essentialism 8–9, 114
expectations 46, 99
   social 36, 64, 80, 83, 101, 169, 176

Fayad, Mona 60, 66
family names *see* last names
female generics 100, 168, 176–7, 180
female terms 64, 102–3, 113–17, 177
feminisation of language *see* female generics
feminist *see also* feminist critique of language
   activism 117–18, 143–4, 173–4, 180
   publishers 57, 81
   research 6–7, 80, 121–3, 126,
   second-wave 4, 100
feminist critique of language 14–18, 21, 27–31, 173, 180
fiction, impact on readers 44–7, 50–1, 103, 167, 178, 182

193

focus group study
    methodology 121–4
    results 128–63
Freud, Sigmund *see also* laughter, liberating 12, 98–9, 118–19, 168

gender *see* sex/gender
genre 3, 9, 46, 172
Gerrig, Richard J. 44–7
Glaser, Barney G. *see* Grounded Theory
grammarians 71
grammatical gender 7
    German 28–30, 34–6, 63–4, 84–6, 93, 104, 108, 156, 160
Grounded Theory 124–8, 132, 152, 165
group membership 35–6

Häutungen 11–12, 52–8, 62–7, 73–4, 110, 168, 178–80
hierarchies, social 17, 84, 113, 122, 163
Hokenson, Jan 80
humour 98–100, 118–20, 148, 168

identity, and sex/gender 63, 111, 138–40
implication
    meaning of a term 15–16, 56, 62, 103,
    impact 20, 29, 113, 138, 174, 177, 181
inclusive language 38–9, 176–8
    and literary texts 10–14, 51–2, 74, 124, 168, 170, 174–6
    contested 4, 38–9, 173
    research 22, 26, 37, 40–3, 181–2
Inventory of Attitudes toward Sexist/Nonsexist Language – General (IASNL–G) 134, 152, 181
Iser, Wolfgang 10, 44–6, 104, 182
Ishiguro, Hidé 53–4, 72–4

Kalverkämper, Hartwig 28–31, 39
Kotthoff, Helga 118–20

Lakoff, Robin 10, 14–18, 23, 27
language *see also* inclusive language
    biased 10–12, 23, 42, 59, 104, 110, 120, 164, 167–9, 183
    definition 9–10
    socialisation 75–6, 177
last names 38, 65–6, 89, 104, 111–13
laughter, liberating 60, 98–100, 117–20
Left Hand of Darkness, The 52–62, 65–7, 73–4, 81, 109–10, 127–8, 168, 178
    reader responses 129–32, 135–44, 151–4, 158, 163–4, 169–73
Le Guin, Ursula K. see also *The Left Hand of Darkness* 3–4, 11–12, 44
Leibniz, Gottfried Wilhelm see also *salva veritate* principle 4, 11, 53–5, 71–4, 168
linguistic relativity principle *see* Sapir–Whorf hypothesis
linguistic visibility 26–7, 32, 176
literary texts, justification 3–4
Livia, Anna 9, 60, 74, 81
Lothane, Zvi 100, 117

male generics 16, 29, 51, 167, 177
    history/etymology 68–71, 90–1

in literary texts 55, 58–63, 73–4, 106–10, 168
research 22–6, 31–7, 41–3
markedness 7, 16–7, 25, 35
Mates, Benson 73–4
McConnell–Ginet, Sally 6–7, 22, 165
McGinn, Marie 76–7, 95
McGowan, Cynthia 68–9, 114–16
meaning
    co-creation of 44–5, 122
    words 9–11, 15, 63, 68–70, 86, 99, 111, 114–15, 135
    names 65–8, 87–90, 111–13
metaphor 130, 137
Moberg, Verne 105, 113

naming *see also* last names 96–7
    in literary texts 65–8, 84, 87–90, 104, 111–13
    sexed/gendered 26, 32–5, 138, 160–2
    occupational 17, 23–7, 30, 36–7, 40, 135–6, 156, 160
narrative studies 3, 44–52, 167
neutral pronouns
    na/nan 11, 78–88, 93–6, 130–3, 139–53, 158–65, 168–71
    person/per 11, 78–85, 90–6, 168
neutral terms *see also* neutral pronouns
    challenges 39–40, 43, 56, 69, 87–90, 94, 97, 107, 169, 176
    history/etymology 90–3
    in literary texts 9, 74, 78–87, 175
    opportunities 11, 78–80, 83–5, 93, 95–7, 171, 178
    reader responses 130–2, 137–65
    research 25–6, 33–6, 41, 171–2
non-binary 43, 94, 178
norms
    fiction highlighting 45, 66, 78–80, 104–6, 111, 170, 173, 177–9
    linguistic 3–4, 19, 39, 55, 59, 153, 158–9, 175, 182
    social 19, 58, 88, 90, 99, 143

Parks, Janet B. *see* Inventory of Attitudes toward Sexist/Nonsexist Language – General (IASNL–G)
parody 60, 148
Partington, Alan 99–100
patriarchy 104–6, 118
Penelope (Stanley), Julia 68–9, 114–17
Piercy, Marge see also *Woman on the Edge of Time* 3–4, 11–12, 77
power
    research 122–3
    social 2, 8, 15–7, 27, 57, 99, 104
prescriptive grammar 71
privileged 15–17, 27, 87, 90, 168
pronouns
    impact of 22–6, 59–64, 82–5, 141–2, 145, 151–4, 158, 165
    neutral *see* neutral pronouns
    she/he 14–16, 28, 39, 63–4, 70–3, 83, 116–17
    they 22–4, 39, 91–2, 149, 168
Pugh, Meryl 59–60, 81

puns 99–100
Pusch, Luise F. 30–1, 37, 93, 104–6, 120, 174, 180

Ragland, Mary Eloise 99, 118–20
reader responses *see also* focus group study, results 2, 4, 44–51, 124, 170, 181–2
research method *see also* focus group study, methodology 1–5, 182
reader, as co-creator of meaning *see* meaning, co-creation of
Redfern, Walter *see also* puns 99–100
reproduction 84
Rhodes, Jewell Parker 59–60
Richter–Schröder, Karin 104–5
Roberton, Mary Ann *see* Inventory of Attitudes toward Sexist/Nonsexist Language – General (IASNL–G)

salva veritate principle 4, 53–4, 71–3, 137, 168
Sapir, Edward *see* Sapir–Whorf hypothesis
Sapir–Whorf hypothesis 18–23, 61, 137
satire 9, 104, 112
science fiction see also *The Left Hand of Darkness/Woman on the Edge of Time* 9, 59, 80–1
semantic derogation 115
semantic shift 68–9, 114–16
sex/gender
  definition 5–8
  gender, social 5–7, 79, 82–3, 87, 107–8, 111–13
  grammatical *see* grammatical gender
  sex, biological 5–8, 61, 64, 66–7, 83, 108, 110
sex/gender and language 8, 14, 44, 51, 93, 173
  focus groups 121, 127, 133–6, 143, 151–4, 161, 165, 169–71
  in literary texts 1–4, 10–3, 51–3, 58, 81, 164, 172–4, 178–82
sexism 5, 80, 100, 105, 134, 171
Shaviro, Steven 94–5
silence 3, 122
singular they *see* pronouns, they
Smith, Mick 95, 142

social categories *see* categorisation, of human beings
social change 4, 18, 28, 38, 143
social context 76–9, 108, 150, 171
  of the reader 45, 87, 103, 109, 163, 170
  and sex/gender 15–16, 30, 40, 92–7, 140–2, 165
social groups 14, 49
social practice 94–6, 142
social status *see* hierarchies, social
socialisation 19, 75–6
speech community 5, 39, 43, 77, 142
Spender, Dale 14–8, 27–8
Stefan, Verena see also *Häutungen* 3–4, 11
stereotypes 25–7, 35, 49, 112, 131, 141, 150
Strauss, Anselm L. *see* Grounded Theory
subversion 99, 104, 157
surnames *see* last names
SYLVAIN–Konventionen 93, 183

Timm, Lenora A. 15, 23
titles
  forms of address 32, 37, 65, 87, 111–12
  occupational 25, 30, 36–7, 87, 135–6, 156, 160, 164
'To imagine a language…' 5, 75–6, 93
Tohidian, Iman 21, 135
Trömel–Plötz, Senta 10, 27–31

violence, against women 84–5, 94–6, 142–3, 149
voting 109, 120

Whorf, Benjamin Lee *see* Sapir–Whorf hypothesis
Wilkinson, Sue 121–3, 134
Wittgenstein, Ludwig *see also* 'To imagine a language…' 11, 75–7, 94–7, 141–2, 146, 175, 178–9
woman, definition 8–9
Woman on the Edge of Time 79, 81–90, 94–6, 110–11, 168, 178
wordplay *see also* puns 5, 12, 99–100, 110, 157, 168–70
world view 19–2, 81, 114–15, 119, 178
  shifts in 47, 100, 108–11, 168

Lightning Source UK Ltd.
Milton Keynes UK
UKHW051851060220
358277UK00005B/458